bef

SPORT / OLYMPICS

OR 5/02

796.48
TOO   HE
         STL

The Olympic Games

A Social Science Perspective

The Olympic Games:

A Social Science Perspective

Kristine Toohey and A.J. Veal

University of Technology, Sydney
Australia

CABI *Publishing*

CABI *Publishing* is a division of CAB *International*

CABI Publishing	CABI Publishing
CAB International	10 E 40th Street
Wallingford	Suite 3203
Oxon OX10 8DE	New York, NY 10016
UK	USA
Tel: +44 (0)1491 832111	Tel: +1 212 481 7018
Fax: +44 (0)1491 833508	Fax: +1 212 686 7993
Email: cabi@cabi.org	Email: cabi-nao@cabi.org
Web site: http://www.cabi.org	

A catalogue record for this book is available from the British Library, London, UK

Library of Congress Cataloging-in-Publication Data
Toohey, K. (Kristine)
        The Olympic games : a social science approach / K. Toohey and A.J. Veal.
        p.   cm.
        Includes bibliographical references (p.) and index.
        ISBN 0-85199-342-7 (alk. paper)
        1. Olympics--Social aspects. 2. Olympics--History.   I. Veal, Anthony James.   II. Title.
        GV721.5.T64 1999
        796.48'09--dc21   99-37882
                                                                          CIP

ISBN 0 85199 342 7

First printed 2000
Reprinted with corrections 2001

Printed and bound in the UK by Cromwell Press, Trowbridge, from copy supplied by the authors.

Contents

List of tables

List of figures

List of appendices

Acknowledgements

The following are acknowledged for permission to use illustrations:

Figures 2.3, 3.1, 3.2, 4.2, 4.4, 5.2, 5.3, 8.1, 10.7: Australian Picture Library

Figures 2.1, 2.2: Kristine Toohey

Figure 9.1: AAP

Figure 10.6: Fairfax Picture Library

Figures 4.3, 5.1, 10.1: Charles Butcher

List of abbreviations

ACOG	Atlanta Committee for the Olympic Games
AOC	Australian Olympic Committee
IF	International (Sport) Federation
IOA	International Olympic Academy
IOC	International Olympic Committee
NOC	National Olympic Committee
OCOG	Organising Committee for the Olympic Games
SLOC	Salt Lake Organising Committee
SOCOG	Sydney Organising Committee for the Olympic Games
USOC	United States Olympic Committee

Preface

This book arises as a result of the decision of the International Olympic Committee, in September 1993, to award the Games of the XXVII Olympiad to Sydney, Australia. The announcement prompted us to develop an undergraduate and post-graduate course on the Olympic Games in the School of Leisure and Tourism Studies at the University of Technology, Sydney (UTS). Building on the long-standing Olympic Games research interests of one of us (Kristine Toohey), a considerable amount of research and teaching activity was subsequently developed at UTS, on the Olympic Games generally and on Sydney 2000 specifically. A book seemed a natural progression.

Despite recent controversies, there is no sign of the Olympic Games fading in terms of their sporting, cultural and economic significance. From their origins in ancient Greece, during their revival at the end of the nineteenth century and through most of their twentieth century existence, the Olympic Games have been more than just another sporting event. While there is an enormous and varied literature available on the Olympic Games, there is no up-to-date publication which seeks to provide a broad, independent, multi-disciplinary account and analysis of this unique phenomenon. It is not possible to provide the definitive analysis of a phenomenon as complex as the Olympic Games in a single, short, book: what we aim to do is to provide an introduction to the various ways in which the Games have been analysed and to raise issues and provide pointers to further study. The 'social science approach' is not intended to involve a heavily theoretical perspective, but rather to reflect the range of interests which observers with a social science background have had, and continue to have, in the Games. We do not seek to provide a detailed account of the sporting achievements of Olympic athletes - this has been done by many authors - our interest is in the Olympics as a social, economic, political and cultural phenomenon.

We would like to thank Alison Burkhardt for assistance with bibliographic matters, Simon Darcy for input to chapter 10, and Averly Whiston for technical assistance with illustrations.

As part of the process of developing this book we assembled a substantial bibliography on the Olympic Games, much of which is included in the references section of the book. The full bibliography is, however, considerably more extensive; it is being continually updated and is available on-line at: www.business.uts.edu. au/leisure/research/olympic.html

K.T.
A.J.V.
Sydney, August 1999

Chapter one:

Introduction

> Olympism is a philosophy of life, exalting and combining in a balanced whole the qualities of body, will and mind. Blending sport with culture and education, Olympism seeks to create a way of life based on the joy found in effort, the educational value of good example and respect for universal fundamental ethical principles. *The Olympic Charter* (IOC, 1995: 1)

> The primary aim of the organisers of sports or Olympic competitions is not sport for its own sake but sport for capitalist profit; or rather, their aim is capitalist profit through sport. (Brohm, 1978: 137)

Every four years, in recent decades, some 10,000 athletes from 200 countries, with a similar number of coaches and officials, as many as 15,000 media representatives and hundreds of thousands of spectators have gathered for two weeks to participate in, report on and watch a sporting event which is in turn viewed on television, listened to on radios and read about in the print media and followed on the Internet by billions of people around the world. Each event has cost enormous sums of money to stage, funded from taxpayers, sponsors and television companies and their advertisers. Sporting records have invariably been broken and national and inter-national heroes created. It is the world's biggest peace-time event.

The history of the Olympic Games begins at least 3000 years ago in classical Greece. In their ancient form, while they celebrated physical excellence, they primarily served a religious purpose. In their modern form, while still ostensibly about physical excellence, the Games play a cultural and economic, and often political, role. The history and global significance of the Games justifies their serious consideration as an object of academic enquiry - indeed, the academic literature on both the ancient and the modern Games is massive and growing (see Burkhardt *et al.*, 1995; Veal *et al.*, 1998). A number of research centres has been established around the world, mostly in universities, specifically to foster research on the Olympic

1

phenomenon, including the International Centre for Olympic Studies at the University of Western Ontario, Canada, the Centre d'Estudis Olímpics at the Universitat Autónoma de Barcelona, Spain, the Centre for Olympic Studies at the University of New South Wales, Australia, and the Olympic Studies Centre at the Olympic Museum in Lausanne.

Most social science disciplines and sub-disciplines have something to offer in the study of the Olympic Games. The largest single group of contributors to the literature on the Olympics has, for obvious reasons, been historians. History is, admittedly, generally seen as part of the humanities rather than the social sciences, but historical work on the modern Games is frequently concerned with social issues, such as the changing status of women, race, community politics, and costs and benefits of the Games. With the growing scale and expense of running the Games, economic analysis has increasingly come into the picture, focusing on such issues as the sources of funding of individual Games and their economic impact on the host city or nation, the funding of the organisation with overall responsibility for the Games, the International Olympic Committee (IOC), and the remuneration of athletes. While in principle, according to the rhetoric of the IOC, athletes who participate in the Games represent just themselves and the 'youth of the world', in practice they represent individual nation states, so politics, political analysis and political debate are never far away from any consideration of the Games. Sociological perspectives arise from such considerations as the question of gender and racial equity in involvement with the Games and in considering the cultural significance of the Games and the role of the media in shaping and portraying their cultural dimensions. Examining the issue of drug abuse in sport, and in the Olympic Games in particular, involves a range of perspectives, including medical sciences, psychology, sociology, economics and politics.

In contrast to most of the existing scholarly publications on the Olympic Games, which have been primarily historical or have been concerned with a single perspective, such as politics or the media, the aim of this book is to encompass all of these dimensions, at least at an introductory level. We seek to provide an overview of the basic socio-cultural dimensions of the Games from both contemporary and historical perspectives. Because of the breadth of coverage attempted, the book does not deal with any one issue in great depth: it seeks to pose questions, examine issues and provide information and sources for further reading and study.

Chapter 2 provides an historical introduction to the original Olympic Games, of ancient Greece. The Games of the classical era were the source of inspiration for the modern revival of the Games in the late nineteenth century, but the precise nature of those ancient celebrations, which lasted for over 1000 years, is the subject of on-going research, including continuing excavations at the ancient site of Olympia. Chapter 3 examines the events leading to the modern revival of the Games in Athens in 1896, while noting that this was by no means the first attempt to revive the Olympics. The revival of the Games at this time was not an isolated event, but was associated with enormous changes which had been taking place in sport and indeed in the wider economy and culture during the second half of the nineteenth century.

In single chapters dealing with each of these historical phenomena, it is not possible to provide definitive accounts, rather, the aim is to highlight the linkages, real and mythologised, between these two periods and the modern day Olympic Games.

In chapter 4 an overview of the modern Olympics is provided. This focusses particularly on the philosophy and *modus operandi* of the IOC, noting the criticisms which this unique body has attracted over the years, many of which were seen to have been vindicated by the scandals which erupted in 1998-1999. The complex worldwide 'Olympic Movement' is examined in this chapter, including the phenomenon of 'Olympism', the structure and functioning of the IOC and an examination of the roles of National Olympic Committees and International Sport Federations. In addition the Winter Olympics, the Cultural Olympiad, the Paralympic Games and similar international sporting events are examined briefly. While reference is made to the bribery scandals which erupted in late 1998 and early 1999, these events are dealt with more fully in chapter 11.

In chapter 5, the issues of politics and nationalism, which permeate the Olympic phenomenon, are analysed. While sport is widely promoted as being 'beyond politics', the chapter examines six different forms of political intervention in the Games, from international terrorism to local pork-barrelling, illustrating the fact that, far from being 'above politics', sport, and the Olympic Games in particular, are quintessentially political. They have been used to promote political philosophies and to achieve sectarian and national political goals. They have themselves been subject to political intrigue and they have been caught up in many of the major international political events of the twentieth century.

Chapter 6 considers the economic and financial dimensions of the Olympics. First, the question of 'political economy' is addressed - in particular the questions which increased funding, commercialisation, sponsorship and professionalisation raise about the role of the Games in the wider economic and political world order. As the second quotation at the head of this chapter illustrates, there is no consensus on such questions. Second, the funding of the IOC is examined, noting its transformation from an insignificant and somewhat impoverished organisation up until the 1970s, to the high-profile, relatively wealthy institution we know today. Finally the chapter examines the financing of individual Games and the measurement of their economic impact on host communities.

The advent of satellite communication has ensured that the role played by the mass communication media has become the single most significant feature which distinguishes the Games of the last three or four decades from those held earlier. Chapter 7 reviews the role the media play in funding the Games and in bringing them to the world. It is the hundreds of millions of dollars generated from television advertising which have transformed the Olympic Games in the last quarter of the twentieth century. Millions may feel that they have a close and intimate knowledge of the Olympic Games, but this is entirely based on print and electronic messages filtered by reporters, editors and producers. The chapter therefore addresses the issue of the extent to which role of the mass media is simply that of passive communicator, ınd the extent to which media organisations use their editorial and financial power to influence the perceived and actual nature of the Games.

The problem of performance enhancing drugs often dominates coverage of international sport, both at the Olympics and elsewhere. At times, drug scandals have threatened the very future of the Olympic Games. With the IOC occupying a key position in the international 'war against drugs' in sport, chapter 8 examines the history of performance enhancing drug use at the Olympics and discusses the complex issues which the practice raises and the past, current and future role of the IOC in seeking to eradicate doping from sport.

Women played no direct part in the sporting aspects of the ancient Olympic Games, or in the initial celebrations of the modern Games. While women have participated in the Olympic Games since 1900, they still account for less than 40% of the participants. The reasons for the restricted role of women are shrouded in myth, intrigue and backroom politics. Chapter 9 examines the history of this phenomenon and considers the equity issues raised by the continued discrimination against women in the Olympics and provides a case-study of the experience of one female Olympian who chose to challenge authority.

Chapter 10 examines in some detail the two most recent summer Olympic Games - Barcelona and Atlanta - as case-studies, and presents a forward look at Sydney 2000. These case-studies demonstrate that, despite certain similarities, each celebration of the Olympic Games is unique, reflecting the social, cultural and physical nature of the host country and city, but also the wider global environment of the time. In addition, the chapter includes, in an appendix, a brief overview of each of the Games of the modern era, with a guide to further reading.

Finally, chapter 11 considers the question of the future of the Games: whether they can survive in their current form and whether current trends in the way they are organised can preserve the proclaimed ideals of the Olympic Movement. It examines the recent bribery scandals which have surrounded the International Olympic Committee and their aftermath, although the saga is still continuing.

The Olympic Games are no longer - if they ever were - just a sporting event: they are also a cultural, political and economic phenomenon. Particular interests see them as a media event, a tourism attraction, a marketing opportunity, a catalyst for urban development and renewal, a city image creator and booster, a vehicle for 'sport for all' campaigns, an inspiration for youth and a force for peace and international understanding. The message of this book is that the Olympic Games do indeed play all these roles, although not always to the extent or in ways that particular interest groups hope or imagine. In fact, it is arguably these added, mainly non-sporting, roles which make the Olympic Games unique, and their continued survival probably depends on their continuing to play these roles.

The quotation from the *Olympic Charter* which opens this chapter demonstrates a number of features of the Olympic Games which, apart from their scale, makes them unique. Other sporting events do not publish manifestoes like the *Olympic Charter* or promulgate a 'philosophy' or 'way of life', with lofty ideals akin to those of a religion, cult or political movement. Neither do other sporting events involve the degree of pomp and ceremonial that surrounds the celebration of each Olympic Games, although it appears that more and more sports are attempting to emulate these features. The Olympic Games are very much part of contemporary world culture, but they are hung about with a curious, at times archaic, set of 'trappings' from the nineteenth century and from antiquity. While they espouse high ideals and values, like any contemporary organisation they are organised by fallible human beings and are faced with a range of worldly problems and challenges which threaten these values, including accusations of excessive commercialisation and the problems of prohibited drug use, politicisation and corruption.

Because of their history, both ancient and modern, and their size and international reach, there is a widespread sense of public 'ownership' of the Olympic Games which does not extend to other sporting events. As a result, the Games are subject to a level of scrutiny, analysis and debate which, while it may be common for single 'national games' in individual countries, is unique at the international level. Extravagant sentiments and hyperbole which are never expressed about other sporting events are commonly expressed about the Olympic Games. For example, Sir Roger Bannister, the first man to run a mile in under four minutes, Olympic athlete and later chair of the British Sports Council, in discussing various reforms for the Games in the 1980s, declared:

> Given a move towards the changes that I have suggested, the Olympic Games should remain one of the great hopes of the world. It is in the deepest interests of the future of the world for them to continue. (Bannister, 1988: 425)

John Lucas, Olympic historian, stated:

> I have abiding faith in the *idea* of a near-perfect Olympic Games as a festival of élite sport, as a peace-filled gathering of the human race in a grand union of the beginning and end of life 'through the endurance of affection, of trust, of friendship, and love'. (Lucas, 1992: 215)

Rod McGeoch, who led Sydney's bid for the 2000 Games, stated:

> The 2000 Olympics will be the greatest peacetime event in Australia's history. It will be something that all Australians will never forget. For many people, it will be the greatest moment of their lives; an event which lives on in their memory. .. Australia is a nation which genuinely does stand for the goals and principles which are the very foundations of the [Olympic] movement. .. It will be one of the most important moments in Australian history when they light the flame at Sydney Olympic Park. (McGeoch and Korporaal, 1994: 307-308)

Such sentiments perhaps explain the sense of outrage when things go wrong, as they did in 1998-1999, or when Olympic Games organisations are found to be no different from other human organisations. Thus Andrew Jennings, trenchant critic of the IOC and its power and abuse of power, states: 'So you thought the Olympics belonged to the world? Wrong. The Olympic Games are *their* exclusive property' (Jennings, 1996: 12). His initial assumption appears to have been that the Games belonged to 'us' in some way, rather than to a self-selected élite, and somewhat secretive organisation. Such sentiments would not often be expressed about international tennis or motor racing.

All this raises our curiosity as to how this unique phenomenon came about, how its constituent elements fit together and combine to create the modern Olympic Games, and whether the Games can possibly meet the many expectations which various stakeholders have for them. This book seeks to explore these issues and throw light on some of the dilemmas. In a rapidly changing world the currency of any writing on social phenomena is fleeting, and the Olympic Games is no exception. As the second millennium closes and the third begins, and as the modern Olympic Games move into their second century, many changes are happening in the Olympic Movement which will ensure that the present soon becomes the distant past and predictions will become reality or mere flights of fancy.

Chapter two:

The Ancient Olympics and their Relevance to the Modern Games

> During the second great Greek revival, 18th- and 19th-century scholars saw what they wished to see regarding life in Ancient Hellas, including the life of the Olympic competitor. That life, seen through the filter of nearly 15 centuries, was frequently described in terms of honour, patriotism, altruism, non-commercial amateur motive, and above all fervent religious belief. (Lucas, 1992: 2-3)

Introduction

One of the reasons why the first modern Olympic Games were revived in Athens in 1896 was their founders' perceptions of certain positive values of sport, which they believed were put into practice by athletes in the Ancient Olympics and which they hoped could be transferred to sport in the late nineteenth century. However, not all their information, and hence ideas, about the Greeks and their athletic festivals was accurate. In reality many of the sports contested in the modern Games have very little in common with their ancient counterpart.

For much of their existence, those who have determined the values, rules and regulations of the modern Olympics have based many of their practices on myths about the purity of the Ancient Games, for example the belief that the Games were not subject to political intervention, commercialism or professionalism and that they were exemplars of peace and equality. It appears that such misconceptions about practices and customs of the ancients were not unique to Olympic revivalists. Hegel, in his celebrated treatise, *Reason in History* (1953: 8), notes: 'in the turmoil of world affairs no universal principle, no memory of similar conditions in the past can help us - a vague memory has no power against the vitality of the present. Nothing is more shallow in this respect than the oft-repeated appeal to Greek and Roman examples'.

This is not to say that the Ancient Olympics were not without merit. Indeed, they have been acknowledged as one of the strongest unifying forces in the ancient Greek world. Like their modern counterpart there were famous instances and practices which exemplified the notion of sportsmanship, just as there were instances of deviance.

Myths

Myths, according to Cheek and Burch (1976:86), are 'the grammar and rhetoric of the social order. They not only regularise the flow of information, but also convey feelings. In doing this they serve the function of bringing together a select few, while concurrently setting this group apart from others'. Roland Barthes, in his seminal work, *Mythologies* (1983), would categorise the hegemony of the modern Games founders' views of the Ancient Olympics as an example of a 'bourgeois norm', in that they assumed that their reality was the correct and natural position and, as a consequence of their power and position, their philosophies initially dominated modern Olympic discourse, whether or not they reflected, or were based on a detailed knowledge of, the recorded history of the Ancient Games.

Myths become regulated by rites, rituals and ceremonies, so it is understandable that such practices have become integral to the modern practices of *Olympism*. This ritualisation in turn becomes embedded in a myth's set of beliefs, so that a paradigm shift occurs and, as a consequence, the myth becomes an 'inherent aspect of social organisation necessary to the regulation of transactions' (Cheek and Burch, 1976:182). Consequently, the more a myth becomes a constituent of dominant discourse, the harder it is to challenge. While some Olympic myths have been debunked in the last 100 years, others survive, thrive and, even today, shape hegemonic practice and policy in international, and especially Olympic, sports.

This has meant that, as these viewpoints became accepted as 'truth', they have then defined what was acceptable and, more importantly, unacceptable within the modern Olympic movement. As the Games have evolved and responded to changes in the twentieth century some of these notions have been challenged and replaced. However, myths have often provided the keystone to the structure and rules of the modern Olympics. Changing these hegemonic practices has at times been a slow and acrimonious process. Indeed, some biases which are still evident and contentious in today's Olympic movement, such as the inequitable participation of women, as athletes and administrators, have these myths as their philosophical basis. Referring to the commonly acknowledged founder of the modern Games, Baron Pierre de Coubertin, Lucas (1992:4) states:

> .. the core of de Coubertin's philosophy is still a part of Olympic ideology and will probably persist for many years. ... Anyone in today's late 20th century who believes that this kind of thinking has been purged from the minds of people connected with the worldwide Olympic Movement is very much mistaken.

Hoberman (1986:1) is less diplomatic about the International Olympic Committee (IOC): 'the Olympic movement does not just overcome its history: it has demonstrated a prodigious ability to forget it'.

History of the Ancient Olympic Games

The earliest records of the Olympic Games indicate that they were held as early as 776 BC (although quite possibly there were earlier unofficial contests at the site) and celebrated once every four years, during the second or third full moon after the summer solstice. At their zenith the games lasted for five days (see Table 2.1). They continued to be celebrated until AD 393, when the Roman Emperor, Theodosius I, a Christian, abolished them because of their links to Zeus. This association meant that their rituals and practices were considered pagan and counter to the new Christian religion of the Roman Empire, which at this time encompassed Greek territory.

Table 2.1. The ancient Olympic programme.

Day	Time	Event
1	Morning	• swearing-in ceremony • prayers and sacrifices • contest for heralds and trumpeters • boys' wrestling, boxing and running events
	Afternoon	• orations
2	Morning	• chariot and horse races
	Afternoon	• pentathlon
	Night	• funeral rites in honour of Pelops • parade of victors • singing • feast
3	Morning	• procession of competitors and officials • animal sacrifices
	Afternoon	• running races
	Night	• banquet
4	Morning	• wrestling
	Afternoon	• boxing • pankration • hoplite race
5		• crowning of victors • feast and celebration

Adapted from Swaddling (1980:37).

Figure 2.1. Entrance to the Olympic stadium at Olympia.

When the Games began, Greek society was preeminent in the Ancient world. Yet, within the area known today as Greece, there was no such thing as a central government, or indeed even a Greek nation. Rather, the region referred to as Ancient Greece was a collection of city states, called *polis*, some of which, at various times, engaged in wars against each other, as well as at other times uniting against common enemies. What united and signified the Greeks was a common language and literature, the acceptance of a common ancestry and celebration of sporting festivals. The Olympic Games were the most prestigious of all these sporting festivals.

The two preeminent city states in the ancient Greek world were Athens and Sparta. Yet neither of these important centres hosted one of the four major sporting festivals of the Greeks. These events, today known as the Panhellenic Games, were held in a four year cycle which is mirrored in today's Olympic Games. Each of these Panhellenic Games honoured a god, awarded token prizes and was held in a permanent, purpose-built location. They are listed in Table 2.2 in chronological order of their believed starting dates.

The Events

The Olympic Games were the most prestigious of all the festivals. Held in Olympia, (see Figure 2.1) in the Western Peloponnesus, in the city state of Elis, a minor and relatively peaceful *polis*, it is believed that the Games began as a single event, a running race, known as the *stade*. The first known victor, Corobeus of Elis, who won the *stade* race, was a cook. This race, which has obvious links to contemporary use of the word stadium, was the distance of one length of the stadium and finished with the contestants facing the sacred *altis* (altar) as a form of honour to Zeus. All races introduced at later dates finished in the same manner. Thus, even the direction of events was based on religious grounds. Many other aspects and rituals of the games also evolved to honour the Greek gods.

Table 2.2. The Panhellenic Games.

Games	Location	God honoured	Prize	Frequency
Olympic	Olympia	Zeus	Olive	Every 4 years
Pythian	Delphi	Apollo	Laurel wreath	Every 4 years, 3 years after the Olympic Games
Isthmian	Corinth	Poseiden	Celery	Every 2 years, 2nd and 4th year of Olympiads
Nemean	Nemea	Zeus	Celery, then pine	Every 2 years, as for Isthmian Games

The Games were originally open only to free born Greek males, who had not been convicted of a crime. Athletes also had to meet other eligibility criteria before being allowed to compete. They were required to swear that they had trained for ten months prior to coming to Olympia and then one month at the training site under the supervision of the *Helenedonakai* (judges).

Although the Ancient Olympics drew crowds of spectators, estimated to be up to 40,000, the facilities were primitive, even by standards of the day. Unlike today's stadia, which are used for many different events, the site at Olympia only saw competitions infrequently, once every four years for the Olympic Games and similarly for the Games of Hera, which were competitions for females, held to honour the goddess Hera, the wife of Zeus. During the intervals between competitions there were perhaps only a few visiting pilgrims and the permanent workers, such as artisans, priests and priestesses, associated with the non-athletic functions of the site. During these extensive breaks, the athletic facilities were, for the most part, deserted and unkempt. One of the first tasks of the Olympic athletes was to prepare the area for competition. Thus, weeding and other associated chores were expected of competitors. The contrast with today's élite competitors, some of whom no longer even stay in the Olympic Village, but in nearby luxury hotels, is marked. Many of the Greek athletes slept under the stars.

One practical concern during competition was that sanitary conditions were also primitive, especially by twentieth century standards, but even in comparison to the Roman stadia, which were in existence in the latter half of the Games' existence. For example, there were open drains. Unlike many other stadia there were few seats at Olympia (hence the word stadia, which refers to standing). A few honoured judges and officials had seats, however the majority of spectators sat or stood on the grassy banks which lined either side of the running track.

Despite their humble beginnings, as the Olympic Games grew in status they became important as a site to demonstrate power and prestige. In a manner similar to today's nationalistic and commercial displays of grandeur, the wealthy who attended the Ancient Olympics were sometimes guilty of conspicuous consumption in their attempts to outdo their rivals through their lavish displays of wealth (Swaddling, 1980). In one such example, 'the Syracusan tyrant Dionysius sent several expensive four-horse chariot teams, beautifully decorated tents, and professional actors to recite poetry he himself had written' (Tufts University, 1997a).

During the early Games, however, crowd numbers were relatively small and so, at this point in their history, facilities were in keeping with the nature of the single event. The relative obscurity of the festival changed over time, as did the influence of the event on Greek society. For example, the Greek calendar came to be measured in 'Olympiads'. The term signified four years and was the principle measure of Greek time. To differentiate Olympiads, each one was named after the winner of the stade race, rather than being assigned a numerical symbol as is our calendar. Not even the athletes of today are afforded that honour.

The number of events at the Olympic Games increased with time (see Table 2.3). The second event to be added to the Games programme was the two *stade* race, or *dialos*. Athletes began at the *altis* end of the stadium, ran one *stade* away and then turned to finish at the starting line. The Greek historian Philostratis explained the symbolism of this arrangement:

> When the people of Elis had sacrificed, then the ambassadors of the Greeks, whoever happened to be there, were expected to offer a sacrifice. That their approach might not be made without ceremony, runners ran a *stade* away from the *altis* as though to invite the Greeks, and back to the same place as though to announce that 'Hellas would be glad to come'. So much then concerning the origins of the two *stade* race. (Philostratis, 1987: 214)

Although some details of the events are known from writings (such as the above), artefacts and engravings, there are many facets of the Games which are still a mystery. For example, the starting lines which have been excavated are made of stone, with two parallel grooves running across them (see Figure 2.2). While there is a belief that there was a starting mechanism, there is no indisputable evidence to determine conclusively how the foot races were started, or indeed how the mechanisms worked. From statues which have been found, for example 'The Runner' (currently in the museum at Olympia), it is believed that runners began from a standing position with their toes in the grooves.

Table 2.3. Olympic events and their introduction to the Games.

Year	Number of games	Event
776 BC	1	Stade
724 BC	14	Diaulos
720 BC	15	Dolichos
708 BC	18	Wrestling and pentathlon
688 BC	23	Boxing
680 BC	25	Chariot race for four horses
648 BC	33	Horse race and pankration
632 BC	37	Stade and wrestling for boys
628 BC	38	Pentathlon for boys (discontinued 628 BC)
616 BC	41	Boxing for boys
520 BC	65	Hoplite race
500 BC	70	Race for mule carts (discontinued 444 BC)
496 BC	71	Race for mares (discontinued 444 BC)
408 BC	93	Chariot race for two horses
396 BC	96	Contest for heralds and trumpeters
384 BC	99	Chariot race for four colts
268 BC	128	Chariot race for two colts
256 BC	131	Colt race
200 BC	145	Pankration for boys

Adapted from Sweet, 1987: 6-7.

The longest foot race, the *dolichos*, was the second known event to be added to the Olympics. Records indicate that it was first held in 720 BC. Scholars believe that it was between 22 to 24 *stades* long (1 *stade* = 192.28 metres) and held entirely in the stadium. Thus, in the ancient Games, there was no equivalent to the modern marathon event.

An Olympic myth surrounds this, one of the premier events of the modern Games. Even the origin of the legendary Marathon run by Phidippides (a.k.a. Philippedes, Pheidippedes or Phiadiples) is clouded in mythology. According to modern beliefs Phidippides allegedly ran from the plains of Marathon to Athens to announce to the Athenians that their army had defeated in battle the Persians, who were under the leadership of Darius (Hopkins, 1966). During this battle the Athenians, led by Miltiardes, killed over 6000 Persians while losing only 192 of their own soldiers.   Herodotus, the 'father of history', notes this. However, like other contemporary accounts, he makes no mention of Phidippides then running to Athens with news of the victory. Instead, he mentions that, before the battle, on behalf of the Athenian army, Phidippides ran to Sparta, a distance of approximately 230 kilometres, in order to seek their assistance in the fight against the Persians. The Spartans' religious practices proscribed their departure until after the full moon and so they declined to assist (Herodotus, 1962). Even this account of Phidippides' run would be regarded suspiciously by modern historians, because of its religious overtones.

Figure 2.2. Starting grooves in the Olympic stadium at Olympia.

> Before they left the city, the generals sent a herald to Sparta: he was Phidippides, an Athenian and moreover, a day-long runner, who made his living in that way. This man, as he himself said and reported to the Athenians, was caught up on the road by Pan. ... This Phidippides, when he was on this errand for the generals and, as he ran, Pan appeared to him, was in Sparta the day after he left the city of the Athenians ... so he delivered the message entrusted to him. (Herodotus, 1962: 105-106)

Herodotus does not mention Phidippides again. Instead, when recording the aftermath of the battle, he describes the Persians' attempts to sail to Athens, attack the city and avenge their defeat. He wrote, 'so they rounded the Cape at Sunium. But the Athenians went as fast as their legs would carry them to the rescue of the city and forestalled the barbarians by getting there first' (Herodotus, 1962: 116).

It is not until the second century AD, in the writings of Lucian of Samosata, that the first mention of Phidippides' alleged run from Marathon to Athens occurs. Lucian refers to the runner as Philippedes in an article, 'A slip of the tongue in salutation', written not as a historical narrative, but rather as an essay dealing with the etymology of the word 'joy'.

The long-distance runner Philippides is said to have been the first who used this word [rejoice] when he announced the victory to the officials who were sitting in session and were concerned with the outcome of the battle: and with the words 'Rejoice; we have won', he expired with this dying word 'Rejoice'. (Lucian, 1905: 3)

An heroic image of the messenger is at the core of this reference (Sweet, 1987). Thus, the sacrificial aspect of the marathon myth originates in this article (Martin and Gynn, 1979).

Plutarch, another Roman and contemporary of Lucian, also notes a similar event, but his tale describes a run by Euchidas, from Delphi to Plataia in 479 BC (Sweet, 1987). Two other sources from antiquity, Pliny the Elder and Pausanias, both mention Phidippides' run to Sparta, but neither mentions a run to Athens (Martin and Gynn, 1979). Consequently, the legend of Phidippides' run to Athens from Marathon is not found in written sources until 600 years after the event was alleged to have occurred. Given this evidence it is difficult to view Phidippides' run as anything other than a myth, yet a marathon race has been included in all modern Olympic Games and is arguably one of its premier events.

The inclusion of the event in the modern Olympics is credited to Michael Breal, a French contemporary of the modern Games' founder, Pierre de Coubertin, who wrote to him, 'if the Organising Committee of the Olympics would be willing to revive the famous run of the Marathon soldier as part of the programme of the Games I would be willing to offer a prize for this new Marathon race' (Breal, cited in Martin and Gynn, 1979: 5). Also interesting, in the Breal proposal, is the offer of a prize for the victor, a practice contrary to Olympic protocol. Although the Athenian organising committee did not give a special prize for the event, the victor of the 1896 Marathon race, Spyridon Loues, a Greek and the only track and field Olympic victor from his country in the first modern Games, reproduced the practices of his ancient Olympic counterparts in receiving rewards from his victory, if not in terms of contesting such an event. He reputedly received cash and gifts in kind from his grateful government and citizens. Over time, the myth of Phidippides' run from Marathon to Athens has become interwoven into the fabric of the modern Games through the staging of one of the most prestigious events in the Modern Olympics.

Although the marathon has no definite links to the ancient Olympic Games there are some events held at today's Games which can trace their origins to their ancient counterparts. This occurred because of the growing importance of the Games to Greek society and a consequent diversification of the programme in the 6th century BC. The introduction of pentathlon and wrestling competitions meant that more sporting facilities were needed. The pentathlon consisted of five events: stade race; long jump; javelin; discus; and wrestling. During the course of the Ancient Games the long jump and discus were only ever held as part of this contest, while the other components became events in their own right. Like so many other aspects of the Games there is conflicting opinion regarding the order of events for the pentathlon. However there appears to be consensus on how the winner was chosen. If an athlete won three events then he was crowned the victor. This meant that, theoretically, competition could finish at the conclusion of the third, fourth or fifth event. If there was no absolute winner then a countback system was used to determine the victor.

Exact details of the long jump are sketchy. Records state that one contestant was reported to have jumped 56 feet. Today's world record is only approximately half of this, so it would appear that direct comparisons between the ancient and modern long jump contests would be inappropriate. One reason why results vary may be the fact that the ancient Greek jumpers carried hand weights, called *halteres*, which they jettisoned in mid-flight. This action was designed to increase the distance jumped. Contestants were accompanied by flautists, whose music was deemed to enhance performance through the rhythm of their tunes. Some modern athletes use 'Walkmans' for similar effect during their warm-ups.

The inclusion of the pentathlon and wrestling events heralded the introduction of combative sports into the programme. As with track races, the list of these sports increased as the Games evolved. Later boxing was introduced. Unlike today's boxing there were no weight divisions or rounds. The fights continued until one athlete was declared the winner by the judges, or one competitor indicated that he conceded. This was done by raising an index finger. Spartans, in keeping with their stoic ideals and image of warlike non-compromise, could not compete in these two events lest one of their citizens concede defeat.

Figure 2.3. Vase painting of competitors in the ancient Olympic Games.

The most brutal event at the Ancient Games was arguably the *Pankration*. Despite modern notions of the peaceful nature of these Games, winners in this event were also the most highly rated athletes. A mixture of boxing and wrestling, it was devoid of most rules. The only limitations were no eye gouging and biting. Apart from these restrictions it was 'open slather' as, replicating the format of the boxing and wrestling contests, there were neither weight divisions nor rounds.

Events for boys were first held at the Games of 632 BC. To be eligible contestants had to be under 18 as well as qualifying for the standard criteria of citizenship and training. Not all events had competitions for boys. One event only contested by men was the *hoplite* race, or race in armour, which was the last running race to be added to the programme. Competitors carried a shield and, at least in the earlier contests, wore a helmet and greaves (leg protectors). The race had obvious connections to military training. Swaddling notes that up to 25 athletes were allowed to enter the event, 'for whom a set of shields was kept in the Temple of Zeus. Presumably this was to ensure that each athlete carried a shield of the same weight' (1980: 44).

Horse and mule events were not held in the stadium, but in the *hippodrome*. The site has not been excavated due to extensive flooding, so little is known about the nature of its events. It is estimated that the length of the races was approximately six *stades*.

Chariot races were the first and major horse events at the Games. Chariots had a single axle and were pulled by four or two horses. Charloteers wore a knee length tunic called a *chiton*. Leather thongs were tied around the wrist and chest. Starting procedures for the races were complicated. This was necessitated because all chariots raced the length of the stadium then turned around a single marker. There was a high element of danger in this procedure as chariots were only lightly constructed, usually of wood, and there were many entrants in the races.

History - Politics

A common twentieth century belief is that a truce was declared throughout the whole of Greece for the duration of the Games and that all wars within Greek territory ceased (Greek Ministry of Culture, 1996). This is now disputed. Instead, some scholars claim that, in the spring of every fourth year, heralds travelled throughout the Greek world proclaiming a truce, in the name of Zeus, only for those spectators and competitors who were travelling to and from the Games. This meant that these travellers had free passage through warring city states (Mandell, 1976).

During the zenith of the Ancient Games, in the fifth century BC, the Games remained fairly peaceful. The Eleans were a small, neutral city state, a lowly position which was orchestrated, to a degree, by the larger city states of Athens and Sparta. The Peloponnesian Wars, however, changed this status, when the Eleans forsook their neutrality and aligned themselves with Athens, banning the common enemy, Sparta, from the Games. According to Swaddling (1980:78) the Games of 424 BC were held with armed troops present for protection against an attack from the

such commercial involvement and the ramifications for Olympic athletes and officials. As the influence of commercialism in the Games has increased, through sponsorship and television rights, those who favour a less commercial Olympics have harked back to the Ancient Games as being 'pure' sport, exempt from the taint of 'filthy lucre'. But herein lies another Olympic myth, for ancient Olympia, once every few years when the Olympic festival took place, was the scene of commercial activity. The stadium was surrounded by concession stands selling food, drink and souvenirs, and artists, sculptors and poets hawked their wares (Swaddling, 1980). An interesting parallel lies between this scene and the 1996 Atlanta Olympics, where commercial excess was one of the strongest points of criticism of the Games by the IOC. Yet, as the above demonstrates, there has always been a commercial aspect present in the Olympics. The difficulty is striking an acceptable balance between sport and commerce.

Like today's athletes, the quest for victory sometimes resulted in instances of cheating. Penalties for offenders were harsh. Contestants and their trainers could be whipped by the *mastigophorai* (whip bearers) for failing to obey the rules. Additionally, heavy fines were meted out for bribery, and, interestingly, '.. as a warning to potential offenders money from such fines was used to pay for bronze statues of Zeus (known as *Zanes*) which were set up along the terrace wall leading to the entrance of the stadium. .. According to Pausanias, there were sixteen of these in all' (Swaddling, 1980: 41).

Women

Pierre de Coubertin, reviver of the modern Games, believed that the Games should be the preserve of male athletes, citing ancient Games practices to reinforce the discriminatory sporting practices of the late nineteenth century. In the main, de Coubertin was correct in his assertions about the place of women in the Greek world. However, in relation to the ancient Olympics he was not entirely accurate, so again this practice touches on the realm of myth. Pausanias, in *Guide to Greece,* interestingly notes that virgins were not refused admission to the Games. It was only married women who were forbidden to compete, or be spectators, at the Games, with the exception of the priestess of *Demeter Chamyne* whose presence was required (Swaddling, 1980: 42). One other married woman, Kallipateira or Pherenike, is recorded to have been admitted to the Games, although the authorities were initially unaware of her sex, as she had disguised herself as a male trainer. Fortuitously, because of previous Olympic boxing victories by her father, brother and son, she did not meet the death punishment suggested for such female transgressors, when her identity was discovered.

Records indicate that, despite these restrictions on women as spectators and competitors, there were female winners at the Games. Such inconsistency was possible because, in the horse races, the prizes were awarded to owners rather than the charioteers or jockeys. Interestingly, this occurrence also demonstrates the degree of professionalism present in the ancient Games, as the charioteers or jockeys were professional athletes. Several women won Olympic victories by this means. The most well known was Kyniska, the daughter of Archidamos, the King of Sparta. To celebrate her victory she erected two statues at Olympia. On one of the statues was the following inscription:

Sparta's Kings were fathers and brothers of mine,
But since with my chariot and storming horses I, Kyniska,
Have won the prize, I place my effigy here
And proudly proclaim
That of all Grecian women I first bore the crown. (Swaddling, 1980: 42)

The Games' Demise

The Games had reached their zenith by the fifth century BC, when belief in the gods' influence on athletic victory was still widely accepted. However, with increased training and specialisation the athletes themselves began to be credited for their sporting successes or failures. Greek society was also changing in other, more direct ways, and later, when the Romans incorporated the Greek mainland into their territory, the end of the ancient Olympic years of glory was signalled. For example, Sulla, a Roman general, sacked Olympia in order to finance his army. He also transferred one Games, those of 80 BC, to Rome. Additionally, some of the Roman Olympic competitors had a different code of conduct, one in antithesis to the modern Games founders' idealised view of the noble ancient Olympian. For example, the emperor Nero wished to compete at Olympia, so he postponed the Games from AD 65 to AD 67, in order for them to coincide with his schedule. Although he failed to complete his event, the chariot race, he was still proclaimed the winner. The aftermath of this debacle was more in line with the true Olympic principles of fair play. 'After his death in AD 68, these Games were declared invalid, and Nero's name was expunged from the victor-lists. His successor Galba also insisted that a 250,000 drachma bribe to the judges should be paid back (Swaddling, 1980: 71).

Although the ancient Olympics later enjoyed a brief revival under some Roman rulers they could never regain their former glory and prestige. In AD 267 a tribe from southern Russia, the Heruli, invaded the area, and fortifications were built to protect the most sacred temple, that of Zeus. The Games, reduced to a few events, lasted for over a century, probably until AD 393, when the Emperor Theodosius I abolished all pagan festivals. If the Games did continue past this point it is unlikely that they extended beyond AD 426, when the Temple of Zeus was destroyed on the orders of Theodosius II. Later invaders pillaged the site and finally, in the fourth century AD, earthquakes and floods covered the area. The site remained virtually undisturbed until 1875 when excavations uncovered the site and the seeds of revival of the Games were planted.

Conclusion

Despite the many myths about the ancient Olympics which have influenced the modern Games, there were some similarities. Coakley details one such likeness between ancient Greek sport and its counterpart in the twentieth century which merits consideration:

> They reflected and recreated the dominant social structural characteristics and patterns of social relations in the society as a whole. The power and advantages that went along with being wealthy, male and young in Greek society served to shape games and contests that limited the participation of women, older people and those without economic resources. In fact the definitions of excellence used to evaluate performance even reflected the abilities of young males. This meant that the abilities of others were by definition sub-standard ... We can see the same things in organised sport today. (Coakley, 1992: 56)

Chapter three:

The Revival of the Olympic Games

I saw the necessity for reestablishing the Olympic Games as a supreme consecration of the cult of athletics practiced in the purest spirit of true sport, proudly, joyfully, and loyally. (de Coubertin, 1988: 103)

Introduction

Ceremonies and symbolism have been utilised throughout history. Rituals have been used as legitimisers, tools and methods by which credibility, a sense of tradition, and at times reverence, are imparted to an institution. Eventually these rituals become so intertwined with the institution itself that they serve to define its place in society. Examples of cultural institutions which use rituals include: religion, the judicial system and government. In sport, the example *par excellence* is the Olympic Movement.

At the Olympic Games ritual is immediately and best exemplified through the Opening Ceremony, the event which receives the greatest media coverage and highest television ratings of any aspect of the Games. However, other facets of the Olympic Movement are also replete with symbolism and ceremony, for example, the medal ceremonies, International Olympic Committee (IOC) Sessions and meetings of the International Olympic Academy (IOA). In addition to their other, more overt, functions these are all devices which have been manufactured by Olympic administrators who have sought to elevate the Games beyond sport into the realm of festival by stamping the Olympic movement with religious and mystical overtones.

Underpinning many of the ceremonial aspects of the Olympic Games is the homage paid to the 'founder' of the modern Olympics, Baron Pierre de Coubertin. Official IOC publications often contain sections glorifying de Coubertin's role in reviving the Games and many scholars credit him as the Modern Games' founder (Lucas, 1988a; Corral, 1994; Kirsty, 1995). But what exactly was de Coubertin's part in reviving the Games? It appears that by examining this question historians have recently discovered more cracks in the columns supporting existing Olympic ideology. For, although de Coubertin deserves credit for instigating the establishment of the International Olympic Committee (IOC) and was instrumental in the staging of the first modern Olympics, he was, in fact, building on the work of others, including individuals in Greece, Germany, North America and Great Britain, who had already managed to stage 'Olympic' style events, albeit on a small scale. But then, it must be remembered that the first Games of the modern era were themselves minimal in comparison to today's extravaganzas. Only 311 athletes from just 14 countries attended the first modern Olympic Games in Athens in 1896. Over 10,000 athletes, from 197 nations, competed in the Atlanta Olympics of 1996. Table 3.1 shows the growth of the Summer Games from Athens to Sydney.

The Interregnum

Even before the ancient Games ended, in about AD 393, the new Christian religion had taught the Western world that the desires of the body were sinful and this, coupled with emphasis on preparing for the afterlife, was counter to the widespread practice of sport until medieval times.

> The spirit of sport however could not be suppressed forever and thus centuries later, the institution of chivalry was grafted onto the code of Christian behaviour. In this way, knighthood, though only to a limited extent, and only when it was expedient, became a revival of the Olympic spirit'. (Messinesi, 1976: 41)

Once the ancient Games ceased the site at Olympia lay neglected. Its ruin had begun earlier, in the time of the Romans, when Sulla sacked the site, and from this time on continued apace. In AD 267, southern Russians, known as Heruli, invaded the area and defensive structures had to be built to keep them from destroying the Olympic Sanctuary. Later, in AD 426, after the Games were abolished, the Temple of Zeus was destroyed by fire. Swaddling (1980) suggests that this may have been deliberately lit, a result of an edict of the Roman Emperor Theodosius II, which ordered all pagan temples in the Mediterranean region to be demolished.

Nature, too, contributed to the demise of the site. Its destructive forces - earthquakes, floods from the river Alpheus and landslides - obliterated all traces of the once magnificent festivals held at Olympia. Hidden and forgotten, it was to be over 1000 years before archaeologists began to excavate the site and thus amplify the public's burgeoning interest in the nascent Olympic Games revivals. The history of the modern Olympic Games' emergence is a story of independent, but inter-connected revivals, culminating in the staging of the Athens Olympics of 1896 (Young, 1996).

Table 3.1. Modern Summer Olympic Games chronology.

Olympiad	Year	Host city	Sports	Events	Countries/ NOCs	Comp- etitors
I	1896	Athens	9	43	14	245
II	1900	Paris	17	86	19	1078
III	1904	Saint-Louis	13	96	13	689
IV	1908	London	21	107	22	2035
V	1912	Stockholm	13	102	28	2437
VI	1916	Not held	-	-	-	-
VII	1920	Antwerp	21	152	29	2607
VIII	1924	Paris	17	126	44	2972
IX	1928	Amsterdam	14	109	46	2884
X	1932	Los Angeles	14	117	37	1333
XI	1936	Berlin	19	129	49	3936
XII	1940	Not held	-	-	-	-
XIII	1944	Not held	-	-	-	-
XIV	1948	London	17	136	59	4092
XV	1952	Helsinki	17	149	69	5429
XVI	1956	Melbourne	16	145	67	3178
		Stockholm†	1	6	29	159
XVII	1960	Rome	17	150	83	5313
XVIII	1964	Tokyo	19	163	93	5133
XIX	1968	Mexico City	18	172	112	5498
XX	1972	Munich	21	172	121	7121
XXI	1976	Montreal	21	198	92	6043
XXII	1980	Moscow	21	203	80	5283
XXIII	1984	Los Angeles	21	221	140	6802
XXIV	1988	Seoul	23	237	159	8473
XXV	1992	Barcelona	25	257	169	9368
XXVI	1996	Atlanta	26	271	197	10332
XXVII	2000	Sydney	28	300	198	10000

† Equestrian events were held in Stockholm because of Australia's quarantine laws.
Sources: Wallechinksy, 1992; Findling and Pelle, 1996; IOC, 1998; USOC, 1999.

There are symbolic connections between the first modern Olympic Games and their ancient counterparts, though, in reality, they evidenced more concrete associations with medieval chivalry and nineteenth century sport, as practised in England. Admittedly the practice code of chivalry can also only claim a slender link to the Games' regeneration. Certainly, the notion of chivalry, exemplified in the fair play ethic, is evident in contemporary Olympic doctrine. Yet, it was more the result of other determinants, occurring later, that actually served to strengthen any philosophic bond between chivalry and the Olympics. The first of these was the advent of public games in the sixteenth century, especially in England, which helped to bring sporting events more frequently into the public domain. Concurrently, the study of Greece by Renaissance scholars was beginning to shed some light, or at least present one version of the accomplishments of ancient athletes, by glorifying their philosophies and their achievements.

In England, at the beginning of the seventeenth century, under the reign of James I, Robert Dover received permission to promote the Cotswold Games as the 'Olympick Games' (Gibbs, 1898). Their celebration was enduring. Most Whitsundays from 1612 until 1852 they were held in Chipping Camden, Gloucestershire. Their varied sporting and cultural program included running, equestrian, jumping, wrestling, throwing, fencing and hunting events as well as chess, poetry, dancing and music. The games were discontinued because of the anti-social behaviour of some participants, an occurrence that would appal Olympic idealists. However, due to renewed interest, the festivities were revived in 1980 and are celebrated each June (British Olympic Association, 1998).

While the Cotswold Games can be seen as an isolated event in the seventeenth century, in the nineteenth century, sporting events with 'Olympic' connections in Europe and North America became numerous (see Appendix 3.1). Events in Greece, England, North America and Germany are discussed in turn below.

Greece

The ideas and ideals of the Ancient Games have been referred to in literature throughout the ages. For example, Shakespeare mentions them in the plays *Henry VI* and *Troilus and Cressida*. Likewise, Milton notes their existence in *Paradise Lost*. Voltaire, Flaubert and Gide also alluded to the Olympics in their works (Mandell, 1976). Young, in his definitive history of the revival of the Games, *The Modern Olympics: A Struggle for Revival,* notes another, more consequential Olympic and literary connection. 'Our modern Olympic movement - even the Olympic idea - seems to have begun as the glancing thought of a poet. He was a Greek, Panagiotis Soutsos, born in 1806 in Constantinople' (1996: 17). His inspiration for a revival of the Games stemmed from a poetic muse. Later, he put his thoughts into action by writing to the Greek Minister of the Interior, John Kolletis, suggesting that March 25 be declared a national holiday. This was the starting date of the Greek War of Independence, in which Greece gained her freedom from Turkish rule. On this anniversary Soutsos advocated that the festivities should include a revival of the ancient Olympics. The Minister believed the proposal had merit and in turn recommended it to the Greek King, Otto. According to Young (1996: 4): 'It is not wholly a coincidence that our own modern Olympic series began - the opening day of Olympiad I, 1896 - on March 25 in Athens'. However, before Kolletis could take any action he was replaced by Rhodartes, who approved only of the idea of marking March 25 as a national holiday (Young 1996). It appeared that the Greek revival plans were stalemated. However, in 1837, a new direction in Greek domestic policy began the process which eventually led to an Olympic festival on Greek soil.

The King created a 'committee for the encouragement of national industry' to promote and foster commercial interests. One of the committee's proposed outcomes was to be a three-day festival whose purpose was to highlight Greek products and individuals and also to recreate some of the events contested at the ancient Olympics (Young, 1996). The individual most credited with establishing these Greek Olympic Festivals is Evangelios Zappas, a wealthy grain merchant. He based his proposal on that of Soutsos and in November 1859 the first of these festivals was held at the Place Louis in Athens (Young, 1996). In addition to a prize of £10, donated by the Much Wenlock Olympian Society of England, victors received wreaths, cash and other prizes from Greek sources (Redmond, 1981). Both Young (1996) and Messinesi (1976) consider these to be the first true Games of the modern Olympic tradition. However, in a cautionary note they also reported that these first Games were not considered to be successful by their organisers.

The Games were able to be held because of the large monetary contribution by Zappas, who also financed further industrial Olympic Games posthumously through his estate. These festivals were held in 1870, 1875, 1888 and 1889, rather than in an Olympian four-year cycle as initially proposed by their benefactor (Young, 1996). The programme expanded during the latter of these games to include swimming, equestrian, shooting and novelty events. Like their English counterparts a class-based approach developed and the last of the Greek festivals was restricted to members of the 'cultured class' (Mandell, 1976). As in the Olympic style festivals concurrently held in Victorian England (which are discussed in the next section), a strict observance of amateurism appeared to be somewhat hypocritical. The games organisers attempted to exclude the lower classes on the basis that their motives for participation were less pure than those who could afford to compete without financial recompense. The awarding of prizes in fact negated this principle.

England

The birth of modern sport is credited to England, dating from the middle of the nineteenth century. Although at this time games and sports were not the prerogative solely of the British, they have been acknowledged as the society that was most influential in developing and moulding them into their current forms (Messinesi, 1976). It was here that many of sports' rules were first codified and their governing bodies formed.

Formative in this evolution of sport were the Greater Public Schools, elite private boarding schools, where team sports were efficiently utilised as agents of social control. As an important component of the curriculum, sport was linked with religion in a concerted effort to help mould 'muscular Christians'. These individuals supposedly exhibited the positive qualities of both sport and religion. Many of the privileged classes who attended these institutions practiced and preached this ethic even after they left school, spreading it throughout the British Empire. The notion of muscular Christianity harked back to the ancient Greek ideal of a 'sound mind in a sound body', with one major variation: essential to its core was the practice of

Christianity, rather than worship of a pantheon of gods. Thus, in many aspects, it was similar to the notion of chivalry, practised in the Middle Ages.

It was believed that some of the virtues required for sound, masculine, muscular Christian practice could be learnt through participating in team sports. These included qualities such as sportsmanship, leadership, teamwork, the ability to be both a good winner and loser, as well as a work (or practice) ethic. One of the foremost and most famous exponents of this doctrine was Thomas Arnold, headmaster of Rugby School. His message was further spread by two of the most popular books of the day, the novels *Tom Brown's Schooldays* and *Tom Brown at Oxford,* written by Thomas Hughes, an ex-pupil of Arnold. These works chronicled the moral and physical development of a youth, Tom Brown, who exemplified these muscular Christian traits, achieving success through practicing this philosophy and the occasional failure and thus moral lesson when he stayed from this doctrine.

Inherent and central to this model of sport was the notion of 'amateurism' - that is, playing the game for intrinsic, rather than extrinsic rewards. Amateurism was a nineteenth century construct which served many functions in Victorian England, not all of them as noble as the ideals it proclaimed. According to Glasser:

> .. one of the primary and original purposes of amateurism as a category of sports was social distinction, that is, to separate the so-called gentleman amateur from the lower classes of society .. any person who competed for money was not only basically inferior, but also a person of questionable character. (Glasser, 1978: 15-16)

One reason proposed for this distinction and classification was the increasing participation of the middle and lower classes in some leisure and sporting activities which had previously been the domain and prerogative of the upper class. To further rationalise the distinction between amateur and professional athletes it was considered by the elite (and thus sports' power brokers) that the latter, 'whose livelihood depended on his success and achievement', could not be 'imbued with the same disinterested sense of fair play' (Messinesi, 1976: 49). Consequently, character development, as a moral outcome of games, was accepted to be exclusively an outcome of amateur sport, but not its professional equivalent. Definitions of amateurism accentuated that its adherents 'competed solely for the love of sport, or solely for pleasure and physical, mental and social benefit that could be derived from athletics' (Glasser, 1978: 18).

This view of amateurism, formed in England and viewed as being 'pure sport', provided the basis of Olympic rules for approximately the first 75 years of its existence together with a misunderstood belief of the practices of the ancient Games, regardless of the reality of under-the-table payments and government subsidies. (See chapter 2 for a more detailed explanation of amateurism in ancient Greece.)

In the nineteenth century the increasing involvement in organized sport by the lower classes was linked to the Industrial Revolution and its associated changes and regulations in work practices. Concomitantly, other leisure activities were generated.

Some of these pursuits were also associated with movements designed to improve character, though these were primarily through more academic pursuits and often subsidised by wealthy patrons. Dr William Penny Brookes in Much Wenlock, a small village in Shropshire, funded one such venture in 1841. The Agricultural Reading Society was formed 'for the promotion and diffusion of useful information. From the society evolved various classes including the Art, Philharmonic and Botany classes and in 1850 Brookes formed the Wenlock Olympian class' (Furbank *et al.*, 1996: 2).

Its first 'Games' were held in October of that year and were an amalgam of traditional country games and athletics. For example: tilting, football, quoits and cricket were contested. According to Furbank *et al.* (1996:3) 'the early Games sometimes included a 'fun' event, once a wheelbarrow race, another year an old women's race for a pound of tea, although it was not usually part of the actual program'. It is important, in the context of future Olympic history, to note that cash prizes were also awarded to victors in some events.

In 1860, the Olympian class withdrew from the Agricultural Reading Society and became a separate entity. In 1860 the Shropshire Olympics were established which rotated around the county. These were not lone ventures. Other Olympic carnivals were also being organised throughout England during this period. In 1862 John Hulley founded the Liverpudlian Olympics, which were also held during the following two years. In 1865 Brookes and Hulley, together with Ravenstein of the German Gymnastics Club in London, formed the National Olympian Association (NOA). 'The aim was to provide a sports association for amateur athletes. Their first festival, held the following year at the Crystal Palace was a great success and attracted 10,000 spectators' (Redmond, 1981:12). Over 200 athletes entered a variety of events in track and field as well as fencing, wrestling, boxing and gymnastic contests. Gold, silver and bronze medals were awarded to place-getters and a special champion's gold medal presented to the most successful athlete. In response, the Amateur Athletic Association (AAA) (now Britain's ruling body) was hastily formed by a London elite who were determined that British sport should be under their control and restricted to 'amateurs and gentlemen', in other words athletes from the public schools and the Universities of Oxford and Cambridge. The NOA faced powerful opposition, but by its very existence, forced the AAA to open its doors to men from the lower classes (Furbank *et al.*, 1996).

In an interesting portent for the amateur issue, that was destined to be one of the most divisive issues of the modern Olympic Games in the twentieth century, the question of eligibility had proved to be contentious, even in these local contests. When the AAA was formed it marked the first time that the word 'amateur' appeared in the title of a sporting organisation. The AAA continued to grow in influence in England and in 1866 and 1867 it too organised Olympic festivals, the first in North Wales and the second in Liverpool. It was a three-day festival which like previous Olympic festivals was popular with spectators (Redmond, 1981). In all, six national 'Olympic Games' were held between 1866 and 1883 in England. Despite the public's approval these games ceased, however the Much Wenlock festivals continued and are in fact still being celebrated.

In an effort to improve his Much Wenlock Olympics Brookes began corresponding with like-minded individuals who were staging Olympic festivals overseas. Foremost of these were his Greek contemporaries. Results of this communication were fruitful, and, as a result of the links forged between Brookes and the Greek Olympic revivalists, the Greek King donated a prize of a silver urn to the winner of the Much Wenlock pentathlon (Redmond, 1981). In turn Brookes sent a cup to winners of the Greek 'Olympic Games' organised by Evangelios Zappas and first held in 1859.

Brookes should be also credited with being one of the first to attempt to internationalise his Olympic revivals. In June 1881, 13 years before the Sorbonne Conference, which led to the emergence of modern Olympics as we know them, a Greek newspaper reported 'Dr Brookes, this enthusiastic philhellene is endeavouring to organise an International Olympian festival, to be held in Athens' (Furbank *et al.*, 1996: 10). The Greek government rejected his proposal. His next international linkage was ultimately to prove more auspicious.

The Frenchman, Baron Pierre de Coubertin had been charged with organising an International Congress on Physical Education, to be held in his country, and, in this capacity wrote to a number of English newspapers appealing for information which would be of benefit to his planning. His strategy was successful. As a result of his requests, William Penny Brookes replied and subsequently corresponded with de Coubertin, who visited him in Much Wenlock, in October, 1890. At this time Brookes was 81 and de Coubertin was only 27. It was here, at the only meeting of the two men, that de Coubertin first heard the suggestion of an international Olympic Games. 'He wrote in an article for the December issue of *La Revue Athletique*: 'if the Olympic Games that modern Greece has not yet been able to revive still survives today, it is due not to a Greek, but to Dr. W. P. Brookes' (in Furbank *et al.*, 1996: 10). After that time de Coubertin gave no further credit to Brookes or Zappas in his writings regarding the Games' revival.

At the Sorbonne Conference of 1894, when de Coubertin received support for his plan to revive the Games, William Penny Brookes was too ill to attend. He died in 1896, before the first modern Games were celebrated. However his place in Olympic history needs to be properly acknowledged, as should the contributions of those other individuals whose national and regional Olympic festivals were precursors to the first international Games.

North America

Beginning in the middle of the nineteenth century, organised sports and games spread from England throughout Europe and North America. Included in the trans-Atlantic sports diaspora was an American version of the Olympic revival movement.

In Montréal, Canada, in 1842, a sporting club called the Olympic Club was formed. This was significant in that it was probably the first time that 'Olympic' featured in the title of a sporting club. In August 1844, the club conducted a two-day 'Montreal Olympic Games'. These games comprised 29 events, including a game of lacrosse between a white team and a first nations team (Redmond, 1981). However, the most popular of the sporting and athletic festivals of that time were the Scottish Highland (Caledonian) Games, which were regularly held throughout the British Empire and other countries, such as the United States, where large numbers of Scots had migrated. The strongest link between the Caledonian Games and the Olympic Games was that each had a track and field programme. They also served a further function in providing a climate conducive to an international Olympic revival, by proving that athletic contests could be popular and enduring, ironically qualities which the early Olympic Games did not necessarily indicate would be their legacy.

The United States also was involved in Olympic-style festivals. In 1853, in New York, a re-enactment of ancient sports in Franconi's Hippodrome included a segment on the Ancient Olympic Games. Its purpose was theatrical rather than competitive and so, 'the Boston Caledonian Games of 1853, the New York Caledonian Games of 1856, or the inaugural sports of the New York Athletic Club in 1868 and its successors had much more in common with other pseudo-Olympics of the nineteenth century than did these 'Olympic Games' ' (Redmond, 1981: 14).

Thus, in North America, as in Europe, during the latter part of the nineteenth century, the foundations were being laid for an interest in a sports festival with an international flavour. Later, one of de Coubertin's greatest allies in his Olympic quest proved to be William Milligan Sloane from Yale University. At the Athens Olympics of 1896 the dominance of the American team was attributed in part to their tradition of athletic carnivals and university sports programmes.

Germany

In 1779, even before the staging of the American Olympic style events, in Worlitz, Germany, an 'Olympic Games' had also been instigated. Predating this:

> ... in 1790 the revolutionary Republican pedagogues of France, Condorcet, Lekanau and Dannou, saw the possibility of a democratic levelling in the revival of the Games. ... Their idea was to hold the 'Olympic Games' in the Paris Champs de Mars. ... to the military exercises were added ... a number of public games revived from the Greeks. (Messinesi, 1976: 52)

Later, in Germany, the Turner movement similarly used sport, specifically a regimented style of gymnastics, to enhance its political agenda. This link between politics and sport in the Olympics proved to be consequential, even in this pre-Games phase. The fitness of the Prussian soldiers was one of the reasons de Coubertin credited Prussia with victory in the Franco Prussian war. France's defeat in this war is acknowledged as one of the inspirations for de Coubertin's interest in sport and an Olympic revival, as the means to re-energise his nation.

The Germans were not the only ones to whom fitness was becoming more important. In central Europe and Scandinavia other gymnastic organisations were formed in the nineteenth century. While these movements had no direct link to the modern Games they were central to the creation of a pro-fitness climate in Europe. By the end of the last century the world was at a juncture where it was receptive to an international sporting festival which celebrated athletic endeavours imbued with links to the Ancient Greeks. De Coubertin provided the impetus to turn receptivity into reality.

Pierre de Coubertin

Pierre Fredy, Baron de Coubertin (see Figure 3.1), was born in Paris, France on January 1, 1863 and died 74 years later in Geneva, Switzerland on September 2, 1937. He was educated, as befitted a French aristocrat of his era, in a classical Catholic tradition, whereby he learnt about and came to admire, many Greek philosophies, writings and practices. Like many of his contemporaries he was also deeply affected and shamed by his country's defeat in the Franco-Prussian War of 1870-1871. He believed that 'the nation had been humiliated by Prussia's ludicrously easy victory over an effeminate, non-sporting, excessively intellectual French population' (Lucas, 1981a: 22). His fervent wish for his country was that it could overcome this deficiency and regain its preeminent position in Europe. He believed that sport was the perfect vehicle to achieve this end. As previously mentioned he came to this understanding of the physical and political potential of sport, and specifically the Olympic Games, in no small part, through his meeting with William Penny Brookes (Young, 1996).

Figure 3.1. Baron Pierre de Coubertin.

His readings of *Tom Brown's School Days* and subsequent trips to England had previously convinced him that Britain's success as a world super power was linked to the sports ethic taught in their elite private schools. De Coubertin believed that if France could emulate this system, then the nation's former glory days could be revived. This patriotic belief was pivotal in his suggestion that the Olympic Games be revived. He first publicly proposed this on 25 November, 1892, in Paris in a speech at the Sorbonne at the Union de Societies Francais de Sport. This suggestion, according to Corral (1994: 20), 'floundered through general incomprehension, despite the enthusiasm with which the idea was greeted. Two years later, in the same place the idea was unanimously accepted'.

Nationalistic sentiments were not the only driving ideals behind his proposals. His belief in the purity of sport also extended to a wider, more altruistic perspective, whereby he believed that international understanding could be enhanced through athletic endeavours – of the purely amateur kind. This was the core of the meeting he called for June 1894, again at the Sorbonne. The main agenda item was the question of amateur athletics, but its most lasting outcome was the tenth proposal on the agenda, the formation of an International Olympic Committee (IOC). A total of 79 delegates from 12 countries and representing 49 sports associations attended the eight day conference.

This Congress of the Sorbonne was held in Paris from 16 to 24 June, and marks the date from which the Modern Olympic Games evolved. National rivalries were in evidence even at this nascent stage of the Olympics and threatened to cause the conference's cancellation. In January 1894, de Coubertin had issued invitations to attend the congress to all the athletic clubs in Europe and overseas for which he had addresses. The response from both the French and English clubs was excellent, however no one from the Netherlands or Switzerland answered his circular. He had invited no German representatives because of enduring bitterness by the French, an outcome of the legacy remaining from the Franco-Prussian hostilities. However, in order to give validity to an 'international' congress and because the German Turner organisations were the largest sporting clubs in the world, de Coubertin realised that German representation would be necessary politically, to give the congress legitimacy in the eyes of the sporting world. Consequently, he visited the German Embassy in Paris to obtain the names of German sport officials.

Before any German club could reply to his invitation the French leader of the Union de Societies Gymnastiques declared that if the Turners were represented then the French gymnasts would withdraw. This was to be the first in a century of threatened Olympic boycotts. To circumvent his problem, de Coubertin invited Baron von Rieffenstein, a German residing in London, to the congress in an unofficial capacity. His diplomacy placated the French and the Congress proceeded without disruption, its enduring contribution to the realm of sport being its decision to schedule the first modern Olympic Games in Athens in 1896 (Warning, 1980).

At the Sorbonne meeting it was decided that the IOC president would come from the host country and so Demetrius Bilelas, a Greek, was elected president of the

15-member IOC, and de Coubertin, general secretary. Bilelas returned to Greece to inform the government of the honour of being chosen as the first site.

This choice of venue was understandable, if unfortunate. Greece was unstable, politically and financially. As a result the modern Games tradition began, as it was to continue in many instances, in an admixture of political and social conflict. Although the Greek people eagerly welcomed the idea of reviving the Games, the Greek Government was not initially so enthusiastic and consequently refused any commitment to them. The Greek Prime Minister, Charios Trikoupis, decided that Greece could not financially afford the honour and wrote to de Coubertin to inform him of this fact:

> Greece had undergone a decade of extreme instability from 1869-1879 and continued to be plagued by domestic unrest and turmoil. Frequent elections, short term governments and the pursuit of irredentism characterised the politics of the period. The attempts ... to rekindle rebellion in Crete brought Greece to the point of bankruptcy. ... By 1893 foreign indebtedness was consuming 33% of the national income. Trikoupis reduced foreign interest payments 70% [and] decided in addition, that Greece would have to balance its budget, which left no room for expenses for items such as Coubertin's festivities. (Strenk, 1970: 33)

De Coubertin saw his Olympic dream being threatened, and departed for Greece to forestall the collapse of his plans. Once in Athens he lobbied successfully with Crown Prince Constantine and persuaded him to provide royal support for the staging of the Games. King George backed his son's position and in 1895, in an unrelated move, the Prime Minister resigned. This removed de Coubertin's main opponent to the Games. The preparations for the Games could now proceed, albeit slowly, due to lack of funds. Collections were made in Greece and amongst Greeks living abroad to obtain monies essential for construction of necessary sporting facilities. The most generous benefactor was Georgios Averoff, a wealthy Athenian businessman, who donated 920,000 drachmae in gold for the reconstruction of the Panathenian stadium (see Figure 3.2) to hold the Opening Ceremony and the track and field events (Warning, 1980).

The Greek Royal Family welcomed the success of the preparations. They realised that the Games offered the chance to increase the prestige of the monarchy while concurrently arousing the national consciousness and identity of the Greek population.

The Games opened in Athens, on Easter Sunday 1896, and were so successful that the early struggles, which had at one point threatened cancellation during the preparatory phase, were all but forgotten. The Olympic's political legacy had begun though and de Coubertin himself wrote: 'in the case of Greece, the Games will be found to have a double affect, one athletic and the other political. Beside working to solve the centuries old Eastern question the Games helped to increase the personality of the King and the Crown Prince' (Strenk, 1970: 33).

Figure 3.2. Crowds flock into the Olympic stadium, Athens, 1896.

It is no exaggeration to acknowledge de Coubertin as the driving force and designer of the modern Olympic Games. He became its second president, serving in this capacity between 1896-1925. However, towards the end of his life he became less involved in the Games' administration.

> The last Olympics de Coubertin attended were in Paris in 1924 .. Coubertin never saw, and so failed to appreciate, the extraordinary transformation the Olympics underwent in the '30s when they arrived at truly spectacular proportion and were drawn to the centre of international political, ideological and commercial life. (Hoberman, 1986: 44)

However, despite his withdrawal from IOC management and his growing financial difficulties he was not forgotten by at least one prominent political figure. Shortly before his death de Coubertin was nominated for the Nobel Peace Prize. His sponsor was Adolf Hitler, a fact which may have been responsible for the nomination's failure (Kirsty, 1995).

Even though de Coubertin's personal influence waned, his philosophies continued to dominate Olympic philosophy. His ideal of Olympism, a fusion of supposed ancient Greek practices and nineteenth century British sporting ideas, internationalism and peace, is still widely articulated in official documents and IOC rhetoric. Its understanding, implementation and even the acknowledgement of its existence by Olympic administrators, athletes and the public seems to be less universal.

Summary

The developments in sport during the nineteenth century, at both national and international levels, provided the impetus which led to the establishment of the Modern Olympic Games, an event based on British sporting ethics and recalling the perceived glories of antiquity. De Coubertin drew on the ideas, philosophies and actions of others to fashion his successful Olympic revival. His drive led to the formation of what was arguably to become the most famous festival of the twentieth century. Like all large socially constructed institutions the Games have been controversial. Since their beginnings the modern Games have been plagued by a plethora of controversies and problems, some arising from the world's contemporary political problems, but others having origins in the beginning of the Games. These issues are the result of the rules and ideals fashioned by the IOC's male élite at the end of the nineteenth century. Problems which have been ongoing, such as the question of women's participation and amateurism, stem from this original modern Olympic philosophy, espoused in the rambling, and at times contradictory, writings of de Coubertin and held to fast by the IOC in the face of a changing world.

 The IOC has based many of its rituals on a quasi-historical veneration of de Coubertin. This serves to perpetuate a symbolism replete with an amalgam of religious, physical and moral qualities which form the basis of the philosophy of Olympism. But to understand Olympism does not necessarily equate to an understanding of Olympic history. Many of those involved with the Olympic movement are themselves ignorant of the meanings of Olympism and its potential. Hoberman states:

> The theatrical qualities of the Games, and the mystical sentiments they inspire, have given rise to a spectacular overestimation of their value to the cohesion of the world community. As a result, Olympic internationalism has been charged with a salvational mission for which it is unsuited. The idea that the Olympic movement has been an important vehicle of moral influence since its inception is an illusion which has thinned for nearly a century. (Hoberman, 1986: 6)

De Coubertin believed that the Games had a moral purpose, although he acknowledged its limitations. What Hoberman suggests is that Olympic idealists expect the impossible. It is unreasonable to hope that a sporting festival can achieve the universal peace that politics has so far failed to accomplish, and it is misguided, or at the very least disingenuous, to promise such a possibility. Horton (1994: 56) takes this point one step further when he suggests that 'today we cling to the ideals of Olympism as philosophical justifications for the continuation of the Games'.

Appendix 3.1: Olympic Games revivals.

Year	Event	Organisers	Country
1662-1852	Cotswold 'Olympick Games'	Robert Dover	England
1679	'Hampton Court Olympics'	Royal court	England
1790	Proposed Olympic Games in Paris		France
1779	Olympic Games, Worlitz		Germany
1819-present	Highland Games		Scotland & overseas
1830s	'Greek Competitions', Poznan	Commercial	Poland
1834, 36	Scandinavian Olympic Games, Ramlösa	Johann Schartau	Sweden
1844	Montreal 'Olympic Games'	Olympic Club	Canada
1849-1895	Much Wenlock Games - annual	W.P. Brookes	England
1853	Franconi's Hippodrome, New York	Commercial	USA
1859, 1870, 1875, 1888	'Zappas Games', Athens	Evangelios Zappas	Greece
1861	Wellington Games	Shropshire Olympian Soc.	England
1862-67	Liverpool Olympics, annual	Liverpool Athletic Club	England
1866	Olympic Festival, Llandudno	Athletic Society of GB	Wales
1866-1868, 1874, 1877, 1883	National Olympiad Assn. Games (London, Birmingham, Wellington, Much Wenlock, Shrewsbury, Hadley)	National Olympiad Assn.	England
1870s	'Olympic Games', Wrzesnia		Poland
1892	Campaign for 'Anglo-Saxon Olympiad'	J.A. Cooper	England
1893	'Ancient Greco-Roman Games'	Olympic Club of San Francisco	USA

From: Rühl and Keuser (1997), Redmond (1988).

Chapter four:

The Modern Olympic Phenomenon

> As a contemporary historical phenomenon, the Modern Olympics have no comparison. Although regarded and interpreted in relation to the social order and political structure of our time, the Olympic games elude classification in a traditional pattern. (Ueberhorst, 1976b: 248)

Introduction

This chapter outlines the major characteristics of the Olympic phenomenon as we know it today. It examines the organisational structure of the 'Olympic Movement', and its various practises and manifestations, including the Cultural Programme and the Winter Olympics.

Olympic Organisation

The Olympic Games involve some 40 different sports (almost 30 in the Summer Games and 11 in the Winter Games). The administration of any one of these sports is complicated, involving multi-million dollar budgets, and local, national, regional and world level development programmes and systems of competition, promotion and regulation. The Olympic Games organisation has to mesh with this complex, world-wide gaggle of sporting organisations to produce major, over-arching sporting events every two years.

The basic structure of the network of international Olympic organisations is summarised in Figure 4.1. At the centre is the International Olympic Committee (IOC), a self-perpetuating body of some 115 members, with virtually absolute power over the Games phenomenon. The various individual sports are represented in the organisational chart by the International Federations (IFs) of individual sports, themselves generally complex organisations, each representing up to 200 national governing bodies. Also represented are the 200 National Olympic Committees (NOCs). With a few exceptions, neither the IFs or the NOCs have direct representation on the IOC. Relationships between the IOC and these bodies are conducted through bi-lateral negotiations and joint meetings.

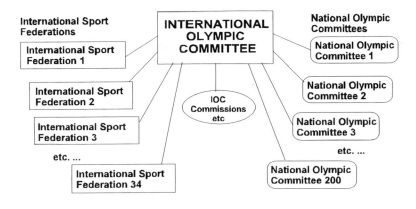

Figure 4.1. International organisation of the Olympic movement.

The International Olympic Committee

Origins

The IOC was founded at the 1894 International Athletic Congress called by Baron Pierre de Coubertin and held at the Sorbonne in Paris. De Coubertin was initially secretary and then president (1896-1925) of the organisation, and for many years the IOC *was*, to all intents and purposes, de Coubertin.

> .. until after about 1908 there was no working I.O.C. Only after that date, and then very slowly, did Coubertin begin to consult the princes, millionaires, and elderly bureaucrats (who thought much the same as him anyway) whose names he had assembled to give the I.O.C. credibility. (Mandell, 1976: 170)

Initially based in Paris, the IOC headquarters moved to Lausanne, Switzerland, when de Coubertin moved his residence there in 1918 (Mandell, 1976: 169, 172), and has remained there ever since.

Terms of Reference

The *Olympic Charter* describes the role of the IOC as follows.

The IOC is the supreme authority of the Olympic Movement. Any person or organization belonging in any capacity whatsoever to the Olympic Movement is bound by the provisions of the Olympic Charter and shall abide by the decisions of the IOC. .. The role of the IOC is to lead the promotion of Olympism in accordance with the Olympic Charter. (IOC, 1995: 1)

The terms of reference of the IOC, as set out in the *Charter*, require it to support and promote:

1.   the development of sport and sporting competition;
2.   the placing of sport 'at the service of humanity';
3.   the regular celebration of the Olympic Games;
4.   peace, the protection of human rights and opposition to discrimination;
5.   the involvement of women in sport as participants and administrators;
6.   sports ethics;
7.   the spirit of fair play and the elimination of violence from sport;
8.   the fight against doping in sport;
9.   prevention of danger to the health of athletes;
10. elimination of political or commercial abuse of sport and athletes;
11. the social and professional future of athletes;
12. the development of sport for all;
13. concern for environmental issues and sustainable development;
14. the International Olympic Academy (IOA);
15. institutions which promote Olympic education. (IOC, 1995: 2)

Thus the organisation of the Olympic Games is just one of the IOC's roles; it also sees itself as promoting a wide range of values and practices related to sport in general and to wider social and political issues. Associated with the mission are the concepts of 'Olympism' and the 'Olympic Movement'. These are discussed further below, but first, it should be noted that the organisation is not just concerned with high ideals: it has a business-like, even commercial, approach to its Olympic 'property'. Clause 11 of the *Charter* states:

The Olympic Games are the exclusive property of the IOC which owns all rights relating thereto, in particular, and without limitation, the rights relating to their organization, exploitation, broadcasting and reproduction by any means whatsoever. (IOC, 1995: 6)

These rights are jealously guarded:

The use of the Olympic symbol, flag, motto and anthem for any advertising, commercial or profit-making purposes whatsoever is strictly reserved for the IOC. (IOC, 1995: 9)

The IOC has not always been financially secure, but in recent years the recognition of the commercial value of the Olympics and its exploitation through a combination of sponsorship and sale of television rights has, as indicated in Chapter 6, provided substantial funding for the organisation.

Membership

The original IOC consisted of 14 men selected, in the main, by de Coubertin. While the membership has since expanded to over 100 (see Appendix 4.1), it remains a self-perpetuating organisation with a somewhat élitist air. New members are appointed by the Committee itself, for indefinite periods, but are expected to retire at age 80. IOC members are deemed to be 'representatives of the IOC' in their respective countries, not representatives or delegates of their country to the IOC. They are intended to be independent and, according to the *Charter*, 'may not accept from governments, organizations, or other legal entities or natural persons, any mandate liable to bind them or interfere with the freedom of their action and vote' (IOC, 1995: 12).

The history of the IOC membership is important for an understanding of its current nature and *modus operandi* (Leiper, 1976). At the end of the nineteenth century and in the early years of the twentieth century, given the lack of the sorts of communication technology which are taken for granted today and the slowness and high cost, by modern standards, of international travel, the successful establishment of any sort of international organisation can be seen as a considerable achievement. To have succeeded without any government subvention is even more remarkable. Such an organisation could only function if its members were independently wealthy and had the time to devote to the enterprise. Thus male members of royal, aristocratic and upper class élites from around the Western world dominated the IOC membership. Such individuals would not have readily thought in terms of democratic or participatory processes; neither would they have travelled third class or stayed in two star hotels. Out of their own pockets, they established an IOC 'style' which was an extension of their own privileged lifestyles, and which has been slow to change. While the membership has widened in recent years, to include, in particular, more former Olympic athletes and sport administrators, the traditional type of member still predominates and, along with them, the élitist and patrician style.

The IOC president is elected for a period of eight years, renewable. In over 100 years of existence, the organisation has had only seven presidents, including de Coubertin (Figure 3.1). Presidents have tended to be long-serving; just four of them having a combined period of office of over 80 years, as shown in Table 4.1. Presidents have been enormously influential in setting the tone and direction of the IOC during their terms of office. In recent years, particularly under the current incumbent, Juan Antonio Samaranch (see Figure 4.2), the office has assumed the status of an ambassador or quasi-head of state, with the courtesy title of 'his excellency' often used.

Figure 4.2: Juan Antonio Samaranch, President of the IOC, 1980 - present

Table 4.1. Presidents of the International Olympic Committee.

Dates	Name	Country
1894-1896	Demetrias Vikélas	Greece
1896-1925	Baron Pierre de Coubertin	France
1925-1942	Count Henry de Baillet-Latour	Belgium
1942-1952	J. Sigfried Edström	Sweden
1952-1972	Avery Brundage	USA
1972-1980	Lord Killanin	Ireland
1980-	Juan Antonio Samaranch	Spain

Critics

An organisation with a profile as prominent as that of the IOC inevitably has its critics. As a non-democratic, non-representative international body, it appears somewhat anachronistic in the modern world, and is therefore particularly subject to criticism for its undemocratic, oligarchic and secretive nature. The organisation's success in recent years in securing substantial funding, together with its power to determine the location of the Games, which can bring millions, even billions, of dollars to successful host cities, have led to scrutiny, and criticism, of its operations.

Some of this scrutiny has been academic and analytical (e.g. Alexandrakis and Krotee, 1988; Krotee, 1988), while some of it, especially recently, has been more sensational in nature.

Lucas (1992: 117-132) identifies five types of criticism of the Olympic Movement, most of it directed principally at the IOC itself. These are: criticisms from a generally left-wing political perspective; criticisms of excessive commercialisation; 'persistent vexation' against the IOC; criticisms of the betrayal of Olympic ideals (particularly the abandonment of amateurism); and criticism related to the encouragement of excessive nationalism - the Olympics as 'war without weapons'. While Lucas notes that the first type of criticism emanates mostly from academic sources (e.g. from Brohm, 1978; Gruneau, 1984; Tomlinson, 1984), the others seem to arise largely in press commentaries.

The most comprehensive critique of the IOC was put forward in the book, *Lords of the Rings*, by journalists Vyv Simson and Andrew Jennings (1992), and in its successor, *New Lords of the Rings* (Jennings, 1996). The tone of these books is indicated by their sub-titles, respectively, *Power, Money and Drugs in the Modern Olympics*, and *Olympic Corruption and How to Buy Gold Medals*. Typical of the accusations of Simson and Jennings is the following statement on the first page of the second book:

> Allegations that bribes have been paid to win gold medals, sex scandals and positive dope tests covered up and Olympic funds diverted to a campaign for the Nobel Peace Prize all pointed back to the secretive leadership of the IOC .. who own and control the Games. They bank substantial profits and live like royalty while young athletes sweat and make sacrifice just to qualify for their heats. (Jennings, 1996: 1)

Of IOC members, Jennings states:

> Some conduct themselves with integrity. Many don't. Some care about sport and its values. Others are more concerned about their wallets. Unfortunately, sports fans know little about them. Individual committee members stay out of the stadium floodlights and conspire to have their disagreements in private. (Jennings, 1996: 11)

In reflecting on the IOC's commercial and proprietorial approach to the Olympic phenomenon, Jennings states:

> If the committee hadn't got the rights to this multi-billion dollar exercise in global marketing locked up and ring-fenced by sabre-toothed attorneys, they could kiss good-bye to their first class flights, five-star hotels, police-escorted limos and fawning hostesses. No more mountains of Beluga caviare, creative expenses claims or free seats at the front row everywhere from Wimbledon to the Olympics'. (Jennings, 1996: 12)

Among the many negative claims made by Jennings and Simson are:

- that information on positive drug tests on athletes at the Los Angeles Games was suppressed (p. 7);
- that bribery was involved in the boxing contest in Seoul in 1988 (p. 9);
- that a senior international sporting official was a member of the East German secret police (p. 10);
- that the IOC manipulates press coverage of its activities (pp. 13-14);
- that information on Samaranch's links with the former fascist Franco regime in Spain has been suppressed (pp. 15, 18-19, 28-33);
- that IOC members gladly accept excessive gifts from potential host cities, in breach of IOC rules (pp. 17-18);
- that Olympic Games events generate controversy and dissent in host communities as well as peace and consensus (pp. 18-27);
- that offers of sexual favours have been used to attempt to influence IOC members' votes in selection of host cities (pp. 39-40);
- that the IOC has 'sold out' the Games to commercialism (pp. 47-54);
- that IOC members are selected on the basis of who will give the President 'least trouble', rather than being the best for the job (p. 56);
- that the IOC has become a 'corpulent bureaucracy' (p. 61).

Overall, Jennings and Simson paint a picture of the IOC as a self-indulgent group of people, prone to political machination, susceptible to personal flattery and over-fond of the creature comforts, especially when provided by others, namely potential and actual host cities.

For a number of years Jennings and Simson were almost alone among the world's journalists in their comprehensive condemnation of the IOC and its workings. Recent revelations and accusations concerning IOC member activities surrounding the selection of host cities for the Games appear to have largely vindicated these lone critics. These recent events are discussed in the final chapter of the book.

Less sensational critics concentrate on more mundane, but perhaps more fundamental, features of the IOC. For example, Alexandrakis and Krotee (1988), argue that the undemocratic nature of the IOC is outmoded. While virtually all other international sporting bodies operate on a representative basis, the IOC continues to appoint its own members on the basis of undeclared criteria, and to insist that its members are representatives of the IOC in their countries, rather than the other way around. While de Coubertin's initial intention was that every country which took part in the Games would be represented on the IOC, as the number of participating countries has grown to 200, this principle has been abandoned. While it might be accepted that a 200-member Committee would be unwieldy, critics question the criteria used to select members, with its over-emphasis on Europe and such idio-syncracies as longstanding members from the 'mini-states' of Liechtenstein and Monaco and three members from Switzerland. The geographical distribution of membership has changed little in the ten years since Alexandrakis and Krotee analysed it, as shown in Table 4.2.

Whether the IOC can, or should, survive in its current form is one of the key issues discussed in the final chapter of the book, concerning the future of the Games.

Table 4.2. Geographical distribution of IOC membership.

Region	IOC members		NOCs	
	% 1988*	% 1998	% 1988*	% 1998
Europe	42	41	18	26
Asia	15	16	24	21
Africa	19	19	29	21
America	20	18	24	24
Oceania	4	5	5	6

Sources: IOC (1998a); * from Alexandrakis and Krotee (1988).

A second major criticism of the IOC is that, in seeking financial independence by means of the sale of television rights and pursuit of sponsorship, the IOC is 'selling out' the Olympic ideal to media and commercial interests. These claims are not discussed further here, but are dealt with in the chapters on finance and economics (chapter 5) and the media (chapter 7).

A further criticism of the IOC is that, despite the responsibility it has assumed for the control of doping in Olympic sports, it has not been sufficiently 'tough on drugs'. It is claimed that, for fear of offending major member nations or particular sporting federations, it has been slow to use its moral authority to demand penalties on offenders and has put insufficient resources into testing. Again, this issue is discussed fully in the relevant chapter on drugs (chapter 8).

Commissions
The IOC operates largely through a number of appointed commissions, or committees, as shown in Table 4.3. While ultimate authority rests with the IOC itself, widespread involvement of sporting and media representatives is achieved by means of the commissions, thus maintaining some semblance of participation, if not democracy. Most of the commissions and their terms of reference are self-explanatory. A few merit particular mention.

Perhaps the most notable of the commissions is the newest, the *Ethics Commission*, established in March 1999 in the wake of allegations of corruption in the selection of cities to host the Games, particularly in relation to Salt Lake City, but extending to other cities and Olympiads as well. The Ethics Commission is 'charged with providing guidance on how the IOC operates in accordance with the best practices of international governance' (IOC, 1999a: 1).

Table 4.3. IOC Commissions etc.

Commission	Functions
Commission for the International Olympic Academy and Olympic Education	Responsible for the IOA, the main function of which is to organise congresses on sport and the Olympics and to promote research on Olympic matters
Eligibility Commission	Advises on which sports should be admitted to the Olympic Games
Athletes' Commission	Membership includes a majority of athletes elected by athletes participating in the Olympic Games, and represents the views of athletes to the IOC
Cultural Commission	Oversees Cultural Olympiads
Olympic Solidarity Commission	Distribution of IOC funds to NOCs, particularly those in less wealthy countries
Commission for the Olympic Movement	Chaired by the President of the IOC, has a wide-ranging remit concerning the future of the movement as a whole
Evaluation Commissions for Candidate Cities	Advises the IOC on bids to host the Games - one is established for each 'Games of the Olympiad' (the Summer Games) and one for the Winter Games. The Commissions visit all bidding cities and evaluate their facilities and capability to organise the Games and report back to the IOC
Coordination Commissions	Established once a host city has been selected, to provide the communication link between the IOC and the local organising committee
Sport and Environment Commission	A new commission concerned with promoting a 'green Games'
Ethics Commission	Established in 1999 in the wake of allegations of corruption in the process of selecting cities to host the Olympics
Olympic Programme Working Group.	Programmes for individual Olympic Games
Women and Sport Working Group	Women's involvement in the Olympics
Sport and the Law Commission	The legal framework within which sport operates
Sport for All Commission	Promotion of sport participation by the general population, adopting the European campaign phrase 'Sport for All'
Medical Commission	Implementation of the Olympic Medical Code, which is concerned with the policing of prohibited drug use (see chapter 8)
Finance Commission	Funding - with Comm. New Sources of Financing
Juridical Commission	Legal advice
Marketing Commission	Marketing advice

Table 4.3. IOC Commissions etc.

Commission	Functions
Joint Mass Media Commission	Television, radio and press - with separate Press, Radio and Television Commissions
Council of the Olympic Order	The Olympic 'honours' medal
Bureau for the Olympic Movement	Development of the Olympic Movement
Pierre de Coubertin Commission	Research on and preservation of the memory of Pierre de Coubertin
Olympic Collectors Commission	Olympic 'collectables'
Int. Federation of Olympic Philately	Olympic stamps*
Int. Federation of Olympic Numismatics	Olympic coins*
Assn. of Collectors of Olympic Memorabilia	Olympic memorabilia

Details of the membership of IOC commissions can be found in the *Olympic Movement Directory* (IOC, 1998).   * A number of Olympic Games have raised a significant proportion of their funds from coin and stamp sales.

Using the Olympic Charter as a foundation document to ensure that the Olympic Movement builds on its core ideals, the Ethics Commission will also:

- promote positive ethics;
- ensure transparency and accountability in the application of ethical standards;
- ensure the standards and rules, contained in the forthcoming IOC code of conduct are clear and applied
- ensure the response to ethical issues is comprehensive, realistic and effective' (IOC, 1999a: 1-2).

Among its activities, the Commission will develop a Code of Ethics and states that it intends to play an active role in ensuring that 'ethical principles are being practiced', including the conduct of independent assessments of compliance and investigation of complaints (IOC, 1999e).

The Ethics Commission is unusual in having a majority of members from outside of the IOC. The membership of eight includes just three IOC members. The external members include a former UN Secretary General, a former US Senator, a former President of the French Constitutional Court, a former President of Switzerland and an Olympic athlete. In view of the serious allegations made against IOC members, the subsequent proving of the allegations and resignations and sackings from the IOC, the whole future of the IOC rests on its ability to restore its moral standing in the world, and the high-powered Ethics Commission is clearly seen as a key element in the strategy.

The *Environment Commission* is also one of the newest, but was created with much less controversy. Its creation signals that, together with sport and culture, 'the environment' is to be promoted as a third key value of the Olympic Movement. Guidelines, and principles for conducting a 'green Games' are set out in a *Manual on Sport and the Environment* (IOC, 1997).

The *Olympic Solidarity Commission* plays a key role in maintaining the world-wide reach of the Olympic Games, being responsible for the distribution of IOC funds to NOCs, particularly those in less wealthy countries, thus enabling them to develop Olympic sport and field Olympic teams (Lucas, 1992: 85-94; IOC, 1996).

The *Commission for the International Olympic Academy and Olympic Education* is responsible for the promotion of the study of Olympism, primarily through the sponsorship of the International Olympic Academy, as discussed below.

Figure 4.3. The Olympic Museum, Lausanne.

The Olympic Museum

The Olympic Museum was established in 1993 at a cost of almost $US70 million. The building, with 11,000 square metres of usable space, occupies a prime site in Lausanne, overlooking Lake Geneva (see Figure 4.3). The purpose of the museum is to be a 'universal repository of the written, visual and graphic memory of the Olympic Games (IOC, n.d.). In Juan Antonio Samaranch's words, the museum is intended to be a 'global source of information on the impact of the Olympic tradition on art, culture, economy and world peace (IOC, n.d.). Pierre de Coubertin had declared his intention to establish a museum to house the IOC archives when the IOC moved to Lausanne in 1915, but little was done until Juan Antonio Samaranch was elected to the presidency in 1980 and declared the establishment of a museum as a prime goal. Some 84% of the cost was provided by 55 individual, institutional and corporate donors. Among the donors were the TOP partners (see chapter 6), such as Coca Cola and Panasonic, Olympic Organising Committees, such as Albertville and Barcelona, and numerous other large corporations. Pound and Johnson (1999) draw attention to the opportune timing of some corporate contributions to the museum fund, noting that: '.. Japanese companies donated about $20 million to the museum project, fuelling suspicion that corporate interests there bought the 1998 Winter Games for Nagano'. They also claim that NBC, which won the US broadcasting rights for the Games up to 2008, donated $1 million to the museum, but NBC is not listed as a donor on the IOC web-site.

The museum also houses the Centre for Olympic Studies and acts as the publishing arm of the IOC. It attracts some 250,000 visitors a year, and in 1995 won the European Museum of the Year Award.

The International Olympic Academy
The International Olympic Academy (IOA) was founded at Olympia, the site of the ancient Olympic Games, in 1961, although the idea had initially been put forward by de Coubertin in 1927. The IOA conducts annual seminars attended by young people from around the world and is complemented by National Olympic Academies in 40 or more countries. As with many Olympic phenomena, the Academy has been subject to much discussion as to its nature and role (Ueberhorst, 1976a; Georgiadis, 1992; Lucas, 1992: 171-182), with one enthusiast even calling for it to be considered the 'Olympic University' (Powell, 1994: 81-95).

The Olympic Movement

The Olympic Games are unique in sport, in having associated with them a declared philosophy, with moral, and almost religious, characteristics, and a recognised 'movement'. The philosophy is know as *Olympism* and is discussed further below. The *Olympic Movement*, according to the *Charter*:

> .. encompasses organizations, athletes and other persons who agree to be guided by the Olympic Charter. The criterion for belonging to the Olympic Movement is recognition by the IOC. (IOC, 1995: 1)

Specifically, the Olympic Movement includes:

> .. the International Federations (IFs), the National Olympic Committees (NOCs), the Organizing Committees of the Olympic Games (OCOGs), the national associations, clubs, and the persons belonging to them, particularly the

athletes whose interests constitute a fundamental element of its actions, and judges/referees, coaches and the other sports technicians. It also includes other organizations and institutions as recognized by the IOC. (IOC, 1995: 3)[1]

The *Charter* also outlines the goals of the Olympic Movement, as follows.

> The goal of the Olympic Movement is to contribute to building a peaceful and better world by educating youth through sport practised without discrimination of any kind and in the Olympic spirit, which requires mutual understanding with a spirit of friendship, solidarity and fair play. (IOC, 1995: 1)

In its web-page, the IOC makes the following statements about the nature of the Olympic Movement:

> Given that the Olympic Movement is a constellation of organizations which are permanent in nature, it generates traditions which, like boundary posts, link the past to the present and provide identity and continuity. Traditions are like roots that provide stability and nourishment: they allow you to grow without abandoning your place or ideals. .. The Olympic Movement uses the activity of sport as the means to achieve its supreme objective, which is no other than to improve the human condition of whoever practises it. .. As the ethical and philosophical code of the Olympic Movement, Olympism can be described as a philosophy of life that uses sport as a means of conveying its educational, pacifistic, democratic, humanitarian, cultural and, today, ecological, principles. (IOC, 1998)

Such sentiments appear to locate the IOC, not just as another sporting body, but as an organisation which transcends sport and links sporting endeavours to such activities as the pursuit of peace and protection of human rights - a role generally associated with the United Nations and its agencies. Indeed, reminiscent of the *Universal Declaration of Human Rights*, the *Olympic Charter* states:

> The practice of sport is a human right. Every individual must have the possibility of practising sport in accordance with his or her needs. (IOC, 1995: 1)

Olympism

The *Olympic Charter* states that Olympism was conceived by Pierre de Coubertin and is defined as follows:

---

[1] Bodies recognised by the IOC are listed in Appendix 4.2.

Olympism is a philosophy of life, exalting and combining in a balanced whole the qualities of body, will and mind. Blending sport with culture and education, Olympism seeks to create a way of life based on the joy found in effort, the educational value of good example and respect for universal fundamental ethical principles. ... The goal of Olympism is to place everywhere sport at the service of the harmonious development of man, with a view to encouraging the establishment of a peaceful society concerned with the preservation of human dignity. To this effect, the Olympic Movement engages, alone or in cooperation with other organizations and within the limits of its means, in actions to promote peace. (IOC, 1995: 1)

The concept of Olympism has been subject to much comment, both from disciples and critics. The quasi-religious or cult-like adherence to the idea is exemplified in the following quotation:

Olympism is all pervading, it is life and the way that life is lived by one person, a group, or a country and is best shown in international relationships. These principles of living are epitomised in the pageantry, panoply, contest and atmosphere of spectator and athlete alike at the celebration of an Olympic Festival.

Olympism enables things to happen for good - but one must believe in it, work for it and allow it to be the driving force within every person. It is easy to believe, for a moment: it is much more difficult to believe, to justify one's belief, to be known for it and to be an example of it.

Many people join in but few lead. Each has to be imbued with the essence of all that is done through study and action - and then, and only then, can Olympism be realised. (Powell, 1994: 81)

The source of these sentiments, a sporting movement, makes them appear grandiose and even somewhat pretentious. How can sport provide a 'philosophy of life'? This is a role normally reserved for religion or political ideology. Should these claims be taken seriously? The temptation is to treat them in the same way that the majority of people treat the claims of extremist cults. But a number of commentators have suggested that the founder of Olympism, Pierre de Coubertin, deserves to be taken seriously as a humanistic philosopher.

Da Costa (1998: 189) argues that, while '.. from today's point of view the unsystematic writings of Coubertin are likely to be seen as superficial, intensely diverse and even contradictory', they can be rendered respectable by being viewed in the context of the eighteenth and nineteenth century philosophical tradition of *eclecticism*. This approach was more inductive than the emerging positivist schools of thought of the time and accommodates an idea such as Olympism, which de Coubertin described as a 'state of mind' rather than a 'system'. The key elements of the state of mind were identified as the relationship between physical effort (sport) and 'eurhythmy' (control) and the search for equilibrium, or the "balanced whole' of body, will and mind' (Da Costa, 1998: 196). Da Costa then seeks to bring the philosophy of Olympism up to date by linking it with contemporary notions of pluralism - suggesting that 'pluralistic Olympism' might take on different forms, depending on 'each specific cultural identity'.

Loland (1994) seeks to explore and add philosophical legitimacy to de Coubertin's ideas by exploring them from the perspective of the 'history of ideas', identifying goals of Olympism, its historical origins and the associated 'unit-ideas' which underpin it. He divides the historical influences on de Coubertin into four. First, the 'French Connection' draws attention to de Coubertin's own upper class upbringing in nineteenth century France and his concerns about France's place in the world, and various influences on his philosophical thinking. Second, the 'Anglo-Saxon Connection' involved the influence of English and American sport, as described in chapter 2. Third, the Internationalist Connection, which, in war-torn Europe, involved concern for international peace. Fourth, the 'Ancient Connection' concerned de Coubertin's idealisation of ancient Greece and its sporting activities. From this Loland attempts to identify 'stable elements in terms of four main goals and to link Olympism to one central unit-idea which seems to found the very basis of the ideology' (1994: 36). The four goals are:

1. to educate and cultivate the individual through sport;
2. to cultivate the relation between men [sic] and society;
3. to promote international understanding and peace;
4. to worship human greatness and possibility.

Loland's conclusion is that these four goals represent, essentially, the goals of western *humanism*. Nevertheless he admits that de Coubertin 'is, of course, not among the strongest representatives of the humanist tradition' (p. 39).

Neither Da Costa or Loland seem to consider the paradox that the unique characteristic of Olympism, its basis in physical activity and sport, is both its strength and its weakness. The strength lies in its popular appeal. The weakness lies in the fact that contemporary Western philosophy is essentially cerebral and is disinclined to take seriously a philosophy which celebrates physical prowess. Indeed, it was the physicality of the ancient Games which is said to have been a reason for their prohibition by a Christian Emperor. This is, of course, in contrast to a number of non-Western philosophies celebrate physical prowess and, albeit in caricatured form, attract popular followings in the West. This suggests that, in the context of Da Costa's 'pluralist Olympism' this Western-based movement may have, after all, more resonance in the East.

While the contemporary world may be ambivalence about embracing Olympism as a whole 'way of life', there seems little doubt that it is seen as a particular way of conducting sport. The moral stance of the Olympic Movement has set it apart from lesser sporting phenomena. In publicly declaring adherence to a set of lofty ideals, the Olympic Movement lays itself open to criticism whenever it deviates from them - an issue we return to in the final chapter.

The Organisation of the Games

Site Selection

The organisation of the Olympic Games is complicated by the practice of choosing a new summer and winter site for every Olympiad. This involves a two-year cycle of location selection, with the Winter Games alternating with the Summer Games, each run every four years. Thus for every Games, a long and elaborate bid process is entered into. The bid process is itself a complex and expensive process, with millions of dollars being expended by hopeful city bid committees. The practice has been for each city entering the bid process to seek to entice as many as possible of the IOC members to visit and view the attractions of the city and its proposed Olympic sites, facilities and plans. In this process, bidding cities are required to conform to guidelines laid down by the IOC (1992, 1999a). An Evaluation Commission of IOC members is appointed to prepare reports on each of the bids for the IOC. Once a candidature is announced, individual IOC members are permitted to make only one visit to bidding cities as the guest of a bid committee, and the value of gifts that may be offered to or received by IOC members is limited to $US150 (Moore and Korporaal, 1998). It is infringements of these rules which gave rise to the IOC crises of 1998/99, discussed further in chapter 11.

At a highly publicised meeting of the IOC - itself a major event for a host city - an exhaustive ballot results in the announcement of the winning city, some seven years before the actual event.

It has been suggested from time to time that a permanent site should be selected for the Games, thus avoiding the continual site-selection 'circus' - but such a proposition has disadvantages as well as advantages, as discussed in Chapter 11.

The site selection process is partly technical and partly political. The technical aspects concern the availability of suitable sporting facilities and other infrastructure, such as transport, accommodation and security, and organisational capabilities of the would-be hosts. Political aspects arise at the local and the international level.

Locally, the question arises as to the extent of community support for the bid, and subsequently, if successful, for the Games themselves. Often a bid is put together by a consortium of business and sporting interests, with only limited input from city, regional or national governments. The extent to which a bid has widespread political support can therefore vary. There have been cases where public opposition to a bid has caused it to be aborted, notably Berlin's bid for the 2000 and Toronto's bid for the 1996 Games (see Kidd, 1992a, b; Lenskyj, 1992, 1994). Once a bid has been successful, continued political and community support for the Games is not necessarily guaranteed, and the question of the public's rights in participating in decisions about preparations for the Games remains an issue (see Ritchie and Lyons, 1990; Haxton, 1993).

International politics inevitably arise in the selection of host cities. The Cold War years saw block voting by western, eastern bloc and third world IOC members, the effects of the long-running South African apartheid issue and boycotts brought about by events such as the Soviet invasion of Afghanistan. The human right records of bidding countries continues to be an issue. These political dimensions of the Games are considered in detail in chapter 5.

Hosting the Games

Once a host city has been selected, the final element of the 'Olympic Family' is established, namely the local Organising Committee for the Olympic Games (OCOG). While financial guarantees for the Games are generally sought and given from city, regional and/or national government, it is the OCOG, in association with the local NOC, which is the body responsible to the IOC for the running of the Games. The extent to which the Games are, in reality, hosted by a *city*, as opposed to a state or national government, varies from case to case - for example, the Moscow Games of 1980 were clearly hosted by the government of the USSR, while the Los Angeles Games were much more clearly hosted by the local OCOG. In the case of the year 2000 Games in Sydney, it is the state government of New South Wales which is the *de facto* host. The OCOG is nevertheless the entity held responsible for the operation of the Games.

The IOC enters into a formal contract - the *host city contract* - with the host city and the NOC, the responsibilities subsequently being assumed by the OCOG. The contract makes clear that the IOC retains a high level of control over the Games, while the host organisation takes full responsibility, particularly financial responsibility, for implementation. Thus the Sydney 2000 host contract states, in clauses 1, 6 and 7:

> 1. *Entrustment of the Organization of the Games*: The IOC hereby entrusts the organization of the Games to the City and the NOC which undertake, jointly and severally, to fulfil their obligations in full compliance with the provisions of the Olympic Charter and of this Contract, including, without limitation, all matters referred to in the appendices to this Contract.
>
> 6. *Joint and Several Obligations of the City, the NOC and the OCOG*: The City, the NOC and the OCOG shall be jointly and severally responsible for all commitments entered into by any or all of them concerning the organization and staging of the Games and shall assume, jointly and severally, the entire financial responsibility for the organization of the Games. All agreements entered into between the City and/or the NOC and/or the OCOG relating to or having any effect upon their financial responsibility with respect to the Games, including the manner in which they share any consideration, surplus or loss relating to the Games, shall be submitted to the IOC Executive Board for approval. ..
>
> 7. *Indemnification and Waiver of Claims Against the IOC*: The City, the NOC and the OCOG shall be jointly and severally undertake to indemnify, hold harmless and exempt the IOC, its officers, members, directors, employees. consultants, agents and other representatives, from all payment in respect of any damages, including all costs, resulting from all acts or omissions relating to the games, including, but not limited to, *force majeure*. Furthermore, the City, the

NOC and the OCOG shall jointly and severally waive any claim against the IOC, its officers, members, directors, employees. consultants, agents and other representatives, for any damages, including all costs, resulting from all acts or omissions relating to the Games, including, but not limited to, *force majeure*, as well as any performance, non-performance, violation or termination of this Contract. This indemnification and waiver shall not apply to wilful misconduct or gross negligence by the IOC, its officers, members, directors, employees. consultants, agents and other representatives. (International Olympic Committee, City of Sydney and Australian Olympic Committee City of Sydney, 1993: 2-3)

The contract specifies only the requirements for running the Games in various appendices to the agreement - in the case of the Sydney 2000 contract, 11 appendices, running to some 350 pages. These provide guidelines for:

- the organisation of meetings, including IOC sessions, and meetings of the IOC Executive Board, IOC commissions, NOCs and IFs and media briefings (Appendix A);
- accreditation to the Games, covering access for athletes, coaches, VIPs, media and Olympic Family (Appendix B);
- transportation for the Olympic Family, including provision, at the OCOG's expense, of individual cars and drivers for IOC members and senior officials, and presidents and secretaries-general of participating NOCs and IFs during the Games (Appendix C);
- the Olympic Village (Appendix D);
- arrangements for the media (Appendix E);
- broadcasting, comprising extensive specification of technical facilities, including numbers and positions of television cameras for different types of venue (Appendix F);
- hotel accommodation for the Olympic Family, estimated to be some 2500 rooms (Appendix G);
- international marketing, relating to IOC international sponsors, including ensuring the availability of 4000 five-star hotel rooms for 'sponsors, suppliers and broadcaster guests and marketing partners' (Appendix H);
- provisions for the IOC Medical Commission (Appendix I);
- provision of insurance cover for Olympic Family (Appendix J);
- Olympic Protocol, concerning a miscellany of matters, such as design of signage, brochures and medals, ticketing and spectator seating (Appendix K).

The Sydney 2000 contract document provides very detailed guidelines on certain matters, such as accreditation and broadcasting, but is curiously brief on other matters, such as the Cultural Programme (five lines), the Torch Relay (three lines) and drug testing (no specific mention, except for reference to provision of facilities for the Medical Commission).

The OCOG is subject to regular review by the appropriate IOC Coordination Commission and, on completion, is required to evaluate its performance in the 'official report' (see Appendix 4.3). The scale and complexity of the Olympic Games is, in part, reflected in the contents of these official reports, which are currently published in three or four volumes of several hundred pages each. For example, the report of the Atlanta Games consisted of three volumes: Volume I deals with planning and organisation; Volume II tells the story of the Games, on a day-by-day basis, from the arrival of the Torch in the USA to the closing ceremony and also examines the post-Games legacy; and Volume III presents the competition results. Volume II runs to 560 pages, with the following 28 chapters (Watkins, 1997):

Prologue

1.	Management and Organisation	15.	Marketing
2.	Accommodations	16.	Medical Services
3.	Accreditation	17.	Olympic Family and Protocol
4.	Atlanta Olympic Broadcasting	18.	Olympic Villages
5.	Centennial Olympic Park	19.	Opening/Closing Ceremonies
6.	Communications	20.	Security
7.	Construction	21.	Sports
8.	Creative Services	22.	Staffing of the Games
9.	Cultural Olympiad	23.	Technology
10.	Event and Guest Services	24.	Ticket Sales
11.	External Relations	25.	Torch Relay
12.	Financial Services	26.	Transportation
13.	Games Services	27.	Venue Management
14.	Logistics	28.	Youth and Education

The seven years between the announcement of a successful bid and the staging of the Games, as well as involving a programme of organisation, construction, marketing and promotion, is also invariably a period of political controversy, cost-blow-outs and embarrassments, uncertainties and set-backs. The organisational 'saga' of each Games is different, although there are some common themes. These differences and commonalities are explored in the case-studies in chapter 10.

Sports Included
The range of sports included in the modern Olympic Games has changed over the years, and continues to change and develop with each Games. Some 34 International Olympic Summer Sporting Federations are recognised by the IOC, as shown in Table 4.4.

We have seen, in chapter 1, that the programme of sports included in the modern Olympic Games has little in common with that of the ancient Games. So how did the modern programme arise? Redmond (1988: 81-82) notes that de Coubertin's experience of various nineteenth century 'pseudo-Olympics', including the Much Wenlock Games and the Highland Games, as discussed in chapter 3, were key

influences on the track and field programme of the first modern Olympic Games in
Athens in 1896. Subsequent developments of the programme have reflected the
interests of host nations, the IOC's view of the commercial value of certain sports nd
the lobbying power of various sporting federations.

Table 4.4. International Olympic Sports Federations.

Summer Games			Winter Games
Archery	Equestrian	Shooting	Bobsleigh and tobogganing
Athletics	Gymnastics	Swimming	Curling
Badminton	Handball	Table tennis	Ice Hockey
Baseball	Hockey	Taekwondo	Luge
Basketball	Judo	Tennis	Modern pentathlon
Boxing	Modern pentathlon	Triathlon	Skating
Canoeing	Rowing	Volleyball	Skiing
Cycling	Sailing	Weightlifting	
Fencing	Shooting	Wrestling	
Football	Softball		

Source: IOC, 1998.

The latest two sports to be included in the Games, due to appear for the first
time at the Sydney 2000 Games, illustrate this diversity of motive. The inclusion of
Taekwondo can be attributed to the influence of IOC Executive Board member Un
Yong Kim, who is also President of the World Taekwondo Federation. The story
behind the inclusion of triathlon, a sport that is less than ten years old, is described
by one journalist as follows:

> According to one version of events, International Olympic Committee
> President, Juan Antonio Samaranch, was watching television at the 1984 Los
> Angeles Olympic games when he saw a triathlon and said: 'get that sport into
> the games'. Mr Samaranch was said to be transfixed by the sight of so many
> glamorous, fit young athletes swimming, cycling and running at will. They were
> the embodiment of the Olympic motto - Faster, Higher, Stronger - and they
> looked fantastic. According to another story, International Triathlon Union
> president Les McDonald used money inherited after his mother's death to fly
> around the world promoting the triathlon cause until Olympic delegates agreed
> that the greatest sporting event in the world could not go on without it. (Evans,
> 1998: 16-17)

Ceremonial

From the beginning of the revival, at de Coubertin's behest, the organisers of the modern Olympic Games sought to replicate the ceremonial nature and religious aura of the ancient Olympic Games, by adopting some of their trappings, but also by adding some of their own (Slowinowski, 1991a, 1993; De Moragas *et al.*, 1996). Among these are the Olympic Symbol, Flag, Motto, Emblems, Anthem, Torch, Flame, the Athletes' Oath and medal ceremonies.

Figure 4.4. The Olympic Flame being lit via the Olympic Rings, at the 1984 Los Angeles Games Opening Ceremony.

The Olympic Symbol is the familiar five Olympic rings, in blue, yellow, black, green and red, representing 'the union of the five continents and the meeting of athletes from throughout the world at the Olympic Games' (IOC, 1995: 3). Despite some attempts to make the link, there is, in fact, no link between the symbol and the ancient Games. It is suggested that, when originally introduced, de Coubertin intended the rings to represent the first five host nations of the modern Games (Greece, France, USA, England, Sweden) - indeed, de Coubertin indicated that the six colours of the symbol (including the white background) included all the colours of these five nations' flags (Van Wynsberghe and Ritchie, 1994). It is even suggested that the original intention was to add new rings for every nation which subsequently hosted a games (Van Wynsberghe and Ritchie, 1994: 125). Regardless of its origins, what is clear today, is that the symbol is the most widely recognised 'logo' in the world, with market research conducted in nine countries showing that, even outside of Games periods, around 80% of the general public identify the rings with the Olympic Games, ahead of commercial logos such as those of Shell and McDonald's (Meenaghan, 1997). Clearly such worldwide recognition has enormous commercial value.

The Olympic Flag portrays the five rings of the Olympic Symbol on a white background. Created by a Greek, Angelo Bolanki in 1912 (Krüger, 1996: 101), it was originally presented by Pierre de Coubertin at the Paris Congress of the IOC in 1914. It is carried at opening ceremonies and is passed on for safe keeping from one host city to the next.

The Olympic Motto is: *Citius, Altius, Fortius*. Created in 1886 by Pierre Didon, a Dominican priest and school teacher, and friend of de Coubertin, it is Latin for 'Faster, Higher, Stronger'. According to the *Charter*, it 'expresses the message which the IOC addresses to all who belong to the Olympic Movement, inviting them to excel in accordance with the Olympic spirit' (IOC, 1995: 2).

Olympic Emblems are designed for each Olympic Games by the host organisation, and incorporate the Olympic Symbol. Such emblems become the logo of the particular Games event.

The Olympic Anthem was introduced in 1958 in Tokyo and is sung at opening and closing ceremonies.

The Olympic Torch and the Olympic Flame are major features of the ceremonial of the modern Olympic Games. While flames were lit at the 1928 Amsterdam Games and the 1932 Los Angeles Games, the ceremony as practised today was introduced in the 1936 Berlin Games, at the instigation of Carl Diem, chairman of the Organising Committee for the Berlin Games (Durantez, 1988: 49). Diem instigated the practice of the torch being lit by the sun's rays on Mount Olympus, in a ceremony conducted by classically attired 'priestesses', then being carried in relay procession to the host country. The lighted torch is carried by a relay of several thousand runners on an extensive international tour prior to the Games, including a nation-wide, highly publicised tour in the host country. The torch's journey culminates in its entry into the Olympic Stadium during the opening ceremony. The torch, usually borne by a local Olympic hero or heroine, is used to light the Olympic Flame - one of the highlights of the occasion. The Olympic Flame burns throughout the Games, and is extinguished during the closing ceremony to mark the end of the Games (Slowinowski, 1991a). While there is no exact parallel in the ancient Olympic

Games, Durantez (1988: 30) points out that torch relay races took place in classical Athens and ceremonies involving lighted torches took place at the Olympic Games, related to the lighting of sacrificial fires in religious ceremonies.

Following the example of Los Angeles, the Torch Relay has now become a money-making aspect of the Games, with members of the public being permitted to pay to carry the torch on part of its journey. Ceremonies and local festivals are held in designated host communities along the route. The relay therefore plays a key role in symbolically 'bringing the Games' to many, often remote, parts of the host country (see also Borgers, 1996; Buschman and Lennartz, 1996; Cahill, 1998, 1999a, b).

The Olympic Athletes' Oath is recited at the opening ceremony by a single athlete, chosen to represent all participants:

> In the name of all the competitors I promise that we shall take part in the Olympic Games, respecting and abiding by the rules which govern them, in the true spirit of sportsmanship, for the glory of sport and the honour of our teams.

The Olympic Creed, attributed to Pierre de Coubertin, states:

> The most important thing in the Olympic Games is not to win but to take part, just as the most important thing in life is not the triumph but the struggle. The essential thing is not to have conquered but to have fought well. (USOC, 1999)

Medal ceremonies in the early modern Games were relatively simple affairs. Medals were presented to the athletes by an appropriate dignitary, generally all together at the closing ceremony; flags of victors' countries were raised and national anthems raised, but there was no victory podium (Barney, 1998). The latter was first introduced at the Lake Placid and Los Angeles Games of 1932. Barney relates that the idea - and directive - came from the IOC President of the time, Count Baillet-Latour, who had seen a podium used at the first British Empire Games at Hamilton, Ontario, two years earlier. At Hamilton victors had simply been presented to the crowd on a two-level podium - at the Lake Placid and Los Angeles Olympics, however, the current practice of actually awarding medals to athletes standing on the podium was introduced.

While the awarding of medals has not been subject to criticism, the raising of national flags and playing of national anthems has been criticised for stimulating a chauvinistic atmosphere which can be seen as being at variance with the Olympic internationalist ideal, as discussed in chapter 5.

Cultural Programme
Each Olympic Games Organising Committee is required by the IOC to organise a cultural programme which should '.. promote harmonious relations, mutual understanding and friendship among the participants and others attending the Olympic Games' (IOC, 1995: 30). De Coubertin's vision for the modern Olympic

Games included a coming together of the arts and sport. This involved not just a cultural programme, but arts competitions, or a 'pentathlon of the Muses' (Bandy, 1988: 166). These were to include architecture, dramatic art, choreography, decoration, literature, music, painting and sculpture - all with a sporting theme. Such competitions were held from the 1912 Stockholm Games through to the 1948 London Games. Their success was, however, mixed: as Bandy (1988: 167) observes, they 'failed to achieve the union of sport and art desired by Coubertin'. So from 1952, the arts have been celebrated at the Games by exhibition and performance only, not by competition.

As Stevenson (1998) points out, despite de Coubertin's aim, the cultural programme has always been subordinate to the sports programme. Since the Barcelona Games in 1992, she notes, host cities have organised cultural programmes which span the four years of the Olympiad, rather than merely being focused on the period of the Games. While offering the potential for greater exposure for the programme, the extended time-period and associated organisational requirements and costs, can also highlight the tendency for the programme to be under-funded, compared with the sports programme. In reviewing the development of the Sydney 2000 programme, Stevenson notes the problem of clashes of interest between official Olympic sponsors and actual and potential sponsors of local arts organisations. The question of sponsorship is considered more fully in Chapter 6. Theatre at the 1984 Los Angeles Games cultural programme has been analysed by Levitt (1990).

The official cultural programmes are, however, not the only association of the Olympic Games with the arts. Over the years, the Games have, for example, spawned a considerable amount of music, as documented by Guegold (1996). Opening and closing ceremonies have become increasingly elaborate over the years, and generally seek to portray the history and culture of the host country through music, dance and spectacle. Watched by billions, the television coverage of opening ceremonies has itself become the focus of research, raising issues as to the extent to which commercial forces undermine the ability of the coverage to convey Olympic ideals of internationalism and participation for its own sake (Larson, 1989; Larson and Rivenburgh, 1991; Rivenburgh, 1991; Gordon and Sibson, 1998).

The Winter Olympics

Krüger (1996: 103) points out that international ice-skating championships first took place in the early 1890s and that the original intention was to include ice sports in the revived Olympic Games. But due to the lack of facilities in Athens, lack of any Greek competitive tradition in the area and, possibly, de Coubertin's ambivalence towards winter sports, they were excluded. Krüger (1996: 104) further relates that winter sports were slow to be introduced because of the tradition of holding the Games in a single city, and few cities were able to host both summer and winter sports. Further, the success of the existing Nordic Games suggested that a winter Olympic Games event was not considered necessary. While ice-skating featured in the 1908 London Games (Onigman, 1976: 227), moves to introduce winter sports into the Stockholm

Games of 1912 were unsuccessful, although they were planned for the cancelled 1916 Berlin Games. Ice skating and ice hockey were included in the official programme of the 1920 Antwerp Games (Krüger, 1996: 104), although only as exhibition sports. Finally, in 1921, the IOC agreed that host countries should organise winter sports competitions as well as summer competitions, and the first official Winter Games took place in 1924 in Chamonix, France. Later the IOC decided that, if the host of the Summer Games was unable to organise a winter competition, then the Winter Games could be awarded to another country. The result of these decisions was the sequence of 18 Winter Games, shown in Table 4.5.

Table 4.5. Winter Olympic Games.

No.	Year	Location	No. of countries	No. of sports	No. of events	No. of competitors
I	1924	Chamonix, France	16	5	13	294
II	1928	St. Moritz, Switzerland	25	6	13	393
III	1932	Lake Placid, USA	17	5	14	307
IV	1936	Garmich-Partenkirchen, Germany	28	6	17	756
	1940	Not celebrated	-	-	-	-
	1944	Not celebrated	-	-	-	-
V	1948	St. Moritz, Switzerland	28	6	24	713
VI	1952	Oslo, Norway	30	5	22	732
VII	1956	Cortina, Italy	32	5	24	819
VIII	1960	Squaw Valley, USA	30	5	27	648
IX	1964	Innsbruck, Austria	36	8	34	933
X	1968	Grenoble, France	37	8	35	1293
XI	1972	Sapporo, Japan	35	8	35	1145
XII	1976	Innsbruck, Austria	37	8	37	1231
XIII	1980	Lake Placid, USA	38	8	38	1283
XIV	1984	Sarajevo, Yugoslavia	49	8	39	1410
XV	1988	Calgary, Canada	57	8	46	1423
XVI	1992	Albertville, France	64	10	57	1801
XVII	1994	Lillehammer, Norway	67	10	61	1737
XVIII	1998	Nagano, Japan	80	14	68	2176
XIX	2002	Salt Lake City, USA	80	15	78	2400

Sources: Wallechinsky (1992), IOC (1998), USOC (1999), Bruce (1999), www.slc2002.org

The Winter Games have not always run smoothly. Onigman, in examining the Winter Olympics over the period 1908 to 1980, notes that they have:

> .. amassed a relatively enviable record of disputes, protests, political posturing, and general confusion .. have been laced with the same kinds of difficulties that have plagued the Summer Games .. difficulties have ranged from eligibility interpretations, choosing referees for a hockey game and granting visas, to embarrassment about the length of women's skating attire and temper tantrums thrown by temperamental participants. (Onigman, 1976: 226)

More recently, controversy over environmental impacts of developments for the Winter Games in sensitive Alpine environments have come to the fore (May, 1995; McIntyre, 1995).

Competing and Related Events

Numerous sporting events have been associated with the Olympic Games, officially or unofficially, over the years, using the Olympic name or image. Other events compete with the Games for prestige, world attention and, today, advertising and sponsorship money.

Unofficial Olympic Games
The earliest example of an unofficial Olympic Games event was the 'interim' Olympics held in Athens in 1906, a small-scale event, nevertheless with royal patronage, which ' .. gave a kiss of life to the Olympic movement, helping to sustain it after the disasters of 1900 and 1904' (Gordon, 1994: 42).

Workers' Olympics
Riordan (1984) provides an account of the growth of socialist and communist workers' sporting organisations which developed in the nineteenth and early twentieth century in opposition to the 'bourgeois' sporting organisations considered to be exclusive, chauvinistic and militaristic. Workers' Olympics, which frequently rivalled the 'bourgeois Olympics' in terms of numbers of participants, countries represented and spectators, were held in: Prague in 1921, Frankfurt in 1925, Moscow in 1928 and Barcelona in 1936. The last of these was aborted due to the outbreak of the Spanish Civil War (see Chapter 10) and was replaced by an event in Antwerp, which attracted 27,000 participants from 17 countries. Butler (1992) describes a similar 'Marxist' Olympics held in Chicago in 1932.

The Paralympic Games
The Paralympic Games, held in each Olympiad immediately following the Summer Games, and in the same location, have their origin in sporting events established for therapeutic and rehabilitation purposes for people with disabilities in the unit for spinal injuries victims in the Stoke-Mandeville Hospital, England, in 1948 (Landry,

1995). While independent of the Olympic organisation, the association of the Paralympic Games with the Olympic Games began in Rome in 1960 (International Paralympic Committee, n.d.; Steadward, 1996).

The Empire/Commonwealth Games
The idea of organising a sporting festival for members of the then British Empire, was first mooted in 1928, following the Amsterdam Games, when the Empire Sports Federation was formed (Gordon, 1994: 130). With a third of the world's land surface coloured pink on British maps, this seemed entirely appropriate. The first British Empire Games, were held in Hamilton, Canada, in 1930, involving six sports and 400 competitors from 11 countries. While modelled on the Olympic Games, they were designed to have a different atmosphere, a policy statement at the time indicating that they would be:

> ... designed on the Olympic model, both in general construction and its stern definition of the amateur. But the games will be very different - free from both the excessive stimulus and the babel of the international stadium. They should be merrier and less stern, and will substitute the stimulus of novel adventure for the pressure of international rivalry. (Commonwealth Games Federation, 1997)

The Games have been held at four-yearly intervals ever since (with the exception of 1942 and 1946), their name changing to British Empire and Commonwealth Games, to British Commonwealth Games and eventually to Commonwealth Games - the Commonwealth being the loosely formed 'club' with Britain and its former colonies as members. The latest Commonwealth Games were held in Kuala Lumpur, Malaysia, and involved 6000 athletes from 71 countries (Commonwealth Games Federation, 1997). The common language arising from the experience of colonial rule certainly reduces the 'babel' of the Games and aids communication, and the games are smaller in scale and are well-known for their friendly atmosphere; however, the historical accident of membership of the British Empire results in a peculiar mix of some 71 Commonwealth countries, so that standards in the various sports are variable.

While the Empire Games were inspired by the Olympic Games, Barney (1998) notes that the Empire Games gave something to the Olympics, in the form of the idea of the two-level victory podium used at the Hamilton Games and copied at Lake Placid and Los Angeles two years later.

World University Games
The World University Games, or *Universiade*, are open to full-time students aged between 17 and 28. They began as a summer event in Turin, Italy, in 1959, with 985 participating athletes from 45 countries. This was followed by a winter games in 1960 in Chamonix, France. The summer games now typically attracts some 6000 athletes from over 160 countries and the winter games 1600 athletes from 50 countries (USOC, 1999).

Regional Games
Various regions of the world hold their own multi-sport events, including the Pan-American Games, the Asian Games and the Pan-Pacific Games. The Pan-American games, for example, date back to the 1950s and now attract some 5000 athletes from more than 40 countries (USOC, 1999).

Gay Games
The organisers of the first Gay Games, which took place in 1982 in San Francisco, originally intended the event to be called the Gay *Olympic* Games, but were prevented from including the word Olympic in their title by court action on the part of the US Olympic Committee. This was despite the fact that, as the Federation of Gay Games (1996) points out, the Olympic title is used by other events, such as the Special Olympics, the Police Olympics, the Nude Olympics, and even the Dog Olympics. The event has been held every four years ever since, in San Francisco again in 1986 and then in Vancouver (1990), New York (1994) and Amsterdam (1998), with Sydney scheduled for 2002. The Gay Games do not impose performance standards on entrants, who represent cities rather than countries. As a result, the number of participants is greater than that of the Olympic Games. In the Amsterdam Gay Games in 1998 some 15,000 participants (42% women) from 68 countries took part in 30 sporting events - and this all on a budget of $US7 million (Federation of Gay Games, 1996).

Single-sport events
The only single-sport event which can match the Olympics in the number of countries competing and in terms of size of television audiences, is the soccer World Cup. However, World championships in individual sports, or groups of sports, such as athletics or swimming, can be as important as the Olympics to athletes involved. Of particular significance is that the Olympic Games practice of involving all member countries in all Games events, leads to participant selection procedures which may not result in a competition between the 'best in the world'. Thus some world championships are seen to provide a higher level of competition in some events. A further issue of potential concern is the question of availability of sponsorship money. There is no guarantee that sponsors will continue indefinitely to see the Olympic Games as the best vehicle for promotional purposes - especially when some competing events can offer a more exclusive arrangement for single corporations.

Conclusions

As the quotation from Horst Ueberhorst, given at the beginning of the chapter, suggests, the Olympic Games are in many ways unique, and therefore defy classification. They are a 100 year old phenomenon with a 2500 year history. But, despite their traditional trappings, they are, in their current form, quintessentially a reflection of the social values and economic and political forces of the late twentieth century. Social theorists are grappling with questions of whether the contemporary world is still 'modern' or has become 'postmodern' and whether it is still 'industrial' or has become 'post-industrial' (Kumar, 1995). The scale, complexity and economic and cultural significance of the Olympic Games place them at the centre of such debates. The following chapters, which deal with issues as diverse as politics, nationalism, economics, feminism, the media and drugs, illustrate this proposition. The broader issues we return to in the final chapter of the book.

Appendix 4.1: Members of the International Olympic Committee*.

Name	Country	Date joined
Grand Duke Jean of Luxembourg	Luxembourg	1946
Alexandru Siperco	Romania	1955
João Havelange	Brazil	1963
Marc Hodler	Switzerland	1963
Prince Alexandre de Merode	Belgium	1964
Mohamed Mzali	Tunisia	1965
Juan Antonio Samaranch	Spain	1966
Jan Staubo	Norway	1966
Augustin Carlos Arroyo	Ecuador	1968
Louis Guirandou-N'Diaye	Ivory Coast	1969
Vitaly Smirnov	Russia	1971
Roy Anthony Bridge	Jamaica	1973
Ashwini Kumar	India	1973
Kéba Mbaye	Senegal	1973
Mohamed Zerguini	Algeria	1974
Peter Tallberg	Finland	1976
Bashir Mohamed Attarabulsi ‡	Libya	1977
Kevan Gosper	Australia	1977
Niels Holst-Sorensen	Denmark	1977
Lamlna Keita	Mali	1977
Shagdarjav Magvan	Mongolia	1977
Philipp von Schoeller	Austria	1978
René Essomba	Cameroon	1978
Tan Seri Hamzah	Malaysia	1978
Richard W. Pound	Canada	1978
Vladimir Cernusak	Slovakia	1981
Nikos Filaretos	Greece	1981
Pirjo Haggman ‡	Finland	1981
Zhenliang He	China	1981
Flor Isava-Fonseca	Venezuela	1981
Franco Carraro	Italy	1982
Phillip Walter Coles	Australia	1982
Ivan Dibos	Peru	1982
Chiharu Igaya	Japan	1982
Prince Faisal Fahd Abdul Aziz	Saudi Arabia	1983
Anania Matthia	Togo	1983
R. Napoleon Munoz Pena	Dominican Rep.	1983
Pal Schmitt	Hungary	1983
Princess Nora von Liechtenstein	Liechtenstein	1984

Name	Country	Date joined
David Sibandze ‡	Swaziland	1984
Henry Adefope	Nigeria	1985
Francisco Elizalde	Philippines	1985
Carlos Ferrer	Spain	1985
Prince Albert de Monaco	Monaco	1985
Kim Un Yong	Korea	1986
Lambis Nikolau	Greece	1986
Anita DeFranz	USA	1986
Jean-Claude Ganga	Congo	1986
Ivan Slavkov	Bulgaria	1987
Anton Geesink	Netherlands	1987
Paul Wallwork	W. Samoa	1987
The Princess Royal	UK	1988
Fidel Mendoza Carrasquilla	Colombia	1988
Tay Wilson	New Zealand	1988
Ching Kuo-Wu	Taiwan	1988
Ram Ruhee	Mauritius	1988
Sinan Erdem	Turkey	1988
Willi Kaltschmitt Lujan	Guatemala	1988
Francis Nyangweso	Uganda	1988
Borislav Stankovic	Yugoslavia	1988
Fernando Ferreira Lima Bello	Portugal	1989
Walter Tröeger	Germany	1989
Carol Anne Letheren	Canada	1990
Shun-Ichiro Okano	Japan	1990
Richard Carrion	Puerto Rico	1990
Zein El Abdin Gadir	Sudan	1990
Nat Indrapana	Thailand	1990
Charles Mukora ‡	Kenya	1990
Antonio Rodriguez	Argentina	1990
Denis Oswald	Switzerland	1991
Jacques Rogge	Belgium	1991
Mario Vazquez Raña	Mexico	1991
Thomas Bach	Germany	1991
Primo Nebiolo	Italy	1992
Sergio Santander Fantini	Chile	1992
Ahmad Al-fahad Al-Sabah	Kuwait	1992
James Easton	USA	1994
Craig Reedie	UK	1994
Mohamad Bob Hasan	Indonesia	1994
Mario Pescante	Italy	1994

Name	Country	Date joined
Gerhard Heiberg	Norway	1994
Arne Ljungqvist	Sweden	1994
Austin L. Sealy	Barbados	1994
Robin Mitchell	Fiji	1994
Alpha Ibrahim Diallo	Guinea	1994
Alex Gilady	Israel	1994
Shamil Tarpischev	Russia	1994
Valery Borzov	Ukraine	1994
René Fasel †	Spain	1995
Jean-Claude Killy	France	1995
Sam Ramsamy	South Africa	1995
Reynaldo Gonzales Lopez	Cuba	1995
Olegario Vazquez Raña	Mexico	1995
Antun Vrdoljak	Croatia	1995
Patrick Hickey	Ireland	1995
Toni Khouri	Lebanon	1995
Vera Caslavska	Czech Rep.	1995
Mustapha Larfaoui †	Algeria	1995
Syed Shahid Ali	Pakistan	1996
Doña Pilar De Borbón	Spain	1996
Ung Chang	N. Korea	1996
Ottavio Cinquanta	Italy	1996
Guy Drut	France	1996
George Killian	USA	1996
Kun Hee Lee	Korea	1996
Gunilla Lindberg	Sweden	1996
Shengrong Lu	China	1996
Julio César Maglione	Uruguay	1996
Tomas Sithole	Zimbabwe	1996
Hein Verbruggen	Netherlands	1996
L'Infante Dona Pilar de Borbon	Spain	1996
Nawal El Moutawakel Bennis	Morocco	1998
Prince Henri De Luxembourg	Luxembourg	1998
Samih Moudallal	Syria	1998
Ser Miang Ng	Singapore	1998
The Prince of Orange	Netherlands	1998
Melitón Sanchez Rivas	Panama	1998
Major General Mounir Sabet	Egypt	1998
Irena Szewinska	Poland	1998

* As of May 1999. ‡ Resigned early 1999.
† Terms end when presidency of Sports Federation ends.

Appendix 4.2: Bodies recognised by the IOC as part of the Olympic movement.

Individual National Olympic Committees - 200

Regional Olympic Committees:
- Association of National Olympic Committees (ANOC);
- Association of National Olympic Committees of Africa (ANOCA);
- Olympic Council of Asia (OCA);
- Pan-American Sports Organization (PASO);
- Association of the European National Olympic Committees (AENOC);
- Oceania National Olympic Committees (ONOC);
- The European Olympic Committees (EOC);

Associations of International Sporting Federations:
- Association of Summer Olympic International Federations (ASOIF);
- Association of the International Winter Sports Federations (AIWF);
- Association of IOC Recognized International Sports Federations (ARISF);
- General Association of International Sports Federations (GAISF).

Appendix 4.3: Official Reports of the Summer Olympic Games.

Athens 1896 Lambros, S. P. and Politis, N. G. (eds) (1896) *The Olympic Games B.C. 776 - A.D. 1896: Vol. 1: The Olympic Games in Ancient Times*, Athens: Central Olympic Committee.

De Coubertin, P., Philemon, T., Politis, N. G. and Anninos, C. (eds) (1896) *The Olympic Games B.C. 776 - A.D. 1896: Vol. 2: The Olympic Games of 1896*, Athens: Central Olympic Committee.

Paris, 1900 Merillon, D. (ed.) (1901) *Concours Internationaux d'Exercises Physiques et de Sport,* 2 Vols, Paris: Imprimerie Nationale.

Peck, F. (1900) *Programme of the International Contests of Physical Exercises and Sports*, New York.

St. Louis, 1904 Sullivan, J. E. (ed.) (1905) *Spalding's Official Athletic Almanac for 1905: Special Olympic Number, Containing the Official Report of the Olympic Games of 1904*, New York: American Sports Publishing.

London, 1908 Cook, T. A. (ed.) (1909) *The Fourth Olympiad: Being the Official Report of the Olympic Games of 1908 Celebrated in London under the Patronage of His Most Gracious Majesty King Edward VII and By Sanction of the International Olympic Committee*, London: British Olympic Council.

Stockholm, 1912 Bergvall, E. (ed.) (1913) *The Official Report of the Olympic Games of Stockholm 1912* (Trans. E. A. Ray), Stockholm: Walstrom and Widstrand.

Antwerp, 1920 Verdyck, A. (ed.) (1920) *Rapport Officiel des Jeux de la VIIème Olympiade*, Brussels: Antwerp Olympic Games Organising Committee.

Paris, 1924 French Olympic Committee (1925) *Les Jeux de la VIIIème Olypiade Paris 1924*, Paris: French Olympic Committee.

Amsterdam, 1928 Van Rossem, G. (1930) *The Ninth Olympiad: Being the Official Report of the Olympic Games Celebrated at Amsterdam*, Amsterdam: J. H. de Bussy.

Los Angeles, 1932 Browne, G. (ed.) (1933) *The Games of the Xth Olympiad, Los Angeles, 1932*, Los Angeles: Los Angeles Organising Committee.

Rubien, F.W. (ed.) (1933) *American Olympic Committee Report: Games of the Xth Olympiad, Los Angeles, 30 July - 14 August 1932. IIIrd Olympic Winter Games, Lake Placid, New York, 4 - 13 February, 1932*, New York: American Olympic Committee.

Berlin, 1936 Berlin Olympic Organising Committee (1937) *The XIth Olympic Games, Berlin, 1936: Official Report*, Berlin: W. Limpert/Berlin Olympic Organising Committee.

London, 1948 Burghley, Lord (ed.) (1951) *The Official Report of the Organising Committee for the XIV Olympiad*, London: McCorquodale & Co. Ltd./London Olympic Organising Committee.

Helsinki, 1952 Kolkka, S. (ed.) (1955) *The Official Report of the Organising Committee for the Games of the XV Olympiad, Helsinki, 1952*, Porvoo, Finland: Werner Soderström Osakeyhtio/Organising Committee for the Helsinki Olympic Games

Melbourne, 1956 Melbourne Olympic Games Organising Committee (1958) *Official Report of the Organising Committee for the Games of the XVIth Olympiad, Melbourne, 1956*, Melbourne: Government Printer/Melbourne Olympic Games Organising Committee.

Stockholm Olympic Games Organising Committee (1956) *Ryttarooliympiaden: The Equestrian Games of the XVIth Olympiade, Stockholm, 1956*, Stockholm: Esselte Aktiebolag.

Rome, 1960 Giacomini, R. (ed.) (1960) *The Games of the XVII Olympiad, Rome, 1960: Official Report* (trans. E. Byatt), Rome: Organising Committee of the Rome Olympic Games.

Tokyo, 1964 Tokyo Olympic Organising Committee (1964) *The games of the XVIII Olympiad, Tokey, 1964: Official Report of the Organising Committee*, Tokyo: Tokyo Olympic Organising Committee.

Mexico City, 1968 Trueblood, B. (ed.) (1968) *Mexico 1968* (4 Vols.), Mexico City: Mexico City Olympic Games Organising Committee.

Munich, 1972   Diem, L. and Knoesel, E. (1974) *The Games: The Official Report of the XXth Olympiad, Munich, 1972*, Munich: Prosport/ Munich Olympic Games Organising Committee.

Montréal, 1976   Rousseau, R. (ed.) (1978) *Games of the XXI Olympiad, Montréal 1976: Official Report*, Montréal: Montréal Olympic Games Organising Committee.

Moscow, 1980   Novikov, I. T. (ed.) (1981) *Games of the XXIInd Olympiad*, (3 Vols), Moscow: Fitzkultura i Sport/Moscow Olympic Games Organising Committee.

Los Angeles, 1984   Perelman, R.B. (ed.) (1984) *Official Report of the Games of the XXIIIrd Olympiad, Los Angeles, 1984*, Los Angeles: LAOOC.

Seoul, 1988   Roh, S.-K. Lee, K.-H. and Lee, B.-J. (eds) (1989) *Official Report: games of the XXIVth Olympiad, Seoul,1988*, Seoul: Korean Textbook Co. Ltd.

Barcelona, 1992   Cuyàs, R. (ed.) (1992) *Official Report of the Games of the XXV Olympiad, Barcelona 1992*, Barcelona: COOB'92 (Barcelona Olympic Organising Committee).

Atlanta, 1996   Watkins, G. T. (1997) *The Official Report of the Centennial Olympic Games* (3 Volumes), Atlanta, Georgia: Atlanta Committee for the Olympic Games/Peachtree Publishers.

Chapter five:

Politics, Nationalism and the Olympic Movement

> Few enthusiasts of élite sport nowadays believe that it can be separated from politics, though there must be many who wish that it could. (Hill, 1995: 1)

Introduction

From their inception to the present, the Olympic Games have been influenced by politics at both intra-national and international levels. Unlike some other influences on the Games, the intrusion of politics has not been felt merely during the period of the Summer or Winter Games, but are a continuing phenomenon occurring, and at times being at their most potent, between Games. Just as other international sporting events are influenced by the ideologies, rivalries and policies of competing nations, it would be unrealistic to expect the Olympics to be an exception and remain immune to external influences.

Although each Olympic Games is unique, some political problems have spanned several Olympiads. These problems have reflected the international relations issues of the day, which, at times, have been so divisive that the Games have been cancelled on three occasions.

Politics

When one talks of politics in sport, it is important to understand the nature of the term itself. Definitions of 'politics' vary, however a common theme is the relationship between power and authority. The origin of the word interestingly dates back to the period of the ancient Olympic Games and is derived from the word *polis*, which meant 'city state', the means by which the Greek community was organised. Politics involves both collaboration and conflict. Cultures must strike an acceptable balance between co-operation and competition, both internally and externally to survive.

Perhaps the most succinct way of describing the political process is 'who gets what, when, where and how'. This is also the most simple and most descriptive definition. It is certainly applicable to the Olympic movement. The relationship between sport and politics is not merely a product of contemporary society but is an ongoing historical association. For example, military training has been closely aligned with physical education throughout history and, as previously mentioned in chapter 1, victories at the ancient Olympic Games were linked to the prestige and favour of the city state.

According to Espy (1979), the link between sport and politics is a strong union for a number of reasons. First, athletes typically represent an organisation which is competing against a similar body. Second, ritual is used to affirm allegiance to that organisation. Third, governments are involved in the preparation of elite athletes and subsidisation of their training and competition. And fourth, because of the institutional nature of sporting governing bodies, there is politics within and between these federations.

Because the Olympics have pre-eminence as an international sporting event, one which is watched in all corners of the world, they have become the perfect medium in which to demonstrate political power and causes. Added to this incentive is the organisational structure and rituals of the Games themselves, although the rhetoric of the IOC suggests the opposite. When Olympic medal ceremonies play the national anthem and raise the flag of the victor's country, when team sports are organised on national lines and when, at the Opening Ceremony, athletes march into the stadium nation by nation, then these practices are overtly creating nationalistic tensions, rivalries and pride.

When investigating the political influences which have impinged on the Games, it is possible to see trends in the types of such intervention. Six categories of political interference appear to dominate the Games. First, internal politics within the nation where the Olympics are being staged have affected the Games. Second, international rivalries, based on either political or ideological disputes, between nations with National Olympic Committees have impinged on the Olympics, as these nations have used the Games as a tool to advance their own agendas. Third, competitors have used the Games as a forum for political demonstrations against their national govern-ments. Fourth, non-participants have used the Games to further their political causes. Fifth, nations with participating NOCs have attempted to equate Olympic success with their social, economic and political superiority (Warning, 1980), and last, the politics within the IOC have impacted on Olympic policy. Each of these forms of political intervention will be examined in turn in this chapter.

Internal Politics of the Host Nation

Even before the first modern Games were celebrated in 1896 this form of political intervention had affected the Olympics. These first Games were awarded to Athens in recognition of Greece's links with the Ancient Olympics. However, the Greek Prime Minister, Charios Trikoupes, decided that his country could not afford the honour and it required the intervention of the Greek Royal Family, specifically Crown Prince Constantine, for the decision to be reversed and for preparations for the Games to continue (Warning, 1980).

The Greek Royal Family welcomed the success of these preparations as they realised that the Games afforded them the opportunity to increase the prestige of the monarchy, while concurrently arousing the national consciousness of the Greek population. De Coubertin himself neatly summed up the political outcomes of the 1896 Olympics: 'In the case of Greece, the Games will be found to have a double effect, one athletic and the other political. Beside working to solve the centuries old Eastern question the Games helped to increase the personality of the King and Crown Prince' (Strenk, 1970: 34).

Paris, France, home of de Coubertin, was chosen to be the site of the Games of the Second Olympiad, and once again internal politics within the organising country threatened to disrupt the Games. Problems began early in 1897. Some French athletic officials were hostile to the Olympics and deliberately hindered their planning. Accordingly, de Coubertin decided to align the Games with the Universal Paris Exposition of 1900. Regrettably, the Exposition's director, Alfred Picart, neither wanted or welcomed the Olympic addition to his festival (Killanin and Rhodda, 1976).

Picart finally agreed to include the Games in the Exposition and with that de Coubertin began the organisation of the Games. A committee was formed and progress appeared to be made. However, because of growing opposition and lack of co-operation, the committee dissolved itself on April 22, 1899, just 12 months before the Games were scheduled to begin. Finally, a member of the original organising committee was appointed by Picart to the position of Director-general of Sporting Contests at the Exposition, thus enabling the organisation of the Games to proceed, although arrangements were still in disarray (Warning, 1980).

De Coubertin found it necessary to undertake a European tour to allay the suspicions of a number of countries, disconcerted by the apparent incompetence of the French officials, who were issuing a constant stream of rules, regulations and memos. In addition, because of the political situation in Europe, he wished to counter German and British fears of demonstrations against their athletes.

Once again, despite all the organisational mismanagement and internal political squabbling, the Games were staged. They ran from May 20 until October 28, although accounts show they were less than successful. Even de Coubertin was quoted as saying: 'There was much goodwill but the interesting results had nothing Olympic about them. We have made a hash of our work' (Killanin and Rhodda, 1976: 30).

Perhaps the most devastating example of internal politics of the host nation intervening in the Olympics occurred in Mexico City in 1968. Mexico was chosen to host these Games despite the fact it was neither a world player in international politics nor an affluent country. In fact, many of its citizens believed that it was wasteful and misguided to outlay such vast sums of money in the name of sport, rather than spending such resources on housing or welfare. Student protests over this issue had become violent in the months preceding the Games, so that three weeks before the Games there were army tanks stationed opposite the Olympic stadium and the road outside the university. Ten days before the Opening Ceremony on October 2, the most violent demonstration occurred. Ten thousand anti-Olympic protesters gathered in the Square of the Three Cultures. Military troops surrounded the square and opened fire on protesters. In the succeeding five hours more than 260 demonstrators were killed and over 1200 injured. The President of Mexico, Diaz Ordaz, called for calm and order as a result of the mayhem and loss of life. There were no further disruptions because of protests and the Games opened on schedule (Warning, 1980).

Disruption at the Munich Games of 1972, because of internal German politics, was also a intrusive force, although not as tragic as the terrorist assault which occurred during these Games. 'Demonstrators wielding iron bars, battled police for three days outside Munich's massive sooty Palace of Justice in what Bavarian officials called a leftist plot to disrupt the Olympics' (Kirshenbaum, 1972: 24).

Montréal four years later, was also the scene of disorganisation, not the least of which was occasioned by the internal politics of the country, especially on the local government level. The main sources of discontent were problems associated with the high cost and construction of facilities needed for the Games

When Montréal first began its planning to host the Games in 1969, Mayor Jean Drapeau estimated the costs at $US120 million. However by 1976 the cost was $US1.6 billion and the deficit alone was $US1 billion. The facts relating to the excessive costs were revealed after the Games, at an official inquiry by the Quebec provincial government, which was initiated to investigate charges of corruption among the official organising committee and officials of Montréal City:

> Drapeau .. and Civic Party politicians visualised the Olympics as a chance to improve their political position and popularity in the city. The Games were, in addition, an opportunity for Montréal to host another international event which would help attract further attention and possible foreign investment to Montréal. Thirdly, the Games would help increase the power of the local French-Canadian ruling elite. Fourthly, local jobs were created for many unemployed French-Canadians. Finally, the Games would express the will of the French-Canadian populace to survive in the face of Anglo-French domination of Canada as a whole. (Strenk, 1970: 27)

There were lengthy hold-ups in building the facilities. Obtaining money from the federal government for construction took much longer than anticipated, putting schedules months behind and necessitating 24 hour workdays at double and triple pay. Contracts were issued without bidding. Drapeau aggravated this situation by volunteering Montréal as the site of the 1974 world bicycling championships. This meant that the Olympic velodrome had to be completed in less than one year instead of the projected three, and was in fact not completed in time. Because of administrative problems and ineptitude similar facilities were not completed in time for the Olympic Games themselves. The most noticeable of the unfinished facilities was the main Olympic stadium. Protests by Montréal citizens occurred before and during the Games because:

> .. the city lacked adequate housing, a water filtration plant, and even enough money to pay striking municipal employees. Drapeau countered such criticism with statements such as: 'The future will be the judge. Every time that a man tries to do something that will last beyond his own time, he has troubles. At the time, I'm sure that no one understood the significance of the Eiffel Tower'. (Strenk, 1970: 27)

Figure 5.1. Lavish facilities provided for the Montréal Games, 1976.

In spite of all the disruptions, the 1976 Games began as scheduled. Unfortunately they were to become the victim of more political disruptions from other sources.

It is likely that, as the Games continue to expand in size and scope, more intra-national opposition to them will occur, because of the ever increasing costs of staging such an event. This form of political intervention has, to a degree, been beyond the scope of the IOC to control. The legal responsibility for staging a Games is with the city that applied for, and was, awarded them by the IOC. If a government has endeavoured to gain international prestige because of building facilities beyond its financial means then it appears on the surface that it must bear the ultimate responsibility for this type of political interference within the Olympic movement. However, perhaps this is too simplistic a viewpoint. If a city did not project magnificent, state of the art facilities and infrastructure upgrades it is unlikely that it would be awarded the Games in the first place. The nature of the bidding process to host an Olympic Games encourages massive government expenditure, which many nations can ill afford, financially or politically. Lack of national support within the host country has the potential to disrupt, and even cancel, the Games but, in the case of Mexico City, the results were more tragic, due to the loss of life.

The problem of host nation/city politics continues: witness the case of Atlanta in 1996. As a result of the Atlanta Committee for the Olympic Games (ACOG) having to raise funds primarily from private sources, commercialism at the Games was rampant. IOC President, Juan Antonio Samaranch, indicated that, in future, it would be necessary for bidding cities to ensure they had the financial support of their national government. This may not necessarily equate with the support of the population. Indeed the bidding process for the 2004 Games resulted in bombs being exploded in Stockholm by protesters opposed to that city's bid, a factor which may have influenced the IOC's decision not to award that city the Games. Instead they were awarded to Athens, site of the first modern Olympic Games.

Opposing Political Ideologies

From the 1894 Sorbonne Congress to the present, and seemingly with no chance of cessation, nations with opposing political ideologies and domestic and foreign policies, have used the Olympic Games as a political lever against their adversaries. The prestige associated with a nation competing at the Games, and likewise the loss of prestige accredited to a Games because of boycotts, has been a weapon applied on many occasions. It is not the ideals of, or opposition to, the Games themselves that have resulted in this type of discord, but the success, prestige and publicity given to the Olympic movement which has exacerbated the process.

Even the conception of the modern Olympics was not without political machinations. As noted in chapter 3, de Coubertin's initial dream of reviving the Games was linked to his wish for France to gain prestige through sport after its defeat in 1871 in the Franco-Prussian War. His trips to England and discussions with William Penny Brookes led him to realise the values of the 'muscular Christianity' ideals practised in English public schools, such as Rugby, and strengthened his belief that sport was educative and had the potential to physically and mentally enhance an individual and a nation. He saw a re-creation of the Ancient Olympics as the medium by which this would occur. The 1894 International Congress of the Sorbonne was the forum where the revival was instigated, although reactivating the Olympics was originally of secondary importance to the question of the promotion of the amateur ideal.

The Olympic Games of 1916 were awarded to Berlin during the Stockholm Games of 1912. The political climate of Europe was tense and this pressure continued to magnify until 1914, when war was declared. The Germans, like their opponents, felt that the war would be short and did not withdraw their offer of, or cease their preparations for, staging the Games. With the continuation of hostilities pressure was exerted by the Allied powers on the IOC and especially on de Coubertin to move the Games either to the United States or Switzerland. De Coubertin resisted such moves until May 4, 1915, when it became known that the German forces had used chlorine gas in the trenches of the eastern front. At this stage the IOC announced that the Games could not be shifted to an alternate site and would, in fact, be cancelled. Thus, for the first time in the history of the modern Games, international politics had influenced the Games to the ultimate extent possible, their cancellation.

The Games of the XII Olympiad, held in Berlin some 20 years later, were also besieged by problems stemming from political and ideological differences, initially involving the issue of discrimination against Jews in Germany under Hitler's regime and escalating from that into a question of a massive boycott to express displeasure at the entire Nazi doctrine.

Hitler assumed power in January 1933, after Berlin had been awarded the 1936 Games. Although originally opposed to the idea of Germany hosting the Games, he quickly perceived that staging the Games would provide a unparalleled opportunity to present Nazi propaganda to the entire world. The question soon became not 'did Germany want the Games?', but did the rest of the world want Germany to host them?

Hitler's domestic political agenda had included the purging of Jews from all positions of power and influence and this included removal of world class athletes from sports clubs and organisations. These athletes were officially declared ineligible for competition within Germany.

In response to this German policy an international boycott of Nazi goods and services was organised, as well as a proposal to move the Games to an alternate site. This movement failed when the IOC reaffirmed its decision to hold the Games in Berlin at its meeting on June 7, 1933. However, to placate the protesters, its president, Count Baillet-Latour, demanded that the Nazis guarantee to uphold to the letter every IOC rule and regulation and, in addition, pledge in writing that there would be no discrimination against athletes on the grounds of race or religion.

Those lobbying against the Germans hosting the Games now changed their strategy and focussed their energies in the direction of organising an Olympic boycott. In 1933 the Amateur Athletic Union (AAU), the principal sports federation in the United States, voted to boycott the Games unless the treatment afforded Jews was improved. It sent its president, Avery Brundage, to visit Germany in order to make a firsthand evaluation of the situation. The Germans accordingly announced that five Jews, including Helen Meyer, Gretel Bergmann, and Rudi Ball, had been selected as candidates for the German Olympic team. Brundage was given VIP treatment on his fact-finding mission, and, upon his return, he stated that he did not notice any difference between the treatment of Jews and other Germans. In light of this evaluation the United States accepted the IOC invitation to the Games (Warning, 1980).

The following year, 1935, General Charles Sherrill, an American IOC member visited Germany and was also favourably impressed by the Nazi regime. Upon his return he stated:

I went to Germany for the purpose of getting at least one Jew on the Germany Olympic team and I feel that my job is finished. As to obstacles placed in the way of Jewish athletes or any others trying to reach Olympic ability, I would have no more business discussing that in Germany than if the Germans attempted to discuss the Negro situation in the American South or the treatment of the Japanese in California. (Kass, 1976: 227)

In 1935 Germany adopted the Nuremberg Laws. These contained a definition of German citizenship that excluded those of Jewish or mixed blood. This automatically excluded all Jews from contention for the German Olympic team. Adverse reaction to these laws was world wide. In New York 35,000 people demonstrated in favour of a boycott. The American Federation of Labor supported the boycott, as did the International Worker's Sport Movement. A 'Committee to Oppose the Olympic Games' was formed in Prague. Russia and Spain announced that they would not participate in the Games. The AAU however stood by its previous decision and voted again to send the United States team to Germany. Brundage, a believer in the fallacy that sport and politics could and should be kept separate, was quoted as saying:

.. frankly, I don't think we have any business meddling in this question. We are a sports group, organised and pledged to promote clean competition and sportsmanship. When we let politics, racial questions, religious or social disputes creep into our actions, we're in for trouble and plenty of it. (Kass, 1976: 229)

And on another occasion he declared:

.. regardless of what country the Olympic Games are held, there will be some group, some religion, or some race that can register a protest because of the action of the government of that country, past or present. (Kass, 1976: 227)

To compensate for the growing world opposition to their hosting the Olympics the Nazis spared no effort or expense in their preparations, both in regard to the facilities and the vast amount of propaganda issued. These preparations successfully overrode the efforts of those trying to abort the Games and consequently the Games of the XII Olympiad were held as scheduled.

The IOC awarded the next Games to Tokyo, Japan. This was regarded by many as an important step in IOC policy, as it was the first occasion that the Games were to be held in an Asian country. However, by 1938, the IOC was in some doubt as to

...sdom of its decision because the Sino-Japanese war had begun. When the IOC could not receive assurances from the Japanese Olympic Committee that the Games would be unaffected by the hostilities they withdrew their offer to the city of Tokyo to host the Games and offered them instead to Helsinki, Finland. The Finns accordingly began their preparations, however in May 1940, the IOC President, Baillet-Latour, issued a statement saying that these Games would have to be cancelled because of World War II. Once again international differences caused the cancellation of the Games.

The Games of the XIII Olympiad, awarded to London, were likewise affected because of the continuation of hostilities and so it was the next Games, those of the XIV Olympiad, once again accorded to London, that were the first Games to be celebrated after a 12 year moratorium.

The choice of London as a site for these Games was controversial from the beginning, both internationally and within Great Britain. London was considered by many to be a poor choice because of the damage the city had suffered as a result of German bombing during the War and strained economic conditions within the country. Also, because of her position as one of the Allied powers of World War II, giving the Games to this city was seen by some as a positive backing of the Allies by the IOC, a supposedly non-political body.

The question of Soviet participation in the Olympic movement was beginning to generate debate in the years immediately preceding these Games. Correspondence between IOC officials Brundage and IOC President Edstrom indicates their reluctance to affiliate the USSR into the necessary international federations. Brundage passed on the sentiments of a colleague in his letter:

> My own guess is that the real object of the Russians is to humiliate the West. .. every time they force a Federation to break its own rules in order to let them compete, Russian prestige is increased and Western prestige is decreased. The trouble at the moment .. is that about half the countries don't want to annoy Russia, and any country which is anxious to obtain a World Championship or a World Congress is reluctant to annoy the Eastern bloc'. (Espy, 1979: 28)

The issue was easily solved when the Soviets failed to form a national Olympic Committee. Under the IOC charter, this meant that they were ineligible to participate. They did, however, send observers to the Games. The question of German and Japanese participation also was not a problem as no national Olympic Committees had existed in either country since the war.

Incidents of international rivalry manifested themselves on numerous occasions before and during the Games. In 1947 several members of the United States Olympic Committee suggested that it would be a nice gesture for the United States to feed all the 1948 Olympic athletes. Not everyone shared this sentiment.

The Soviet magazine *Ogonyk*, interpreting the gesture as provocative, denounced the offer as a 'Pork Trick', made to bring profits to American capitalists on their 'canned pork' and to provide an excuse in case the United States team was defeated. The magazine predicted that the United States track and field and swimming teams would lose and argued that by offering food to European athletes and United States could later claim, if it lost, that the feed had enhanced the physical power of the European athletes. (Espy, 1979: 30)

Another incident at these Olympics, caused because of international rivalry, occurred when an Italian reporter accused the British government of barring him from entering the country to cover the Games because he was a Communist. The official British reply was that 'after careful interrogation they had determined he was a possible saboteur' (Espy, 1979: 30). In addition, Rumania withdrew from competition because of the failure of the Olympic Organising Committee to include Russians and East Germans as part of its membership.

The 1952 Games were awarded to Helsinki as compensation for the cancelled 1940 Games which they were to have hosted. These Games were held at the height of the Cold War and this, as with all previous international conflicts, created problems both before and during the Games. The key issue was the question of recognition of a team from Germany

Before World War II, Germany had one national Olympic Committee, however, because of the post-war split of the country, committees were formed in both East and West Germany. Subsequently each approached the IOC for recognition. Under IOC regulations only one committee from any country could be recognised as the Olympic representative of that country. Each of the German states had only received recognition from a smattering of countries and neither from the United Nations. Rivalry between the two Germanies was intense. The IOC decided to give provisional recognition to the West German committee, although its Soviet delegate insisted that, as there were two states, there should be two separate committees. As a final compromise an agreement was drawn up wherein the two sides would attempt to form a single team, and the formation of a German Olympic Committee would be left to the Germans themselves. The East Germans refused to take part in this compromise, and, as a result, no East Germans participated in the Games. Similar to this recognition problem with the Germans was the question of whether to recognise Communist China or Nationalist China (Warning, 1980).

Since 1936, a tradition had been established whereby an Olympic torch had been ignited in Olympia, Greece, and carried by a relay of runners to the site of a Games, lighting the Olympic Flame which would burn for the duration of the Games. The most direct route for the torch bearers to Helsinki would have necessitated travelling through a section of Estonia. Requests were made to the Soviet government to allow passage through this Soviet territory. All requests were refused and consequently the Finnish organisers had to route the runners over the Arctic Circle, through Sweden to Finland and Helsinki via the southern corner of the country, a far more circuitous route. The supposed reasons for the Soviets' actions was that Estonia, which had only been a Soviet territory since 1944, had not been adequately integrated into the Soviet system and consequently was not open for world view (Warning, 1980).

Another established Olympic tradition broken at these Games concerned the Olympic Village. The USSR participated in the Olympics for the first time in these Games, and were allowed to set up their own separate encampment for their officials and athletes instead of sharing facilities with other athletes, a system which had been established at Los Angeles during the 1932 Games and perpetuated ever since.

Originally the Soviets had planned to fly their team in from Leningrad each day. They rescinded this decision contingent upon the agreement that the Eastern bloc countries could be housed in a separate Olympic village. The Finns acceded to this request and converted what was meant to be the women's quarters, at Andinum, for the exclusive use of the athletes from Bulgaria, Czechoslovakia, Hungary, the USSR, Poland, Rumania, and the non-competing People's Republic of China. At first Communist athletes maintained a complete isolationist policy, however as the Games progressed, interaction with Western athletes became more commonplace.

The 1956 Games were awarded to Melbourne, Australia, and were held in a period of great international tension. Two major world political crises, one in Hungary and the other around the Suez Canal had brought the world to the brink of war. The Suez region has historically been a troubled area and the year 1956 was no exception. In early October, Egypt seized the Suez Canal, the main shipping route between Europe and the Pacific Ocean. Israel counterattacked and was aided in her efforts by Great Britain and France. Egyptian attitude towards the Olympic Games in the light of these circumstances was that 'nations guilty of cowardly aggression should be expelled from the Games' (Killanin and Rodda, 1976: 69). When no action was forthcoming from the IOC, Egypt withdrew from the Games in protest. Lebanon, joined in the boycott. Avery Brundage, the President of the IOC, commented, 'we are dead against any country using the Games for political purposes, whether right or wrong. The Olympics are competitions between individuals, not nations' (Killanin and Rhodda, 1976: 69).

The Hungarian situation also resulted in an Olympic boycott. Mass unrest in Poland and Hungary developed during October, 1956 into the most significant revolt against the regime in Moscow since the defection of Marshall Tito of Yugoslavia. To counteract this the Soviets sent massive amounts of troops and equipment into Hungary. Yet, the revolts continued and on October 25, the Soviets fired on unarmed crowds in Budapest. In spite of this, the dissension continued and, in retaliation, on November 4, Soviet forces attacked Budapest, crushing all opposition.

When the revolution began, the Hungarian Olympic team was gathered in Budapest for training. They were scheduled to leave for Australia on October 28, in order to have three weeks in Melbourne before the Games to acclimatise. On October 23 many of the athletes marched in the massive demonstrations, and the Hungarian officials fearing reprisals, endeavoured to gather the team together. It took almost two days for the team to assemble.

Many of the athletes had been involved in the fighting and, as they came to the hotel, many without their baggage they told us how they had manned machine guns and barricades, fought secret police and Soviet troops and helped carry wounded. Our faces were flushed with pride and pleasure as we went to Prague where we were to leave by air for Australia. The Czechs put us up in a boarding school... the atmosphere was explosive and only the warning from Czech authorities that we could not cross the border from Hungary kept many from returning. We were told the border was closed. .. Five days after our arrival in Prague our team leader Gyula Hegyi. .. who is head of the Nationalist Sports Council called us together and told us emotionally, 'We must go to the Games'. (*Sports Illustrated*, 1956: 22)

While the athletes were in Prague, 17 of their coaches, trainers, masseurs, and technicians had left Odessa on October 8, on the Russian ship 'Gruzia' with the Russian team bound for Melbourne. At first, relations were friendly, however, as a knowledge of early events in the revolution were known there was a certain distance between the athletes from the two nations. One Hungarian commented to *Sports Illustrated*: 'there was no clash between Hungarians and Russians but this was due to the fact that at no stage of the voyage were we aware of what really happened in Hungary' (*Sports Illustrated*, 1956: 23). The Soviets had monitored incoming news broadcasts and only filtered through certain information.

The main body of Hungarian athletes were not involved in this situation as they flew from Prague to Melbourne. Here they were greeted by hundreds of ex-patriot Hungarians who had settled in the city. These crowds carried armfuls of flowers and the Hungarian flag of green, red, and white from which the Communist symbol was conspicuously absent but to which black streamers had been attached.

Like their counterparts on board ship, these Hungarian athletes had been so closely supervised in Prague that no team members knew of the latter attacks on Budapest until their arrival in Melbourne. After some indecision the athletes chose to compete in the Games, however, not under the flag of 'Red Hungary'. Other nations took more drastic measures. The Dutch Olympic team withdrew in protest and their Olympic Committee donated 100,000 guilders to Hungarian relief. The Spanish team also withdrew rather than compete against the Soviets. The Swiss team withdrew then reconsidered. On attempting to re-enter the Games however they found that it was too late to reapply (Toohey, 1990).

For the first recorded time in Olympic history, open fighting between athletes occurred during the competition. It occurred between Hungarian and Soviet athletes and was, in fact, a manifestation of the political situation in Hungary. It took place during a water-polo game between the two countries.

The game was a minute old when Russia's Peter Mchvenieradze hammer-locked a Hungarian player and wound up in the penalty box. With the battle continuing below the water and belt lines, the Hungarians gained a 2-0 lead by half-time. Just after the second half began, a Russian smacked Hungary's Antol

Bolvari in the right eye and the ball was all but disregarded as fighting broke out all over the pool. Like barracudas, the contestants flailed at one another underwater, sending up whirlpool proof of titanic struggles beneath.

The closing whistle was still reverberating when the Russian back, Valantine Prokopov, slammed an elbow into the eye of the Hungarian centre, Irwin Zador, opening a deep gash. Zador struggled from the water and into the arms of a teammate, Hungarian born spectators rushed towards the pool for revenge, the Russian team formed a protective knot, and the police quickly stepped in to enforce peace.

Miklos Maryin, youngest of the Hungarian poloists, decided: 'They play their sports just as they conduct their lives, with brutality and disregard for fair play'. But Maryin and his teammates had the consolation of victory: Hungary 4, Russia 0. (*Sports Illustrated*, 1956: 23)

While the Olympic procedures intensify existing rivalries between competing nations, it is the media and most especially the participating nations which must also take a fair share of the blame. The press embellishes stories, and, by concentrating on national rivalries, they accentuate and may exacerbate existing political conditions. Indirectly, the media has aided political intervention in the Games because of its extensive coverage of and fascination with the Olympics throughout the world. If there was not such an widespread publicising of the Games then governments, groups and individuals would not use the Games as a means of exposure and publicity for their causes.

Primarily the responsibility for political interference in the Games must rest with the participating nations themselves, for it is the federal governments of participating NOCs and their policies which have provided the greatest number of instances of politics within the Olympic movement. Nations have evidenced this form of interference within the competitions themselves, or beforehand to politically embarrass others. They have used the Olympic movement as a form of leverage against nations whose internal policies may be ideologically opposed to theirs. Most notable instances of this type of interference have been those involving the expulsion of South Africa and Rhodesia from the Olympic Movement.

During the 1960s many countries had curtailed their sporting links with South Africa as well as Rhodesia because of their apartheid policies. In 1968 they were formally suspended from the Olympic movement for a number of reasons, one of which was that apartheid contravened Section 3 of the Olympic Charter, which forbade discrimination on the basis of race.

Despite their expulsion from the Olympic movement, and for a period of time following this, South African rugby and cricket teams continued to compete overseas in defiance of a United Nations General Assembly request to all its members to suspend sporting link with the country (United Nations, 1968: 22). By 1976, however, South Africa was almost entirely ostracised by sanctioned sporting bodies. Yet, not all countries adhered to the UN request, for example a New Zealand rugby team disregarded world opinion and travelled to South Africa to compete against the South Africa team the Springboks.

As a result of this tour, African countries refused to participate in the Montreal Games unless New Zealand was expelled. According to Ludwig (1976: 6), '.. the African countries found in the boycott issue, the only area of agreement likely to unite Kenya, Uganda, Zambia and Zaire'.

It was under the auspices of the Supreme Council for Sport in Africa (SCSA) the IOC was asked to ban New Zealand. However, the IOC supported New Zealand's participation in the Games, based on the fact that rugby was not an Olympic sport and, as such, the New Zealand Rugby Federation, which sanctioned the tour, had no direct affiliation with the New Zealand Olympic Committee. New Zealand maintained its right to participate in the Games, refusing to withdraw and, as a consequence, 30 African and Middle Eastern countries boycotted the Games (Warning, 1980).

The effects of the boycott have been widely debated. While many of the boycotting nations were small and their athletes had little chance of success, the large number of countries which were united on the issue demonstrated the degree of solidarity regarding the ostracising of South Africa, and the increasing opposition to apartheid.

The notion of the boycott as an efficient and forceful political weapon was again utilised in the following Olympiad. This time it was the United States which instigated a boycott to embarrass the Soviet Union, the country in whose capital Moscow the Games were to be staged.

In December 1979, the Soviet Union invaded Afghanistan. In response, Jimmy Carter, the President of the United Nations, called on the nations of the world to impose sanctions on the USSR and to specifically boycott the forthcoming Olympic Games which had been awarded to Moscow. Not all countries immediately rallied to his cause, even close US allies were at first reluctant. For example, the Australian Prime Minister, Malcolm Fraser, stated 'the Games .. are an international event - not a Russian event - and should be seen in that context' (Australian Parliament, 1980: 29). However Carter was not discouraged by the initial lack of support. He continued to lobby US allies and support for his cause slowly increased.

Ironically, while becoming involved in this process, some leaders appeared confused or even hypocritical about their participation in the boycott movement and its relationship to politics. For example, Malcolm Fraser commented: 'the government places a great deal of importance on being able for the future to re-establish the Olympic ideal in a way which will enable the athletes of the world to compete free of partisan politics of one kind or another' (Australian Parliament, 1980: 97).

When the Australian Olympic Federation announced in April it was sending a team to Moscow, Fraser, who by this time was firmly in the Carter boycott camp, acted in a manner contrary to his previous statements about the separation of sport and state. The government withdrew all its funding for the Australian Olympic team to travel to Moscow. Like some other countries, such as Great Britain, the Australian team's presence at the Games was funded by private contributions. Eventually 26 nations boycotted the Games, most notably the US, West Germany, the People's Republic of China, Japan and Canada (Loder, 1997). This, according to Kanin (1981: 108) was 'the most extensive diplomatic effort ever connected with an Olympic celebration and demonstrated unequivocally that nations saw the Olympics as an effective tool to try to influence the foreign policy of other nations, those with opposing political ideologies'.

The following Games, held in Los Angeles were not immune from these same forces. This time it was the Eastern bloc countries boycotting in retaliation for the previous Olympics. Officially they cited smog and safety concerns for their athletes as the reasons for their non-attendance, however the chance to inflict an embarrassment upon their capitalist hosts, similar to the one they had experienced, was certainly on their agenda.

Since this time Olympic boycotts have not assumed the same importance. The IOC has instituted penalties on NOCs which boycott (see IOC, 1995), however this penalty does not necessarily address those who instigate the boycotts, namely national governments. It also fails to acknowledge the price that NOCs and athletes have paid in defying their governments' wishes and attending the Games. While the *Olympic Charter* suggests that NOCs 'seek sources of funding which will enable them to maintain their autonomy in all respects' (IOC, 1995: 55), this is a simplistic solution for some NOCs, especially those in third world countries.

Some NOCs, for example, the United States Olympic Committee and the Australian Olympic Committee, have been quite successful in accumulating capital, to allow a degree of independence from their governments, however even in these countries, Olympics sports and athletes may still be dependent on their governments for funding to maintain training programmes and subsidies. Thus, while such NOCs can distance themselves from governments in terms of receiving funds for travel to a specific Games, they may still be reliant on the same governments for grants for Olympic athletes to develop their athletic skills in the period between the Games.

The nexus between government and sport exists on many levels and this makes it possible for governments to use the Olympic Games as a tool to punish other governments for their politics and ideologies. Events such as the Soviet invasion of Afghanistan thus become a part of Olympic history even though, on the surface, there are no obvious links.

Nationalism

A victory in an Olympic event means, on the most obvious level, that, on a given day, in a particular event, an athlete or team was the best in the competition. Be that as it may, there are multifaceted levels of meanings in such outcomes. One of these sub-textual messages occurs when nations have used Olympic victories in an attempt to substantiate the relative advantages of their social, political and economic ideologies.

There is a fine but discrete line between the use of the Olympics as a political tool to embarrass opponents and the phenomenon of nationalism. The main difference lies in the fact that the former can occur throughout the entire period of an Olympiad, while nationalism generally arises as a result of outstanding Olympic performances, the national medal tally for particular Summer or Winter Olympic Games, or hosting a Games with the purpose of highlighting national superiority. Another difference between the two phenomena lies in the fact that national rivalry is directed at a particular nation or nations, whereas claims of superiority need not necessarily have a particular government as a target.

The 1908 Games held in London were the first to exhibit national rivalry to an extent that was disruptive to the Olympic movement. Originally the Games were to have been staged in Rome, however the Italians let it be known that they could not continue their offer and in 1906 London was assigned the Games in their stead.

The major display of national rivalry in these games was between the American and British participants and officials. This mirrored a general cooling in Anglo-American relations. This rivalry was very much in evidence and disrupted the staging of the athletic events. An American official, James Sullivan, exemplified the American attitude: 'They [the officials] were unfair to the Americans, they were unfair to every athlete except the British, but their real aim was to beat the Americans. Their conduct was cruel and unsportsmanlike and absolutely unfair' (in Killanin and Rhodda, 1976: 37). The two most blatant examples of cheating occurred in the 400 metres and the marathon. In the former the US victor was disqualified and in the latter officials assisted the drugged and collapsing Italian, Dorando Pietri across the finish line so that he would beat the fast finishing American, Johnny Hayes. After American protests about the blatant support the Italian received, Hayes was declared the winner (Warning, 1980).

In response to the criticism of partiality and bias in their judging, the British Olympic Committee subsequently published a book entitled, *Replies to the Criticism of the Olympic Games* (British Olympic Committee, 1909). It was a 64 page publication setting out quotations of charges from the Americans on one side and 'dignified' replies from the British on the other. As a result of this publication, athletic associations between the two countries were temporarily broken off . The scandal of biased judging forced the IOC to alter its policy in regard to officials. From these Games on, judges came from a variety of countries, rather than exclusively from the host nation (Warning, 1980).

The overt displays of rivalry began at the Opening Ceremony when the British neglected to display the American flag. During this ceremony the United States replied in kind by refusing to dip their flag to the King and Queen of England on the principle that 'this flag dips to no earthly King' (Warning, 1980: 31). This established a tradition which American teams have upheld ever since.

Perhaps the most overt example of a nation attempting to use the Olympics to illustrate its superiority occurred 28 years later, at the 1936 Olympic Games. At these Olympics the Nazis attempted to demonstrate to the world that their policies had raised Germany from the devastating effects of reparation payments and then the Great Depression, while at the same time highlighting the greatness of the Aryan race. Their attempts at the latter confirmed how this policy can be a double edged sword.

The fact that Berlin was awarded the Games in 1931 itself had a political underpinning. The decision by the IOC was an attempt to aid Germany in its restoration after its defeat in World War I (Loder, 1997). When Adolf Hitler came to power in 1933 he was initially opposed to hosting the Games, however his opposition was transformed to support when he perceived the propaganda potential of sport. Strenk (1970: 28) notes: 'here was a chance to show the world how modern and progressive Germany was .. to demonstrate that Germans were happy and prosperous under the Nazi system, and to divert public attention away from other areas of Nazi policy such as campaigns against the Jews'.

The Germans were thorough in their preparations in order to achieve these aims. For example, the excavations at the site of the Ancient Games, at Olympia in Greece, were reopened by the Germans in 1935 and a special exhibit was arranged, which toured throughout Germany, showing Olympic artefacts and German cultural exhibits.

The Games themselves highlighted German technology, with a number of new types of recording apparatus being introduced, for example, electronic timing, electronic starting pistols, photo finish equipment, machines to record 'touches' in fencing, the broadcasting of results on television and short wave radio and wire photos (Warning, 1980).

Figure 5.2. Berlin, 1936: arrival of the Olympic torch, against a backdrop of Nazi flags.

The host city, Berlin, was cleaned up. Special police units patrolled to price gouging. Violence directed against Jews was temporarily curtailed and propaganda adorned the buildings. In describing his government's policy aims an assistant to propaganda Minister Goebbels stated:

> It is the aspiration of the Nationalist Socialist regime to bring visitors here in the largest possible number. .. In this we see the effective defence measures against the lying reports about Germany rampant abroad. .. Every German hotelier, taxi driver represents the Nationalist state to the foreigner. Therefore they all have the duty to behave themselves accordingly and not to shame the Fatherland. (Strenk, 1979: 31)

Although these measures served to create a favourable impression of the German government, their master plan was not entirely successful. The weak link was on the Olympic field of play. Inherent in the German's scheme to demonstrate Aryan superiority was the premise that their representatives' performances would be superior. This would demonstrate that German efficiency in the community and industry was transferable to human achievement in sport. With the spectacular victories by black athletes (whom the Germans derogatorily termed 'auxiliaries'), notably by Jesse Owens, these hopes were negated. The Nazis' plans, while not wasted, did not achieve their desired goals and Hitler's government had to be content with global acceptance of German efficiency, rather than Aryan supremacy.

The USSR competed in the Olympics for the first time in 1952, during the Cold War period. Both the Soviets and their political rivals, the US, perceived Olympic competition in nationalistic terms. Before these Games the Soviet press, especially the newspapers *Pravda* and *Izvestia,* was instrumental in extolling their athletes to perform at their best so that their performances would reflect well and bring honour to the Communist system. It was during this time that steroid use increased, partly as a result of systemic pressure in Eastern bloc countries and, in retaliatory moves, Western athletes seeking to negate such advantages by also using similar substances.

The athletes thus played an active role in nationalistic rivalries and many believed in the superiority of their nation state. The 1968 Olympics provide another example of this. Wayne Brauman, a United States wrestler, writing in the *New York Times*, accused the Soviet Union and Romanian teams of trying to broker an athletic deal:

> If the United States 158-pounder let the Rumanian pin him then the United States 198-pounder would be allowed to pin his Russian opponent. .. They thought we were crazy when we turned them down .. and after they went on to pin both of us anyway, they thought we were crazier.
>
> International athletics is a totally political thing .. Avery Brundage might not like to hear anyone say that of all other countries. Most of them resent the United States... because we're number one in the world. And sports is one area

where they can demonstrate their superiority over us. ('Wrestling star hits at politics', 1972)

Interference by Those Not Involved in the Games

With the increasing media coverage of the Olympic Games and its subsequent availability to more of the world through the advent of satellite TV, the Games have become a vehicle for individuals with no affiliation to the Games to draw attention to issues also unrelated to the Olympic movement. Even before extensive TV coverage, protesters had disrupted the Games with the same purpose, although, obviously, their audience was smaller. Those who were present at the Opening Ceremony of the 1952 Games in Helsinki were witness to such an event when Barbara Rotbraut-Pleyer, dubbed the 'Peace Angel' by the press, disturbed the proceedings.

> A rather plump lady, partly veiled and wearing what appeared to be a flowing white nightdress, was able to get on the track, complete half a circle of it, and actually ascend to the rostrum and begin with a speech with what sounded something like 'Peace'. .. But lack of breadth, because of her girth and exertion, and the timely action of one senior Finnish official who did not know she was not part of the official ceremony stopped her at this point. She was removed by the police who later announced that she was a mentally deranged German girl who had come to address 'Humanity'. (Killanin and Rhodda,1976: 64)

While this incident appears to be somewhat bizarre, harmless and even rather amusing, other protests have not been so innocent. One of the most tragic incidents in Olympic history is of this genre and occurred in 1972 when Palestinian terrorists invaded the Olympic village:

> Before the Munich Games began, and during their first days, West German authorities were aware of reports which indicated that there would be political demonstrations connected with the Olympics. None of these reports indicated that Israeli athletes would be the target of the demonstrations, however, German authorities had met with an Israeli diplomat to discuss security arrangements for athletes in the Olympic Village. (Warning, 1980: 49)

The Israeli team was housed at Connolly Strasse 31 in the Olympic Village. These premises also housed athletes from Uruguay and Hong Kong. On 5 September, Palestinian terrorists, belonging to a group called Black September, infiltrated the village and took ten Israelis hostage in their quarters. In the initial raid an Israeli wrestling coach was killed. For the next two days the ten hostages, who included both athletes and officials, were held captive while the terrorists and German officials negotiated terms for their release. The Black September group demanded the release of over 200 political prisoners held by the Israelis.

Additionally, they sought safe passage for themselves and their hostages to an airport of their choice in the Middle East (Warning, 1980).

In keeping with her country's determination not to negotiate with hostages the Israeli Prime Minister, Golda Meir, announced that Israel would not accede to any of the terrorists' demands. Similarly, Avery Brundage, President of the IOC, declared that the IOC was opposed to the forcible removal of Olympic athletes from the Olympic Village. The Egyptian President, Alwar Sadat, was notified of the attack and implored to intervene. He announced that the Egyptian government knew nothing of the attack and had no intention of becoming involved.

Meanwhile, the West German government decided to implement a plan to free the hostages on German soil. Consequently, the terrorists and hostages were allowed to leave the Olympic Village and proceed to Furstenfeldbrock Airfield, where an attempt was made to free the hostages. When the Palestinians realised that they had been ambushed they detonated hand grenades which they threw into the helicopters containing the hostages. All of the Israelis died in the melee (Groussard, 1975).

As a result of the deaths, teams from four nations (Egypt, Israel, Algeria and the Philippines) withdrew, as well as individuals from the Dutch and Norwegian contingents. The Israeli Government called for the cancellation of the Games, however the IOC decided against this course of action, based on the argument that the Games would, in the future, then be more susceptible to further violence (Warning, 1980). The IOC instead decided to cancel all competition on 7 September, and a memorial service for the dead athletes and officials was held. When addressing the service, IOC President Avery Brundage stated:

> Sadly in this imperfect world, the greater and more important the Olympic Games become they are open to commercial, political and now criminal pressures. The Games of the Twentieth Olympiad were subject to two savage attacks. First we lose the Rhodesian battle against political blackmail ... We only have the strength of a great ideal, I am sure the public will agree that we cannot allow a handful of terrorists to destroy the nucleus of international goodwill we had in the Olympic Movement - The Games must go on. (Groussard, 1975: 422)

This statement was considered by many to be inappropriate, because the question of Rhodesia's participation was a separate issue and the linking of the two problems was seen to be, at the very least, undiplomatic. The following day Brundage issued an apology 'regretting any misunderstanding of words' and the Games continued, one day behind schedule (Kirshenbaum, 1972: 26).

Another, less violent and less well known protest was undertaken by Irish demonstrators wishing to draw world attention to their protests against British rule in Northern Ireland. The protesters rode bicycles into the British road cycling team during competition.

The following Games in Montreal in 1976 were also not immune from political demonstrations, despite tight security measures adopted in the aftermath of the

Munich massacre. Canadians, who were Ukrainian immigrants, used the Games to demonstrate for an independent Ukranian Olympic team, instead of the present status as members of the Soviet team. These demonstrations were non-violent. The protesters attended many events and waved Ukrainian flags, chanted political slogans and burnt a Soviet flag which they had removed from an Olympic flagpole (Takac, 1976).

While the Olympic Games hold pre-eminence in the sporting world they will continue to be an attractive target for terrorists. While the lessons learnt from Montreal have meant that security for athletes and officials has been adequate, the Atlanta Games of 1996, evidenced a new form of terrorism, directed towards spectators, in the form of a bomb blast.

Several bomb threats had been received by the Atlanta Organising Committee for the Olympic Games (ACOG) during and before the Games. Before the Games the spectre of violence had been raised when a Georgian based militia group's headquarters had been raided, after reports that the group intended to disrupt the Games (Hinds, 1996). Pipe bombs were discovered and seized in the raid.

The bomb attack occurred in Olympic Centennial Park, a recreation area created especially for the Games, where athletes and the public could meet and enjoy and consume activities and products designed by Olympic sponsors such as Coca Cola and Swatch. The bomb, hidden in a knapsack, exploded early in the morning of Saturday, 27 July. Fragments of the bomb were thrown as far as 80 metres from the site of the explosion.

One woman was killed by the blast, a reporter died from a heart attack directly attributable to the bomb and another 110 people were injured. After the bombing a telephone conference between ACOG, the White House and Georgian state officials was held (Hinds, 1996). As in 1972, the authorities decided that cancelling the Games would equate with a victory to terrorism. US President, Bill Clinton, declared, 'We cannot let terrorism win' (Hewitt, 1996: 11) and François Carrard, the IOC Director General echoed Avery Brundage's 1972 comment when he announced 'the Games must go on' (Magnay and Hinds, 1996: 7). As a mark of respect for those killed or injured in the blast all Olympic flags were lowered to half mast and there was a minute's silence at all Olympic venues (Loder, 1997). The Olympic competitions continued, however Centennial Park was closed for three days and when it reopened, on July 30, security measures to enter the precinct were far more stringent. The official report of the Games of the XXVI Olympiad gave the incident only a relatively brief mention and put a spin on the outcome that could be considered to be somewhat insensitive when it stated:

> .. this tragedy brought together in a universal appeal to continue the Olympic Games in the spirit in which they were started. .. The 40,000 people who participated in the park's emotional reopening demonstrated their unwavering support of the celebration of the Olympic Games'. (Watkins, 1997: 87)

The person or persons responsible have not to date been found. As a result of these acts of terrorism and the threats of violence at other Games, for example Seoul in 1988, Olympic security measures have become increasingly sophisticated. With the instance of terrorism now also directed towards spectators, this task will become increasingly more complex and difficult for organising committees at future Games. The global and public nature of the Games makes them an attractive vehicle for terrorist groups, or even individuals, to gain media publicity for their causes. This is a form of political intervention which can never be underestimated by OCOGs or the IOC. It would be in their best interests and that of humanity for the Olympic Games to be recognised for their sporting achievements, not because of violence.

Interference by Athletes

At various times athletes have used the Olympics to protest against conditions in their own countries. Just as terrorists see the Olympics as the medium to advertise their cause, so too athletes have seen this potential to reach large audiences and simultaneously embarrass their government.

The first such example of this form of intervention occurred at the 1968 Mexico Olympics and involved US athletes. Initially, this demonstration began in support of South Africa's expulsion from the Olympic Movement, however, even when this issue was resolved to the protesters' satisfaction, their demonstrations continued. Their cause shifted to highlight the inferior treatment of black athletes in the US.

It was in July 1967, at the first National Conference on Black Power, held at Newark, New Jersey, that a boycott of black athletes at the Mexico Games was first proposed, in conjunction with a boycott of professional boxing to protest against the World Boxing Association stripping Mohammad Ali of his crown. By November the proposed boycott was gaining momentum. It was led by Harry Edwards, a sociology professor at San Jose State College, California and endorsed by Martin Luther King (Warning, 1980).

The protesters released a set of demands which would have to be met before their boycott would be lifted. Included in this was the demand that Avery Brundage resign as President of the IOC because of his racist beliefs, and that a black be appointed to the United States Olympic Committee. Brundage replied, in his characteristically blunt manner, that if the black Americans boycotted the Olympics they would not be missed (Lapchick, 1975).

The assassination of Martin Luther King in April 1968 added to the resolve of the protesters and increased their ranks, however a vote of black athletes at the Olympic trials indicated that only about 50% were against competing. An official boycott was called off and a decision made to stage a protest at the Games instead (Lapchick, 1975). The first sign of trouble at the Games occurred when Tommy Smith, a 200 metre sprinter said that if he won his event he did not want Avery Brundage to present him with a medal. In their heats of the 200 metres Smith and fellow American John Carlos wore black knee-length socks instead of their uniform issue as a sign of their protest.

On 15 October Smith and Carlos finished first and third respectively in the final of this event. During the medal ceremony Smith wore a black glove on his right hand and a black scarf on his neck and Carlos a black glove on his left hand and beads around his neck. While the US anthem was played Smith and Carlos raised their gloved hands and refused to look at their flag being raised. As a result of this demonstration the IOC applied pressure on the USOC and the two athletes were expelled from the US team (Warning, 1980). Despite IOC warnings further demonstrations occurred by US athletes, and, although not as powerful as the Smith and Carlos incident, enabled protesters to feel that their demonstrations were successful in gaining the attention of the world press for their cause. Similar protests by blacks at the Munich Games resulted in the expulsion of a further two athletes, Vince Mathews and Wayne Collet. However, the press attention was focused on a more tragic protest at these Games, which resulted in the death of 11 Israeli athletes.

Figure 5.3. Black Power salute, Mexico City, 1968.

Because the Olympics enjoy pre-eminence as an international sporting event and festival, they have become the ideal medium for nations, groups and individuals to appropriate and thereby demonstrate and exploit their political power and causes. The overtly political organisational structure and rituals of the Games themselves exacerbate the event's political construction. They draw upon and provide symbolic capital to various interest groups, despite the fact that the rhetoric and philosophy of the IOC suggest the opposite and portray the movement in terms of its potential as a mechanism for achieving world peace, reconciliation and concord

IOC Politics

Since before the Sorbonne Conference, when there were political decisions made regarding whether or not invitations should be sent to a German representative, politics, overtly and more commonly, covertly, have been a facet of the internal workings of the IOC.

The Olympic movement has been rated by some political analysts as a very successful organisation (Hoberman, 1986). Aligned to this perception is its increasing popularity with the general public throughout the world and concomitant attractiveness to a variety of political interests that wish to harness the passions it creates (Houlihan, 1994). Ironically, the IOC has fostered such manipulation because it 'has continually seen the Olympic Games as a sporting event with a philosophy that placed the Olympics above such mundane preoccupations as politics' (Leiper, 1981: 105). In other words it has created a political agenda while maintaining its aloofness from such quotidian affairs. Houlihan (1994: 111) suggests that this has had negative repercussions for the movement because, 'such inherently contradictory practices are obviously difficult to sustain while not enabling other organisations to exploit their ambiguities. .. The Olympics therefore provide a conveniently adaptable context for the furthering of interests'.

The structure of the IOC was discussed in detail in chapter 4. What must be remembered from this detail in terms of the IOC's own political context is the fact that it has been structured as a self-electing, self-regulating association, and until 1981 it consisted entirely of men. Even today it still has primarily selected its power base from Westernised nations. Its executive has usually been selected from individuals who are professionally powerful, members of the nobility, moneyed, or a combination of these three criteria. Sitting at the top of the Olympic food chain is the IOC President, whose influence throughout the world of sports is supreme.

The current IOC President, Juan Antonio Samaranch, has had to deal with a plethora of political issues through which, until late 1998, he has invariably adroitly manoeuvred the organisation, to a greater status. The most consequential of these has been the period of rapid transition for the IOC in commercial terms. When Avery Brundage retired as IOC President in 1972 the organisation had borrowed money on its forthcoming Munich television rights return in order to remain operational. The term of Lord Killanin's presidency, from 1972 to 1980, saw IOC assets grow to $US5 million (Miller, 1996). Because of the substantial increases in television rights since that time and the successful TOP strategy, as discussed in chapter 6, even these figures seem small when compared to the current IOC assets.

Juan Antonio Samaranch was born in Barcelona on 17 July, 1920. His first Olympic role came in 1954, when he was appointed to the Spanish Olympic Committee. In 1965, he was proposed for IOC membership at its session in Madrid, however, as five new members had already been accepted at this session, a decision as to his status was deferred (Pound, 1994). The wait was relatively short. The following year, at the 56th IOC Session, in Rome, he was appointed as an IOC member. Interestingly, in light of his subsequent presidential rulings on IOC membership tenure, the result of this delay made him subject to the determination that members who were appointed post-1995, were required to retire at the age of 72. In a less than open manner, the ruling was later changed, allowing him to remain at the helm until after the 2000 Games (Pound, 1994).

In 1974 Samaranch was appointed as a Vice-President and, when three years later he was appointed Spanish Ambassador to the Soviet Union in Moscow, he was perfectly placed to campaign for the up-coming IOC Presidency. His lobbying was successful and, during the IOC Session held in Moscow in conjunction with the Games, he was elected its seventh President (Miller, 1996).

Decisions as to the awarding of IOC membership have often been the result of political manoeuvring. One of the IOC's fiercest critics, Andrew Jennings, in his book *The New Lords of the Rings* documents how both Samaranch and Brundage adopted a dictatorial style of leadership. He comments, 'Brundage dominated the Olympic Committee; he selected new members, arbitrarily took the big decisions and devolved little power' (1996: 32). Of the current IOC President he says, 'Samaranch selects new members who won't cause him trouble. He nominates and the committee rubber stamps' (1996: 56). In terms of the politics of gender he adds, 'it's an Olympic family dominated by men; ninety three percent of it, average age sixty three... Women were excluded until 1981' (1996: 67). This issue is discussed in more detail in chapter 9.

· Conclusion

From their inception to the present, the modern Olympic Games have been influenced by politics at both intra-national and international levels. Just as other international sporting events organised similarly along national lines (such as the Commonwealth Games and the Soccer World Cup) are influenced by the ideologies, rivalries and policies of competing nations, and become political currency, it would be unrealistic to expect the Olympics to be an exception to this exchange. Yet, we still hear that hackneyed and illusory phrase 'politics should be kept out of the Olympics', ironically often voiced by politicians. According to Clarke and Clarke:

> This is a proposition which assumes that politics and sport are two clearly separated fields of life. .. But to describe politics in this way is to leave out a different level of political relations. These relations lie outside the formal arena

of party politics, and operate in the maintenance of social patterns of power, domination and subordination throughout the whole of society. It is this aspect of politics that is involved in 'managing' a society composed of divided and conflicting classes and groups. It is... a level of political activity that stresses the importance of ideology, particularly, in the role of presenting a divided society as if it was an harmonious unity. (Clarke and Clarke, 1982: 62)

The IOC states that, 'the goal of Olympism is to place everywhere sport at the service of the harmonious development of man, with a view to encouraging the establishment of a peaceful society concerned with the preservation of human dignity' (IOC, 1995: 10). This mission, itself a hotly contested claim, can be literally and figuratively hijacked by Olympic protocol itself, which is highly ritualistic and replete with political symbolism and overtones. When, during the Olympic medal ceremonies, national anthems are played and the flag of the victors' countries are raised, when team sports are organised on national lines and, during the Opening Ceremony athletes march into the stadium nation by nation, these practices are overtly creating nationalistic tensions, self-regard and rivalries. Such discords do not dissolve at the perimeters of the Olympic venues. Indeed, it is often events outside the Games' control and jurisdiction and the media's subsequent interpretation and mediation of them that precipitate and serve to incite the Olympics' political tensions:

Athletes (and sometimes spectators) are the living, breathing representatives of national or racial characteristics. .. sporting competition is invested with, and helps to keep in circulation, a whole repertoire of national and racial mythologies- myths of 'their' strangeness, difference, peculiarity, which help to reinforce the ethnocentrism of our own culture. These may .. draw on past or present resentments, hostilities and conflicts of their own experience- experiences which lie outside sport. (Clarke and Clarke, 1982: 66)

There is prestige associated with hosting an Olympic Games. The Nazis capitalised on this, and, in recent Olympiads, nations hosting the Games have endeavoured to stage a more spectacular festival, with more grandiose facilities, than the preceding Olympics. Today it is prohibitive to all but developed countries to host the Games for, although the Olympic Games is awarded to a city rather than a country, it is generally impossible for any city to bear the financial burden without assistance from national or regional governments. The 1968 Mexico City Games demonstrated that a developing country's citizens thought that such a high level of expenditure on a sporting event was unwarranted, while the citizens of Montréal were faced with excessive tax increases because of their city government's insistence upon using the Olympics as a showcase for the city.

Apart from the collapse of the Cold War, there are few indications that there will be any diminution in political intrusions into the Games. Various proposals have been put forward in an attempt to minimise political interference by reducing their political significance, including the idea of establishing a permanent site for the

Games, as discussed in chapter 11, or splitting the Games into a series of smaller-scale world championships. However, the effect of implementing such proposals would be to diminish the overall significance of the Games - a price which the Olympic movement is unlikely to be prepared to pay.

Chapter six:

The Economics and Financing of the Games

> The staging of a hallmark event can provide a significant boost to the economy of a city or region in which it is held. Such an event can generate substantial expenditure within both the public and private sectors of the economy and the impact of this expenditure is distributed widely throughout the economy. Unfortunately, hallmark events can also generate significant economic costs that often get forgotten in the euphoria surrounding an event. A common legacy of many past events has been a huge debt and a great deal of under-utilised infrastructure. (Roberts and McLeod, 1989: 242)

Introduction

In cities and countries which host the Olympic Games, the question of their cost, particularly to the public purse, arguably attracts as much attention from the media, governments and the public as the sporting aspects of the event. This is not surprising, since the sheer scale of the modern Games generally results in significant government involvement and considerable government expense, raising inevitable questions about the use of public funds. In this chapter three related dimensions of the Olympic Games are considered, namely the political economy of the Games, their financing and their economic impact. *Political economy*, as the term implies, involves both economic and political concerns: it addresses questions about the role of the Olympic Games in national and international economic and political systems. *Finance* is more specifically concerned with the question of money. In this chapter, the discussion of finance is divided into two parts: the funding of the Olympic Movement as a whole and the financing of individual Games. *Economic impact* is concerned with the effects of the Games on the host community, in terms of increasing local incomes and job creation.

Political Economy

The main contributions to discussion of the political economy of the Olympic Games have come from Marxist and neo-Marxist writers, such as Brohm (1978) and Gruneau (1984). *Marxism* sees the basic dynamic in capitalist society, or western market economies, as arising from the clash of interests between the capitalist (bourgeois) class, which owns the 'means of production', and the working class (proletariat), which owns nothing but its labour power, which it must sell to the capitalist to live. Marx argued that, as capitalism developed, opportunities for profitable investment of capital would become increasingly scarce, so capitalists would continually seek to reduce the wages paid to workers in order to maintain profitability and growth. Since such a situation is clearly unstable, Marx predicted that the system would inevitably fall apart, as a result of increasingly severe crises, such as depression and wars, or as a result of violent revolution on the part of the workers, or a combination of the two. In the first half of the twentieth century, in the face of wars and depressions, Marx's predictions seemed increasingly plausible but, as the second half of the century has unfolded, they have looked less and less plausible. Where do the Olympic Games fit into such a scenario? To answer this we should consider the later development of Marxist ideas referred to a *neo-Marxism*. Neo-Marxism, while retaining Marx's basic analysis, modifies the basic ideas in order to explain why capitalism has managed to survive so long, despite its contradictions and periodic crises. Neo-Marxist analyses depict the modern phenomenon of sport, including the Olympic Games, as one example of the opportunities which have been exploited to prolong the life of the capitalist system. In its search for investment opportunities, international capital has 'discovered sport', including the Olympic Games.

With the collapse of the Marxist Communist regimes of Eastern Europe and the Soviet Union in the late 1980s, and with the increasing market orientation of remaining Marxist regimes, such as China and Vietnam, western Marxist thinking has experienced a crisis of its own, since capitalism and the market system seems increasingly triumphant around the world. Thus the Marxist and neo-Marxist analysis of sport and other phenomena seems less relevant today. Nevertheless a considerable amount of writing on the Olympic Games over the last two or three decades has been imbued with Marxist and neo-Marxist ideas, and the critique offers a perspective which is largely absent from other writing, so it is appropriate that it be considered here. Gruneau's writing on the Games is typical of this genre (1984, 1989; Gruneau and Cantelon, 1988). His paper on 'Commercialism and the modern Olympics', presents the following sequence of observations and arguments.

Firstly he notes, with obvious displeasure, that the 1984 Los Angeles Games, which was being planned at the time he was writing, received substantial sponsorship funds from major US companies, such as McDonald's, Coca Cola, Mars and Budweiser. He observes that the companies involved used sponsorship of the Games to project an image of public-spiritedness and wholesomeness through association

with the positive images of youth and sports and notes that 'many people' objected
to 'such obvious commercialism'. But, he argues, this is nothing new:

> .. the Los Angeles Games are in no way a significant departure from practices
> established in earlier Olympics. Rather, I believe the 1984 Games are best
> understood as a more fully developed expression of the incorporation of
> sporting practice into the ever-expanding marketplace of international
> capitalism. (Gruneau, 1984: 2)

Elaborating on this historical perspective, Gruneau first observes that, by the end of
the nineteenth century, when the Olympics were being revived, industrialisation and
urbanisation in Britain and other industrial nations had created a market for spectator
sports, which could be exploited by business interests. This was exemplified by the
Games of the early part of the twentieth century, which were associated with trade
fairs, designed to promote capitalist trade and commerce (the Paris Universal
Exhibition in 1900, the St Louis World Fair in 1904, the Anglo-French Exhibition
in London in 1908). The notion that the Olympic Games represented the ideal of
sport for its own sake, untarnished by commercialism, was already, according to
Gruneau, a doubtful proposition.

This association with commercialisation was, however, taking place alongside
the creation by the British middle and upper classes of the idea of *amateurism* in
sport. Gruneau sees amateurism as an expression of class supremacy and an effort
to keep the working class in its place, but he does not remark on the paradox of parts
of the bourgeoisie apparently developing ways of commercially exploiting sport
while another part of the same class was simultaneously instituting the decidedly
non-commercial phenomenon of amateurism, except to say, in passing:

> *Amateurism notwithstanding*, sporting competition became clearly drawn into
> the universal market during the latter half of the nineteenth century. (Gruneau,
> 1984: 4, emphasis added)

Later in the paper, however, Gruneau recognises the 'lingering anti-professional
traditions of amateurism' as part of the 'resistance to sport's absorption into
capitalism's universal market' (p. 12). So amateurism, oddly, plays two contradictory
roles in the Gruneau's neo-Marxist critique: it is both a reinforcer of class division
(and therefore of capital) and a form of resistance against the power of capital.
Further paradox is added to the discussion when other critical writers discuss the
recent *removal* of amateurism from the Olympic ideal - here the rise of the
professional athlete is seen as further evidence of the encroachment of capitalism
into the field of sport (see, for example, Lawrence, 1986: 212).

As, in the course of the twentieth century, the Games increased in scale and
prestige, Gruneau notes, they came to be recognised as a means for nationalistic
promotion and were used to boost the fortunes of whichever regime or economic
system held sway in the host city or country at the time. Thus the Los Angeles

Games of 1932 projected the 'American Dream' of prosperity based on free-enterprise and the Berlin Olympics of 1936 sought to promote Nazism. Further, the Games of the post-Second World War era became a pawn in the Cold War political and economic rivalries between East and West. Eventually, Gruneau observes, by the 1960s the Olympic Games were:

> .. increasingly intertwined with a powerful international bloc of financial, travel, retail, and media interests; potential profits were tied to the growing size and visibility of the Games. (Gruneau, 1984: 8-9)

In the 1970s, Gruneau argues, the growing scale of the Olympics produced an 'economic crisis of the Olympics', culminating in the celebrated $1 billion deficit of the 1976 Montreal Games. This in turn resulted in few cities wishing to host the Games, so that Los Angeles, with its private sector-funded solution, was the only city to bid for the 1984 Games. The Los Angeles Games are seen as the culmination of the process of commercialisation and commodification of the Olympics. While this involves exposure to the masses through the media, Gruneau sees the Games as essentially élitist, rather than democratic:

> What kind of sport is the Los Angeles Olympic Organizing Committee and its corporate sponsors supporting? .. My answer is that it is a highly specialised, élite sport that is being supported here, and not a form of recreational sport for the broadest possible number of participants. Furthermore, the presence of the great corporations is a statement in itself: such sponsorship signifies the omnipresence of corporate capital in our lives, even to the extent of dominating our games. Throughout this century sport has become progressively more commodified - to the point where, at its highest levels, it now stands before us as a simple division of the entertainment and light consumer-goods industries. (Gruneau, 1984: 12)

Gruneau then introduces the neo-Marxist idea of 'resistance' - the notion that the working classes and other oppressed groups under capitalism engage in various forms of opposition to the oppressive, controlling forces of capital. In the case of the Olympic Games, however, resistance has most frequently taken the form of protests against public expenditure thus contributing to the emergence of Games events increasingly dependent of private, commercial funding. Such 'resistance' to the onslaught of capital would therefore seem somewhat counter-productive:

> .. there has been a considerable degree of resistance to sport's absorption into capitalism's universal market. Not only the lingering anti-professional traditions of amateurism, but also community and trade union groups have objected to the excesses and spending priorities of the Olympic circus. In the late 1970s considerable popular resistance focused on the use of public revenues to build elaborate facilities and to offset Olympic deficits. Yet the result of this

resistance was to clear the way for the 'Hamburger Olympics' [Los Angeles] and another stage in the commodification of international sport. (Gruneau, 1984: 13)

He then notes a further paradox: the role of the state in sport. On the one hand the state generally appears to provide 'non-market', subsidised, 'welfare' orientated sports services, including providing support for the non-commercial ideals of the Olympics. This can be seen as anti-commercial or anti-capital. But, on the other hand, the state can be seen to be *supporting* capital (or the 'accumulation' of capital) - by promoting a commercialised Games, by underwriting any deficits which may arise and by generating business for private firms - for example in the form of contracts for the building of stadia. And ultimately, in a capitalist economy, the state is itself dependent on a thriving commercial sector for its income. Ultimately, he sees the state as part of the:

.. growing bloc of shared interests in high-performance sport, complete with elaborate centralised facilities, state and commercial sponsorship, and a complex infrastructure of sports scientists, coaches, technical personnel and bureaucrats. .. Sports policies in most capitalist countries .. are so tied into the bloc of vested interests supporting the Olympic movement that they cannot be easily opposed. (Gruneau, 1984: 14-15)

Finally Gruneau returns to the issue of resistance, this time to advocate it as a concern for the left of politics:

Yet this situation is far from immutable. People dissatisfied with the messages embodied in the 'Hamburger Olympics' can still struggle to relocate sport on the welfare rather than the accumulation side of modern state policy. But for there to be a popular mobilisation - in trade unions, community groups and political parties - in support of a non-market sporting practice, such a practice must be seen to be a legitimate concern for the left. (Gruneau, 1984:15)

Thus it can be seen that the Olympic Games touch on most of the concerns of Marxism and neo-Marxism - class conflict, commodification, global market power, the role of the state and the question of resistance and the struggle of the masses against the powerful forces of capital.

Other commentators have also addressed these issues from a critical stance, including Nixon (1988) and Lawrence (1986), who also focus on issues arising from the Los Angeles Games, and Whitson (1998), who brings the discussion up to date in focussing on the concept of globalisation and gender issues. While not developed in a theoretical way, and not within a neo-Marxist framework, the critique of the Games by Simson and Jennings (1992; Jennings, 1996), referred to in chapter 4, is also concerned, in part, with political economy. Basically, the Simson and Jennings thesis is that the personal pursuit of money and power by those involved with the organisation of the Games, has resulted in the Games being transformed from a traditional non-profit phenomenon into an international marketing, money-making, enterprise. To the extent that certain IOC processes, such as the selection of cities to host the Games, are shown to be tainted by corruption, as current highly publicised events would indicate, this would add strength to the arguments of critics of whatever ideological persuasion.

The literature on the political economy of sport, and the Olympic Games in particular, has focused primarily on the West, but it should also be noted that sport and the Olympics can be seen as having played an important part in sustaining the Communist regimes of Eastern Europe and the Soviet Union and continues to play such a role among those that remain, such as China, Vietnam and Cuba. While the role of sport under these regimes may be viewed as serving primarily political and nationalistic goals, as discussed in Chapter 5, there is also an economic dimension, in that communism or socialism represents a type of *economic* system as well as a political ideology. Thus the success of athletes from the 'second world' was intended, along with the success of such phenomena as space and nuclear programmes, to demonstrate the superiority of the Communist economic system. However, as with these non-sport endeavours, there is evidence to suggest that success was achieved only at inordinate financial expense, which probably distorted the very economic system it was intended to celebrate (Riordan, 1993: 51-2).

Funding the Olympic Movement

As we have seen (chapter 4), the Olympic Movement comprises a large, worldwide, multi-faceted network of organisations, with the International Olympic Committee (IOC) at its heart. The IOC is not a government or United Nations organisation - so how is it funded? In the early days of Baron de Coubertin, as noted in chapter 4, IOC members were wealthy men (they were all *men* until recent times), who paid their own way and provided for the minimal requirements of the organisation largely out of their own ample pockets. For many years the IOC was therefore run by wealthy people but was itself a relatively poor organisation, with no assured independent source of income.

Two things changed this situation dramatically. The first was the growth and popularity of the coverage of the Games on television and the subsequent growth in the value of the broadcasting rights. The second was the advent of sponsorship, in the form of The Olympic Programme. These are discussed in turn below.

Broadcasting Rights
As indicated in Table 6.1, the value of the broadcasting rights for the Olympics has grown rapidly from around a US$1 million in Rome, in 1960, to some US$700 million for the Sydney 2000 Games. Even making allowances for inflation, the growth is still dramatic, showing a 60-fold growth. The key factor in this pattern of growth was the advent of satellite broadcasting, which enabled television signals to be beamed instantly around the world. Prior to the 1970s, pictures could only be

broadcast internationally by means of relatively costly and slow physical transport of film and video-tape.

Table 6.1. Value of Summer Olympics broadcasting rights.

Games	Year	Value, $US millions	
		Current prices	1998 prices*
Rome	1960	1.2	12
Tokyo	1964	1.6	13
Mexico City	1968	10	83
Munich	1972	18	105
Montréal	1976	35	121
Moscow	1980	88	214
Los Angeles	1984	288	511
Seoul	1988	407	529
Barcelona	1992	636	705
Atlanta	1996	900	900
Sydney	2000	1100	1100

Source: Brunet, 1995 ; Cashman, 1999   (*Using Australian price Index).

The broadcasting rights for the Olympic Games are owned by the IOC, not the local Games organisers. Only a portion of the proceeds from the sale of the rights to a particular Games event - usually some two thirds - is passed to the local Organising Committee. The rest, an estimated US$100 million per annum, is distributed to NOCs, via the Olympic Solidarity programme or retained by the IOC.

Clearly the Olympic Movement is significantly dependent on income from broadcasting rights and particularly, since as much as 80% of the revenue derives from the USA (Slater, 1998: 56), on the American networks. We do not propose to explore the issue of the possible direct effects of this dependency here, since the media are discussed in detail in chapter 7. The broadcasting companies which pay these large sums are mostly commercial organisations which must generate audiences which will in turn attract advertisers, to recoup their outlays and produce a profit. In fact, the picture is more complex than this. Olympic broadcasters do not always make a profit from their investment. As Hill puts it:

.. the sums paid for television rights in the Olympics are not always rationally determined. Indeed, paying huge sums for them has always been seen by television companies as a loss leader, and [quoting Klatell and Marcus] 'the networks have allowed the Olympics to become so emotional an issue, so much a matter of pride and self-importance, that they no longer measure it by any reasonable business standard normally applied to programming decisions'. (Hill, 1995: 78)

There is, however, no sign of this source of funding drying up. Television companies continue to compete to pay increasingly large sums of money for the Olympic broadcasting rights, even signing contracts for several Olympiads in advance.

The Olympic Programme/Partners (TOP)

The Olympic Programme (TOP) was established in 1985 and later changed to The Olympic Partners programme. TOP was devised by International Sports and Leisure (ISL), a marketing and management company jointly owned by the sports clothing manufacturer Adidas and a Japanese advertising agency, Dentsu. The connection with Adidas is considered highly significant by Olympic historians, because of the involvement of the owner of the company, Horst Dassler (Hill, 1995: 80-89; Jennings, 1996: 47-54). Dassler developed his influence in the Olympic Movement and other national and international sporting organisations through generous sponsorship deals and used his position to promote Adidas products. As early as the 1968 Olympic Games, it is claimed that 83% of medal winners used Adidas shoes and equipment (Hill, 1995: 88).

Table 6.2. The Olympic Partners, 1997-2000.

Company	Category
Coca Cola	Soft drinks
Visa	Credit card
McDonalds	Restaurants
Panasonic	TV, audio and video technology
IBM	Computers and results technology
Xerox	Photocopying, facsimile, printing
Kodak	'Still imaging' - photographic
Time Inc. (Sports Illustrated)	Publishing
John Hancock	Insurance
UPS (United Parcel Service)	Mail services
Samsung	Wireless communication

TOP operates by selling to sponsors world-wide rights to use the Olympic logo in advertising and promotion for the period of an Olympiad. Sponsorship rights relate to product categories, such as soft drinks, computers or credit cards. The *Partners* for the 1997-2000 Olympiad are listed in Table 6.2. TOP companies contribute sums of the order of $US40 million each over the Olympiad - giving a total of some $US400 million. Part of the Partners' support is generally provided 'in kind' - that is, in the form of goods and services rather than cash. For example, IBM provides the electronic scoring system for the Games. Some of the statistics from TOP sponsors are impressive, for example, at the Nagano Winter Games: Coca Cola provided some four million products at venues; IBM provided 500 technology specialists; Panasonic 3000 monitors for the International Broadcast Centre; and Xerox provided 2000 document machines producing more than one billion copies (IOC, n.d.).

Because the commercial presence of the companies varies from country to country, and because NOCs may have existing national sponsorship deals with other companies which may conflict with TOP companies' expectation of exclusivity, negotiations take place with each NOC, concerning how the system will operate in their countries and what proportion of the TOP funds each NOC will receive. Proceeds are divided between the NOCs (20% of the total), the Summer and Winter Games (70%) and the IOC (10%) (IOC, n.d.; Hill, 1995: 84).

The exceptional feature of Olympic sponsorship, including TOP and local sponsorship of individual Games events, is that the initial sponsorship payment delivers very little by way of direct exposure for the sponsoring companies. In order to capitalise on their initial payment, TOP companies generally spend substantial additional sums of money bringing their association with the Games to the public attention. While this is often the case in sports sponsorship (Crompton, 1996), it is particularly apparent in the case of the Olympic Games since, for example, no advertising is permitted at Olympic venues and there are no 'naming rights' for the Games as there are for many other sporting events. While all the current TOP companies are US or Japan based, in joining TOP they are purchasing a world-wide license and the cost of 'taking the message to the world' can be substantial. Including the Olympic logo on such things as packaging, letterheads and existing advertisements is a marginal cost, but in most cases, specific advertising and promotional campaigns are developed so that the link between the company's name, sporting success and the 'spirit' of the Games is made clear to the consumer and potential consumer over the four years of the Olympiad.

At the beginning of the chapter we noted the criticism by Gruneau and others of the 'selling out' of the Olympics to commercialisation. While the extent of the 'selling out' is debatable, the extent of the dependency of the IOC and the Olympic movement on the world of commerce is beyond dispute: the list of TOP companies reads like a 'who's who' of international capitalism. Virtually all other non-profit international organisations depend for their funding on public subscriptions and/or contributions from governments. This does not, of course, protect them from outside influences. In the case of the Olympic Games there have been times when it has seemed that they would become wholly dependent on governments for funding; at other times broadcasting fees have become dominant. The TOP scheme has enabled the IOC to avoid these situations. The accompanying air of commercialisation is, nevertheless, distasteful to many. John Lucas, writing in 1992, was of the opinion that the commercialisation of the Olympic Games was a temporary phenomenon. He wrote:

> The Olympic Movement, especially the IOC, is bedazzled by its newfound avenues of financial opportunity and will continue exploring them for some years to come. By the millennial year 2000, the IOC will have accumulated in properties, investments, credits, and cash sufficient billions of dollars so that it can 'ease off'. It will pull back appreciably from this financial focus and be able

at last to devote nearly all of its vast power, influence, and new wealth to educational and altruistic efforts at an even higher level and through a more universal presence than are now possible. (Lucas, 1992: 80)

Clearly Lucas was somewhat premature in his predictions. The Olympic Games are ultimately dependent for their success on public support and the goodwill of governments, but the unique achievement of the IOC and the Olympic Movement - sellout or no sellout - is to manage to juggle the demands of 'Olympism', international capitalism, the media, governments and popular support to achieve a degree of financial independence.

Before examining the funding of individual Games events, it is worthwhile noting the complex financial relationships between the worldwide movement and the IOC, the International Sporting Federations, the National Olympic Committees and individual Olympic Games events. The major sources of funds, broadcasting rights and world-wide sponsorship funds, are controlled by the IOC, albeit with the majority of the income being passed on to the other organisations in the system. This is represented diagrammatically in Figure 6.1. Perhaps the most important feature of this system to note is that, ultimately, all the resources come from the public who follow the Games through the media and purchase the, mostly non-sporting, goods and services of sponsors and advertisers.

Funding Individual Games

Just to assemble a bid for an Olympic Games costs many millions of dollars. Included in the bid document presented to the IOC must be a detailed budget on just how the Games event is to be financed (IOC, 1992). Key decisions must be made early on in the process as to what new sporting facilities and other items of infrastructure to construct. A key decision is then what to include and what to exclude from the 'Olympic Budget'. For example, a host city may choose to refurbish its airport to coincide with the opening of the Olympic Games, but the refurbished airport will be enjoyed for many years after the Games is over - so to what extent should this be seen as an *Olympic* cost? This argument can even be raised in relation to sporting venues, since they also will continue to be used and enjoyed by local citizens after the Games. In practice host cities or governments have to consider the *net* costs of running the event - the difference between costs and revenue. In general it is considered that this difference will be negative - that is, the Games will cost the host money, rather than make a profit. The huge costs of the 1976 Montréal Games (Iton, 1978, 1988; Wright, 1978) created the impression that this net cost would inevitably be substantial, even crippling. As a result, few cities were willing to bid for subsequent Games - in fact, Los Angeles was the only bidder for the 1984 Games. When the Los Angeles organisers demonstrated that the Games could be run at a profit (Lawrence, 1986; Nixon 1988), competition among cities to host the Games increased dramatically.

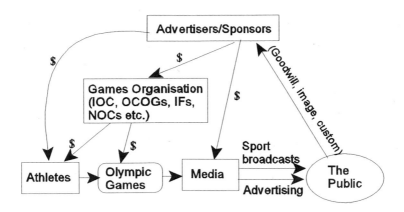

Figure 6.1. Commercial structure of the Games.

Costs

So what does it cost to run an Olympic Games, and where does the money come from to meet these costs? The estimated gross cost (before taking account of any income) of the Barcelona Games at the time of the bid was some US$1.1 billion but the final cost was US$1.4 billion (Brunet, 1993: 37). The Atlanta Games are estimated to have cost US$1.5 billion (Humphreys and Plummer, 1992). In the case of the Sydney 2000 Games, the estimated cost at the time of the bid in 1993 was US$1.02 billion (Darcy and Veal, 1994); by 1996 additional construction costs and designation of additional items as 'Olympic' costs, had increased the budget by US$350 million (Olympic Coordinating Authority, 1996); and by 1998 it was being claimed that the budget was US$1.5 billion.

The main cost headings for a typical individual Games event are as listed in Table 6.3. The major element is accounted for by the provision of sporting facilities, which typically amount to at least half of total costs. The involvement of the private sector in the provision of such facilities illustrates the point that their costs can only be partially attributable to the Games event. A private builder and operator of a stadium clearly considers the flow of income and expenditure over the lifetime of the facility; the initial capital cost is an investment, which must produce an on-going return to the investor. Table 6.4 gives hypothetical examples of how a company investing in a $500 million stadium might view the investment over perhaps a 30 year lifetime for the stadium. It indicates that a considerable profit would need to be generated every year to justify the investment. The two weeks of Olympic competition would probably make only a small contribution to the total revenue stream. It indicates that government subsidy, as a contribution to building costs, or as a contribution to annual operating costs, may be a necessary ingredient, even for a so-called 'private enterprise' stadium.

Table 6.3. Individual Olympic Games: cost headings.

- Preparing the bid
- Building new or refurbishing/adapting existing:
  - sport venues
  - infrastructure (e.g. transport facilities)
  - athletes'/officials' village
  - facilities for the media
- Training volunteers
- Staffing and servicing the Organising Committee
- Organisation of the Torch Relay
- Support for athletes' and officials' travel
- Hosting athletes and team officials (during Games)
- Hosting the Olympic Family (IOC, IFs, NOCs etc.) (before and during the Games)
- Cultural Programme

Table 6.4. The economics of a stadium.

	No subsidy	Capital subsidy	Operating subsidy
	$ million		
a. Building costs	500	500	500
b. Government capital subsidy	0	200	0
c. Government operating subsidy (p.a.)	0	0	25
d. Return required on capital (15%)	75	45	75
e. Depreciation (5% p.a.)	25	25	25
f. Total annual surplus required (d+e-c)	100	70	75

Source: hypothetical.

Financial calculations come into play in relation to the construction of the athletes' and officials' village. A residential complex for some 15,000 people, if newly constructed for the Olympic Games, clearly is expected to have an 'after-Games' life. In the case of the Atlanta Games, the accommodation was destined to house university students. In the case of Barcelona and Sydney the accommodation was and is destined for the private sector. This means that the developers can expect to recoup their capital outlay quite quickly, as the housing units are sold. In the case of Sydney, it was felt that the local housing market would not be able to cope with some 5000 townhouses and flats at one time, so a proportion of the housing consists of demountable, temporary buildings - a proportion of the residential suburb will therefore be developed at a later date when the market is seen to be able to cope.

Finally, in considering the costs of organising the Games, it should be noted that substantial items of expenditure do not appear in the officially published accounts. Among these are the costs of public services, the costs of team preparation and sponsors' expenditure.

The various public services, such as police, ambulance and other emergency services, which a host city must lay on to cope with additional visitor numbers can be substantial. In addition, the presence of numerous high profile visitors and the world-wide media focus raise security issues which require contingency plans involving armed forces and other security services. Almost 200 NOCs send teams to the Games, ranging in size from a handful to hundreds of athletes and officials. While it may be difficult to disentangle Olympic-related expenditure from the costs of sport generally, it is likely that the worldwide aggregate costs of preparing these 200 teams and 10,000 athletes for the Games, dwarf the costs borne by the Games host organisers. To capitalise on their sponsorship investment, sponsor generally need to spend many more millions of dollars on advertising, promotions and hospitality. While some economic impact studies have made estimate of the expenditure of Games sponsors over and above their payments to the IOC or the organising committee, but this is not an exact science and not all the expenditure takes place in the host city. Overall, therefore, it should be borne in mind that the true costs of the Games are much higher than the immediate costs of the host organising committee and government.

Income

Table 6.5 lists the main sources of income for Games events. The largest single item is the 70% share of television fees which accrues to the host city. We have already seen that the IOC has become proportionately less dependent on television for its income, particularly with the advent of sponsorship, in the form of TOP. In the case of individual Games, however, the degree of financial dependence on television fees varies. The implications of this for individual Games are discussed in chapter 7.

Figure 6.2 shows the pattern of income sources for a number of summer Games, from 1964. It shows in particular the growing importance of television fees and sponsorship. The contributions of governments in recent Games vary quite markedly, from zero in the case of Los Angeles to some 25 per cent of the total in the case of Seoul. Special lottery funds have also been highly significant for some Games.

As Preuss (1998) points out, the Olympic Games have generally been run at a profit, even though published accounts have, in many cases, indicated significant losses. The confusion arises over how to treat major facility and infrastructure investments which often accompany the Games. Re-calculating the profit and loss statements for all the summer Olympic Games from Munich in 1972 to Atlanta in 1996, Preuss demonstrates that, by separating out these investment items, all these Games, including the notorious Montréal Games, can be shown to have made a substantial profit, ranging from $US240 million (Barcelona) to $US800 million (Seoul).

Table 6.5. Individual Olympic Games: income headings.

- Television fees
- Sponsorship - Local
- Sponsorship - TOP funds
- Ticket sales
- Lottery
- Sale of merchandise/coins/stamps
- Government subsidy/donations

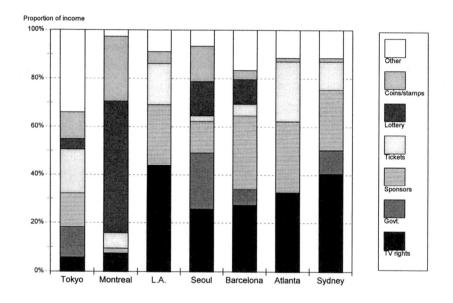

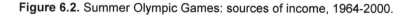

Source: Brunet (1993); Darcy and Veal (1994)

Figure 6.2. Summer Olympic Games: sources of income, 1964-2000.

Local sponsorship arrangements generally follow the pattern of the international, TOP, sponsorship deals, that is, sponsors are offered 'exclusive' sponsorship rights in certain categories. It can be seen from Table 6.2 that a number of categories remain for local sponsorship, including such areas as banking, air transport, land transport, television coverage, clothing, training and telecommunications. As with TOP sponsors, local sponsors often provide support 'in kind' as well as in cash.

A key aspect of the resourcing of an Olympic Games event is volunteer labour. The ability to generate volunteer support is a key aspect of cities' bids for the Games, indicating enthusiasm for the Games on the part of the host public as well as offering cost savings. Typically, at the time of the Games, several tens of thousands of volunteers will be involved, in marshalling, providing advice to the public and assisting with numerous, often menial, but necessary tasks.

Economic Impact

One of the main reasons why cities and nations and their governments bid to host the Olympic Games is the promise of positive *economic impact*. That is, it is anticipated that the Games will bring increased incomes and jobs to the host city, region and country. For many individuals and organisations involved with promotion of the Games this is, in fact, their primary motive. Just how significant are these impacts? The economic evaluation of sporting events is a complex process which has itself spawned a small academic and consultancy industry (see, for example: Burns *et al.*, 1986; Syme *et al.,* 1989; Hall, 1994).

Economic impact is different from the financial assessment of income and expenditure discussed above. Economic impact is not concerned with profit and loss of the event itself, but with the effect of the event on jobs and incomes in the general local, regional or national economy - thus even a loss-making event can have a significant economic impact. Economic impact is also different from cost-benefit analysis, which seeks to take into account all effects of an event, even those which do not formally appear in any financial balance sheet. Cost-benefit analysis is discussed briefly at the end of the chapter.

Assessing the economic impact of an event such as the Olympic Games involves four steps:

1. identifying all the expenditure items which are attributable to the event, that is, expenditure which would not have taken place without the event;
2. measuring these expenditure items;
3. estimating the *indirect* effect of these expenditure items;
4. converting aggregate expenditure into an estimate of jobs.

These steps are discussed in turn below. They are discussed in general terms only. Actual examples of economic impact studies in action are presented in the case-studies in chapter 10.

Identifying Expenditure Items
Identifying relevant expenditure items is not as straightforward as it might seem. For example, expenditure by the Organising Committee which is funded from international television fees or sponsorship is clearly additional expenditure which would not have taken place without the Games. But expenditure which is funded from local ticket sales or local commercial sponsorship is not 'additional expenditure' because it is likely that if the local ticket buyers or sponsors had not bought tickets to or sponsored the Games, they would have spent their money locally in some other way - there is no gain to the local economy as a result of the Games.

The exercise is complicated by the *geographical area* chosen to study. For example, if the national government gives a special grant for the Games to the Organising Committee, this is 'extra' income for the host city or region, but it is not extra income for *the country*, since it can be assumed that if the government had not given the grant for the Games, it would have spent the money anyway, somewhere in the country. Thus economic impact can be assessed at the level of the host city, the host region or province or the host country.

Table 6.6 lists the items which are typically included as relevant expenditure items in a national level economic impact study of an event such as the Olympic Games. *Direct expenditure* items arise directly from the event. *Induced expenditure* items arise indirectly. One item is the additional tourism which may arise as a result of the additional exposure the host country or city receives in the media as a result of the Games. A related *induced* item is the additional international events, particularly sporting events, which are attracted to a city as a result of hosting the Games. These events are attracted as a result of the 'glamour' associated with an 'Olympic city', but primarily as a result of the availability of high standard sport competition venues.

Table 6.6. Economic impact expenditure items - national level study.

Direct expenditure

1. Expenditure financed from fees for international broadcasting rights
2. Expenditure financed from international sponsorship income (inc. TOP)
3. Expenditure of international broadcasters in host country
4. Expenditure of foreign athletes and officials in host country
5. Expenditure of international spectators to the Games
6. Expenditure of international sponsoring organisations (over and above sponsorship fee)

Induced expenditure

7. Expenditure by foreign tourists drawn to host country as a result of heightened profile
8. Expenditure arising from additional international 'spin-off' events (e.g. sport, congresses) which take place as a result of the Games

Measuring Expenditure

How are data on these expenditure items collected? Table 6.7 gives an indication of typical data sources which would be used. Some items are relatively easy to ascertain - for example the first two items, on television and sponsor income, should be available from the Games Organising Committee. Other items usually require some sort of research study, possibly involving surveys of relevant organisations and individuals or use of existing data sources on tourist expenditure patterns.

Table 6.7. Data sources for expenditure items.

Item	Data source
1. International broadcasting rights fees	Organising Committee/IOC
2. International sponsorship income	Organising Committee/IOC
3. Expenditure of international broadcasters	Study 1*
4. Expenditure of foreign athletes/officials	Study 2*
5. Expenditure of international spectators	Study 3*
6. Expenditure of international sponsors	Study 4*
7. Expenditure by additional foreign tourists	Tourism Commission
8. Expenditure from 'spin-off' events	Tourism Commission

* Specific research projects.

Assessing Indirect Effects

When a visitor or construction company spends money in a city the initial sum spent is called *direct* expenditure. However, the impact on the local economy does not stop there. The recipients of this expenditure - for example construction workers or employees of hotels or restaurants - spend the money they receive. This expenditure goes partly to local businesses, such as shops and service providers. These businesses in turn pay wages to their staff and buy supplies, again partly from other local businesses. The initial expenditure therefore circulates in the economy, creating additional personal and business income. The process does not go on for ever because expenditure 'leaks' out of the system, in savings, taxes and expenditure paid to organisations outside the study area. The overall effect can, however, be measured by economists, and is known as the 'multiplier' effect. Thus, for example, a 'multiplier' of 1.9 may be calculated, which would indicate that an initial £1 million expenditure would result in total expenditure - direct and indirect - of £1.9 million.

Estimation of jobs

Estimates of levels of expenditure can be converted into an estimate of 'jobs created', by dividing by a suitable wage or salary level. For example, the £1.9 million expenditure given in the example above would convert to 670 one-year jobs if an average wage/salary of about £15,000 were assumed. Since much of the indirect expenditure is scattered in small amounts around many organisations in the host economy, not every pound works to create specific jobs. In some cases it may result in payment of overtime, or increased hours for part-time workers or increased profits. It is also notable that, given the nature of a sporting event such as the Olympic Games, the jobs created are likely to be short-term. Construction jobs may last a year or two, as would jobs with the Organising Committee, and some of the jobs created in the tourism industry would last as long as the positive effects on tourism lasted, but many jobs would be just for a few months, or even days, at the time of the event. However, in some cases, the effect of a burst of economic activity generated by a major sporting event, can have the effect of 'kick-starting' the local economy, so that the effect is self-sustaining and has a continuing impact after the event is over. It is believed that this was experienced to some extent in the case of the Barcelona Games of 1992 (Brunet, 1993).

Examples of measurement of direct and indirect expenditure and multipliers for recent Olympic Games events are given in the case-studies in chapter 10. It can be seen that measurement of these economic outcomes can be quite complex and therefore quite costly to implement. Since they involve research, often involving the use of survey data, the results are often far from certain and are open to challenge and debate.

Cost-benefit analysis

Cost-benefit analysis is a more complex process than economic impact analysis: it seeks to assess, and if possible measure in money terms, all the impacts of an event, not just the obviously economic effects. Examples of additional effects which cost-benefit analysis might seek to measure include negative factors, such as noise disturbance to residents, traffic congestion and accidents and increased accommodation costs, and positive impacts, such as environmental enhancement, city image boosting, possible increased sport participation (and hence health benefits) among the population and general community enjoyment of the event. Each of these items poses challenges to the researcher and calls for a significant research project in its own right. For example, measurement of the effects of traffic congestion would involve either detailed monitoring of traffic volumes and speeds before and during the event or surveys of residents to discover the effects of the event on their travel times. Total time lost due to traffic delays and congestion can then be valued using some sort of valuation of time (e.g. the average wage rate) and costs of vehicle fuel. The cost of traffic accidents is routinely assessed by transport organisations, in terms of medical costs and pain and suffering (valued by using sums arrived at in typical court awards).

The 'general community enjoyment' of the event should be particularly noted. Economists call this the 'psychic' value of the event. We are often told that the host city, and even the host country, experiences a 'party' during the Olympic Games and that a general boost to the overall sense of well-being is experienced as a result of successfully hosting the Games. Thus even those not directly involved, as spectators, athletes, workers or volunteers, may obtain some benefit from the Games. Economists have devised ways of discovering how much this enjoyment is worth to people in monetary terms - sometimes simply by asking people in a survey. Thus, for example, in a country of 50 million population, if the average person feels that the Games gave them £20 worth of enjoyment (e.g. the equivalent of going out to a show), then the 'psychic value' of the event to the community would be £1 billion. In one example of such an assessment, in relation to the Adelaide Formula One Grand Prix, it was found that the psychic value of the event to the population far outweighed all the costs of staging the event (Burns *et al.*, 1986).

Economic Decision-making

There can be no doubt that financial and economic considerations lie as close to the heart of the Olympic phenomenon as do sporting values. Since the 1980s, cities and nations have vied with each other to host the Games largely because of their hoped-for economic effects. It is the money generated from television rights and sponsorship which has transformed the Games over the last half of the twentieth century, from an event dominated by the amateur ideal and government and voluntary funding to the professional and commercially orientated phenomenon of today. Much of the controversy surrounding the Olympic Games arises from financial and economic factors. Even apparently non-economic issues, such as the problems caused by the use of prohibited drugs, have strong economic or financial dimensions, brought about by the professionalisation of sport.

Bids by cities to stage the Olympic Games invariably give rise to detailed studies of their likely costs and economic benefits, usually commissioned by the bidding organisation (e.g. City of Calgary and Alberta Tourism and Small Business, 1985; Canadian Ministry for Fitness and Amateur Sport, 1986; National Institute of Economic and Industry Research, 1990; Brain and Manolakos, 1991; Heinemann, 1992; Humphreys and Plummer, 1992). However, despite the widely acknowledged importance of financial and economic factors to the Olympic Games, and their significance in cities' decisions to bid for the Games, it should be noted that political considerations are generally more significant and more powerful in influencing the decision-making process. Information about the finances and economic impact of a Games event some seven or eight years in the future must inevitably be speculative. Projected outcomes must depend on a number of assumptions, particularly about likely levels of income from broadcasting rights and sponsorship and about the costs of constructing facilities. Further, decisions about just what to include in the Games budget and what to exclude are open to political manipulation, despite the bid guidelines provided by the IOC (1992). Thus a government or group of business people or sports administrators who are politically committed to bidding for the Games can make a number of assumptions and decisions on the budget which produce favourable projected outcomes. The politics determines the economics, not the other way around. Thus, despite the analytical techniques available to aid in making 'rational' decisions, the decision to pursue a bid is, more often than not, driven by political rather than economic considerations - even if economic arguments are used by the proponents. But the Olympic Games are not unique in this respect: they are simply at the pinnacle of a class of events which, because of their scale and profile, have been called 'hallmark' events (Hall, 1994). Because of their profile it has been argued that they are subject to a certain type of decision-making - 'hallmark decision-making' (Veal, 1994: 68).

Post-Games evaluations may, however, be having a long-term effect on the quality of decision-making. A data-base of studies is beginning to be established (e.g. Iton, 1978; Economics Research Associates, 1984; Brunet, 1993; Wilcox, 1994). Such studies are taken into account by bidding cities and now provide a basis for making plausible, as opposed to hopeful, assumptions about likely patterns of income and expenditure.

Conclusions

There can be no doubt that economics and funding have become dominant issues in the organisation of the Olympic Games and in the discourses surrounding them. The scale of the resources involved has increased markedly over the last quarter of a century. However, despite the impression given by some commentators, the economic forces did not create the Games, it is the Olympic phenomenon which has generated and attracted the resources. Masses of people are interested in and attracted by sport, and, in one form or another, such interest and attraction has a long history and seems to be universal. It is on the basis of this interest and attraction that the mass media are able to deliver audiences which generate advertising revenue and sponsors are able to justify spending their millions of dollars. Nevertheless, while economic forces did not create the modern Olympics, it can be said that they have transformed them. Whether the transformation is out of all recognition, and whether it is evil or benign is a matter of personal opinion.

Chapter seven:

The Olympics and the Mass Media

Whatever else the Olympic Games have been, they are now the ultimate media festival. (Whannel, 1984: 30)

Introduction

The *propaganda* model of media (Herman and Chomsky, 1988) asserts that the media echo, maintain and propagate the viewpoints of post-modern societies governments and/or industrial elites. They are active and willing accessories in defining and shaping the hegemonic order of contemporary cultures. While there may be occasional criticisms of these power brokers in the mainstream mass media, public debates about their defects and agendas are to a great extent curtailed and controlled. Dissension and discord is,

> .. managed and contained and the public is not provided with a full view. .. Views incompatible with the interests of corporate and government elites are attributed to special interest groups. .. A supply of experts is 'bought' in to add legitimacy to media messages that serve élite interests. (Lenskyj, 1997: 3)

As an example of this, the Australian Centre for Independent Journalism, in writing about the role of the media in Sydney during its bid for the 2000 Games, believed that journalists who were critical of the Bid Committee were labelled as being unpatriotic, inaccurate or even eccentric (Australian Centre for Independent Journalism, 1993).

The propaganda model thus has currency when examining the relationships between the media and the Olympic movement. While it is a variety of government and commercial elites whose interests are best served through the perpetuation of the Olympic Games' current elevated status in the sporting world, none of these has greater cause for self interest in maintaining the *status quo* than the International Olympic Committee (IOC).

Gruneau, examines this theme of cultural/sporting and media hegemony, specifically in the context of relationship between the institutions of sport and the media. He states:

> Television's elaboration and selection of preferred emphases and meanings, its favoured narratives, its 'management' of contradictory themes and values (e.g., between unbridled individual success and obligations to team, nation or community), can all be seen as part of a complex process through which *some* understandings of sport, the body, consumer culture and the pursuit of excellence are naturalized while others are marginalised, downgraded, or ignored. (Gruneau, 1989: 7.28)

This chapter examines the multi-faceted relationship between the Olympics and the mass media from the viewpoint of Herman and Chomsky's propaganda model, with one basic difference. While, in 1988, they argued with legitimacy that community radio and television rather than mainstream media sources were the key to affecting change, by 1998 the changing nature of information technology meant that the Internet had now usurped this function. Within existing power structures it now has the ability to be the most potent vehicle by which dissent about current Olympic policies and practices can be aired without censorship.

The Relationship Between the Olympics and the Mass Media

In 1956 Avery Brundage, president of the IOC is quoted as saying: '.. the IOC has managed without TV for sixty years, and believe me- we are going to manage for another sixty' (quoted in Lyberg, 1996: 350). Despite Brundage's prediction, the Olympic Games have now become reliant on television. Technological advances in the mass media, especially television, have enabled the Games to expand and become more accessible to viewing audiences throughout the globe (see Table 7.1). For example, the cumulative number of television viewers for the Atlanta Games was estimated to have been in excess of 19.6 billion.

The growth of the television audience has resulted in both positive and negative outcomes for the Olympic movement. It has enabled substantial amounts of funding to be channelled to the IOC and some, in turn, to Olympic sports, NOCs and Olympic Solidarity. It has allowed viewers throughout the world to share in the pageantry, victories and achievements of outstanding athletes. It has, in many ways, been responsible for the growth of sponsorship for Olympic athletes and teams and thus, indirectly, for the positive accomplishments which have resulted from this. On a less favourable note, it is also accountable for the problems and excesses which have ensued as a concomitant of this accompanying increase in commercialism.

Table 7.1. Growth of media coverage of the Olympics.

Summer Games		No. of countries with coverage	Winter Games		No. of countries with coverage
Year	City		Year	City	
1936	Berlin	1			
1948	London	1			
1952	Helsinki	2			
1956	Melbourne	1	1956	Cortina	22
1960	Rome	21	1960	Squaw Valley	27
1964	Tokyo	40	1964	Innsbruck	30
1968	Mexico City	n/a	1968	Grenoble	32
1972	Munich	98	1972	Sapporo	41
1976	Montreal	124	1976	Innsbruck	38
1980	Moscow	111	1980	Lake Placid	40
1984	Los Angeles	156	1984	Sarajevo	100
1988	Seoul	160	1988	Calgary	64
1992	Barcelona	193	1992	Albertville	86
1996	Atlanta	214	1994	Lillehammer	120
2000	Sydney	220*	1998	Nagano	160*

Source: IOC, 1998: 32. * Estimate.

The negative consequences of the alliance between television and the Olympic movement have caused some critics to question the influence of television networks, especially those from the USA, in applying pressure to schedule some Olympic events to boost their viewing audience, rather than at a time that is most suitable for athletes. On a more global scale, the growth of the Games, as a consequence of the expanded television audience, has led to concerns about gigantism of the Olympic movement. Likewise, over-commercialisation is accepted as a by-product of the Games' success and is linked to television's ability to reach a world audience.

While critics perceive these to be problems, on the other hand, the IOC and the broadcast industry appear to be content with their alliance, at least outwardly. Its symbiotic benefits flow to both partners. Nevertheless, it is important to analyse the ramifications of television on the Games, not only in terms of the impact on the Olympic movement itself, but also because of the implications for the ultimate consumer, the viewing audience.

Not all Olympic events, and indeed not all Olympic sports, are shown by each broadcaster, thus limiting television viewers' choices. Not only is content restricted in this manner, it is further altered, especially in larger events, by directors segmenting or fragmenting sports coverage. Verbal commentary further interprets and modifies the Olympic experience for the home viewer, while slow-motion replays distort the sense of time. Camera angles can provide visual images that spectators viewing the event live do not have the opportunity to witness. The underwater cameras at the swimming, those at the top of the diving platform and those in bull's eye of the archery targets, all direct the viewer's attention in a manner unique to television. Linked to this, it is interesting to note the pattern that has emerged at recent Games of many athletes themselves watching and immediately reliving their victories on the giant screens at the stadium. There is no question that the visual and auditory images received live in the Olympic venues and the experiences in the living room are vastly different.

What the majority of the world's Olympic audience see via the medium of television, is a mediated Games, enhanced, compacted, interpreted, interrupted and replaced with a distortion of time and space, often complete with the signage and advertising that is banned from Olympic venues (courtesy of the commercial breaks). While the 'clean stadium' approach at all Olympic venues has enabled the IOC to claim that it has set limits on its policies regarding commercialism, it is interesting to note how television has allowed, not so much a bending of this rule, but clever uses of it.

After his 200 metre victory at the Atlanta Games, Michael Johnson was seen proudly giving television interviews adjacent to the official timing equipment. The *Swatch* company, the Olympic Partner (TOP) sponsors in the 'time keeping' category, received worldwide publicity when their label was clearly visible right beside Johnson's head. Athletic shoe and apparel companies likewise appear to benefit immensely from television exposure. Remaining with Michael Johnson as the example, Nike, which was not an official Olympic sponsor, received a substantial return on its investment in the manufacture of Johnson's signature 'golden' shoes, through the publicity they received in the media both before and after his 1996 Olympic victories. Of course, expectations of media coverage can be a two-edged sword, especially for TOP sponsors. Reebok was the official sports shoe of the 1996 Games, yet was outsmarted by ambush marketer Nike's clever choice of sponsored athletes, whose successes, personalities and images made them both crowd pleasers and televisual.

The Nature of Olympic Television Broadcasts

Olympic broadcasts are different to most other sportscasts, understandably so because of the extended length of the Olympic Games in comparison to most sports events. It is much harder to maintain viewer interest consistently over a 16 or 17 day period than for a single three hour contest. A direct result of this need to retain audiences throughout the Games has been the evolution of a new Olympic sub-genre of sportscasting, one which has emerged in the networks' effort to build a larger share of the sports audience market, beyond the traditional sport demographic of the

18-35 male. For example, the American broadcaster, NBC, deliberately scheduled its 1996 broadcast to cater more for a female audience. Dick Ebersol, President of NBC Sports and Chairman and Chief Executive Officer, NBC Olympics Unit, when describing the network's previous telecasts of the Seoul and Barcelona Games, commented 'every minute we showed boxing we lost a minimum of 25 percent of the audience. The Olympics are driven by female-appeal sports, and we lost all the women' (Hruska, 1996: 8).

In order to cater for this previously under-acknowledged and under-appreciated viewing audience for its Atlanta coverage NBC 'used its muscle to alter the schedule so events that appeal to women will extend throughout the Games' 17 days (Hruska, 1996: 9). Consequently, the swimming programme was extended by an extra day and the gymnastics programme was similarly extended by two days, with an additional closing 'Champions Gala', based on the figure skating exhibition, which had been a successful feature of the Winter Games. To further attract the female demographic NBC devised a strategy of presenting the Olympics as a story, rather than sport. Ebersol explained 'You lose this special audience if you treat the Olympics as a normal, results driven sporting event on TV' (Hruska, 1996: 9). Yet, it could be legitimately argued that the heart of the Games broadcasts should be the presentation of sport.

After all, the Olympics is, in reality, a series of sporting events. The deliberate manipulation by television to alter this has in many ways detracted from the essence of the sport experience for the television viewer. As a result, the viewer has a television package wherein the host city, targeted athletes and celebrities with no Olympic connections, become featured actors in an Olympic story, which at times has all the makings of a soap opera. They receive star billing for short segments, of approximately 2-5 minutes, which focus on their history, past triumphs or adversities, their Olympic dreams and aspirations and sometimes long bows are drawn to even establish a relationship to the Games (which may be considered to be tenuous at best). This additional coverage allows a unsophisticated form of plot development to occur, whereby there may be multiple story lines, ones that at times have overshadowed the sports competition. Indeed, while these vignettes are being broadcast over the airwaves, Olympic sports themselves are being conducted, and obviously these are not receiving air-time.

This additional, 'human-interest' material allows Olympic sport to merge with other genres of television programming so that Games coverage becomes at various times; infotainment, drama, current affairs, news, and even as previously mentioned a soap opera. Meadow proposes three hypotheses to explain why Olympic broadcasts have mutated from purely sporting programmes into these other formats, designed to target the widest possible audience. The first hypothesis suggests that as, 'the Olympic replaced so much of the ordinary broadcasts, the conventions of all other programmes were included under the Olympic broadcast umbrella' (Meadow, 1989: 6-7). His next two hypotheses relate to the expectations of the viewing audience. Meadow maintains that the public desires the style of Olympic broadcasts to mirror its regular diet of programmes. Broadcasters have conformed to these wishes, by providing a mode of delivery that ends in a climax. Meadow lastly suggests that Olympic television is designed to appeal to the nationalistic biases of the audience, by presenting some homegrown athletes as superior to their foreign opponents.

Whatever the networks' intent it is commonplace that during prime time viewing the television broadcasts often become a smorgasbord or *potpourri* of segmented highlights. As one Australian Television producer, Bob Kemp, of Channel 10, commented:

> .. the Americans used the policy that they need to change their perspective of what they're looking at, at least every four or five minutes because they think that's the attention span of their average viewer. I give the average viewer audience more credit than that - in Australia anyway. (Goldlust, 1987: 99)

Ironically, in the subsequent Olympics, the 10 Network offered Australians a format similar to the one being criticised. The average length of a segment during the whole of their 1988 Olympic broadcast was less than six minutes (Toohey, 1997).

Many of the Olympic glamour sports do not receive regular television coverage, apart from 16 days every four years, when the Summer or Winter Games are on. Ken Sutcliffe, one of Australia's most respected sports commentators, noted 'the Olympics by and large are minority sports well packaged and they're successful because they provide the combination of character, courage, fashion, speed and danger' (*Proceedings of the NSW Olympic Academy*, 1995: 23).

Another appeal of Olympic broadcasts as television programming, suggested by Meadow (1989) above, is their nationalistic focus. Olympic networks can, to a large degree, individualise their coverage to suit their audiences' perceived needs, by choosing which feed they take from the host broadcaster. Thus, the choice of sports and events that Great Britain viewers are presented with may be vastly different to the Olympic television coverage shown in Japan. Networks tailor and may even supplement the host broadcasts by providing their own footage to suit their potential audience and to target their nation's most popular athletes. This individuality, of course, is seen as critical to a ratings success, and is one of the main reasons that networks bid for Olympic broadcast rights.

Despite ratings successes networks have been accused of taking their nationalistic focus to jingoistic excess and concentrating almost exclusively on own nation's athletes, while ignoring heroic performances of foreigners. The 1996 NBC American coverage was heavily criticised for this. The problem is exacerbated in such situations, when the network involved holds the broadcast rights for the country in which the Olympics are being held. There are many international visitors who travel to the Games but who are who are also interested in seeing events on television which may feature their nation's top athletes (who may be world or Olympic champions) and for which they do not have tickets.

Many of the international press were similarly unimpressed with NBC's 1996 coverage, as the network concentrated on American competitors, ignoring some events in which there were remarkable performances by foreign athletes, for example, the 1500 metres freestyle, in which Kieren Perkins won a consecutive gold medal, but had no US place getters, was not broadcast. Such critics considered this domestic focus to be a self indulgent exercise in national self aggrandisement.

Commentators may also play an active role in this nationalistic and even at times xenophobic process, as it is often their commentary that provides or accentuates the political focus of the broadcast, while casting aspersions on their national rivals. For example, the Chinese female swimmers were the objects of intense media scrutiny in Atlanta because of their suspected drug use, as was the Irish champion Michelle Smith. While neither the Chinese swimmers nor Smith returned positive samples, the media suspicions, especially in the case of Smith, detracted from their achievements and provided a forum for disgruntled athletes to voice their opinions. Since this time events have supported the accusers. Nevertheless the fact remains that these accused athletes passed the IOC drug testing procedures during the Games. This, in turn, reflected poorly on the IOC's current doping policy.

Thus, while the television media has the potential to truly internationalise the Olympics, in line with the Olympic Charter, this potential is restricted by networks' tendency to focus primarily on what they consider to be the glamour events and also on their own country's athletes. Consequently, some Olympic sports and champion athletes do not receive due media recognition. Concurrently, the Olympic message becomes modified, subsumed or altered in exchange for national prestige.

While networks may believe they are providing their audience with a format, focus and a nationalistic perspective that the viewers want, this is not always the case. Australia's Network 10 kept a tally of viewer complaints regarding their broadcast of the 1988 Olympics. 'Too much concentration on Australian athletes was the third highest complaint, yet not enough focus on Australian athletes also featured high on the list at number four' (Toohey, 1990). The Olympic networks need to be in tune with their viewers' requirements because of the huge financial outlay they expend to secure broadcast rights. Table 7.2 illustrates escalating costs of securing television rights since 1960.

History of Olympic Television Coverage

Television cameras first captured Olympic images at the 1936 Berlin Games, when a closed circuit television system broadcast Olympic events within the Berlin city vicinity to an audience estimated at more than 162,000. It was at the next Games, not celebrated until 1948, because of the Second World War, that a financial return for broadcasts was first arranged. The BBC agreed to pay 1000 guineas to the organising committee to show events on television. 'Reports at the time indicated that the BBC later pleaded desperate poverty, but, as they were all gentlemen, when the BBC paid up the organisers never cashed the cheque' (IOC, 1998: 25). Nevertheless, the fundamental principle of seeking broadcast rights fees was established.

Table 7.2: Television rights holders and fees - USA and Australia.

Year	City	USA Company	Fee, $US millions	Australia Company	Fee, $US millions
1960	Rome	CBS	0.4	Aust. TV Pool	not known
1964	Tokyo	NBC	1.5	Aust. TV Pool	not known
1968	Mexico City	ABC	4.5	Aust. TV Pool	not known
1972	Munich	ABC	7.5	Aust. TV Pool	not known
1976	Montreal	ABC	25	Aust. TV Pool	not known
1980	Moscow	NBC	87	Channel 7	1.4
1984	Los Angeles	ABC	225	Channel 10	10.6
1988	Seoul	NBC	300	Channel 10	6.8
1992	Barcelona	NBC	401	Channel 7	33.8
1996	Atlanta	NBC	456	Channel 7	30.0
2000	Sydney	NBC	715	Channel 7	45.0

Source: Sydney Olympic Broadcasting Organisation, 1997: 20.

At the 1952 Helsinki Games the American television network, NBC, sought to obtain exclusive coverage of the Olympics, however because of strong opposition within the broadcasting community this did not eventuate and all networks received free and equal access (Wenn, 1993).

The first live broadcast of a Winter Olympics occurred at the Cortina 1956 Games. There was an interesting sidelight to this media milestone when the final torch bearer tripped over a television cable, placed on the ice surface of the Olympic stadium, dropping and temporarily extinguishing the Olympic flame. This new technology obviously still had some minor hiccups (IOC, 1998).

On a more serious note, the Melbourne Olympics of 1956 provided a turning point in the relationship between the IOC and the media. Some members of the IOC had already recognised the potential financial windfall that television rights could provide, however, there was debate within the organisation on whether such an initiative was in keeping with the Olympic ethos, because of the possible taint of commercialism. The IOC President, Avery Brundage, an apostle of the amateur ethos, was sceptical of becoming involved with marketing television rights, however other Olympic officials took a more pragmatic approach.

The 1956 Melbourne Organising Committee had begun discussions with NBC in 1954, regarding potential television rights, however the US network was not particularly interested. Australia's location meant that broadcasting to its American audience would not be easy and there would be a large time lag between the events and their coverage. This era was before the advent of satellite television, so all footage would have to be flown (rather than beamed as it is now) to the USA.

Following NBC's rejection a tentative agreement for exclusive film rights was reached with a London firm, Associated Re-diffusion. As with the previous Olympics this proposal caused controversy.

The television networks argued that the Games were a news event, rather than entertainment, and, as such, should be available gratis to all broadcasters. They requested nine minutes of free coverage every day (Wenn, 1993). This was not acceptable to the Melbourne Organising Committee, which argued in turn that such an understanding would be detrimental to the potential sale of an official Olympic film. Negotiations between the television networks and the Organising Committee broke down, and, as a result, the networks boycotted the Games. Consequently, there was only limited television coverage of the Games overseas.

In learning from these issues the IOC took a more proactive stance before the next Games and formalised its broadcasting procedures. In 1958, Rule 49 of the IOC Charter was altered to allow the television rights to be negotiated by each organising committee. At this time the IOC did not receive the resultant revenue, however in 1968 after the financial returns from television escalated, the IOC decided that it had the prerogative to the revenue from television rights and that any resultant windfall should be channelled directly to it. The IOC would then determine its distribution.

It was not until the 1960s that the IOC began to accurately realise the economic potential of television. The first sign of this occurred in 1960, when broadcast rights of the Rome Olympics were sold to the American Broadcasting Commission (ABC) group for $US4 million.

Despite the realisation of the potential pot of gold to be gained from television, not everyone in the IOC executive was in favour of wholeheartedly embracing this new source of revenue. Some even saw it as a potential millstone. During the 1960s, the IOC President, Avery Brundage, became increasingly less enthralled with the lobbying of the IFs and OCOGs to increase their share of the potential windfall. Consequently, in an effort to satisfy all partners, in 1966, the IOC devised a new television revenue sharing formula, known as the 'Rome Formula' (Wenn, 1995).

This revised allocation of money to the IFs and OCOGs did not satisfy their demands. Be that as it may, on this point, as with so many others, Brundage refused to negotiate. Wenn (1995) argues that he adopted a non-conciliatory approach for two reasons. He believed that the sporting bodies might expend the money in a way that might be to the detriment of the IOC and also that future Olympic Organising Committees would need this large cash infusion in order to stage the Games effectively.

Brundage's strategy was, however, flawed. In a move to circumvent the 'Rome Formula' ruling, OCOGs began to negotiate separate 'technical services' contracts with television networks to increase their share of revenue. In 1969, the Munich Organising Committee led the way when it signed a tentative contract for US$13.5 million with ABC for the US television rights. Only US$7.5 million of this was designated as a rights payment. The rest was allocated to the OCOG as recompense for its technical services, such as installations and facilities (Wenn, 1995).

Bitter negotiations between Willi Daume, the Munich Organising Committee's President, and the IOC Finance Committee, resulted in a compromise which greatly reduced Munich's portion of the money. Yet, another media precedent had been set and, accordingly, this practice of separate media contracts has continued to the present. For example, for the 1996 Games ACOG signed a technical services contract of US$5 million with the European Broadcasting Union in addition to the broadcast rights agreement (Spa *et al.*, 1995: 21).

The escalation of the television revenue rights for the Games is, in many ways, directly related to advances in broadcast technology which have enabled the Olympic Games to be seen by more of the world's population. For example, in 1960 the Olympics were able to be televised live to 18 European cities and shown only hours later in Japan and North America (IOC, 1998b).

Some key improvements which have been critical to increasing the Olympic television audience include the advent of satellite broadcasts (first used in the Olympics in 1964) and the introduction of colour television, initially used in Olympic broadcasts in 1972. Other, smaller, but nevertheless important, techno-logical advances, which have enhanced the appeal of Games broadcasts include slow motion replays and small cameras (cams) placed in key positions at events. Also, in 1972, it was decided that no final was to overlap another, giving broadcasters the opportunity to televise all medals being won if they so chose (IOC, 1998b).

These television advances in turn led to increased commercialisation in the Olympic Games and a concomitant diminution in the belief of the sanctity of amateur ethos that had dominated the Games' philosophical platform since their revival. Wenn argues that there were three main causes for the advent of the interdependence between the commodification of the Games and Brundage's failure to control the Olympics to maintain his idealized amateur version of the Olympics:

> First, international athletes who discovered that sports equipment manufacturers were willing to supply them with funds for services rendered (with the display of their brand name equipment to a worldwide service). .. Second, Brundage's colleagues .. coveted commercial television revenue. They believed that the money would assist the IOC in executing its mandate to spread the Olympic message throughout the world. .. Third, Brundage had few options in his quest to temper the financial ambitions of the IFs, NOCs and representatives of the Organising Committees. .. It was predictable that the Organizing Committees would attempt to maximize their share of the income. (Wenn, 1995: 14)

Following Brundage's resignation and Lord Killanin's election as President of the IOC in 1972, the organisation became increasingly reliant on television revenue. In 1974, when the IOC received 98% of its income from television it formed a Television Sub-committee, to which it appointed representatives from the media. This has evolved to become the Radio and Television Commission which currently has seven of its 20 members drawn from the ranks of the media.

In 1984, for the Los Angeles Olympics, 156 nations acquired the broadcast rights, resulting in an estimated 2.5 billion viewers worldwide. The continuing technological progression of the medium resulted in the introduction of the 'super slo-mo' and the multilateral picture during these Games (IOC, 1998b).

Television audience interest in the Games has continued to increase since its modest 1936 debut. During the 1992 Barcelona Games the major broadcasters were showing about 17 hours per day of Olympic coverage. It was estimated that the typical viewer watched the Games an average of 11 times (IOC, 1998b).

Preliminary results of audiences for the Nagano Winter Olympics indicate that they set a new record for the number of countries televising the Games and that the cumulative global audience equalled Lillehammer's 10.7 billion viewers, despite the time zone differences for the advantageous markets of Europe and North America. The most significant increase in audience numbers understandably was in the Asia-Pacific region, where there were smaller time differences. For example, in Australia, the cumulative audience increased by 90%, to an estimated 40 million viewers (IOC, 1998c).

As a result of increases in the revenue needed to secure broadcasting rights some television networks, realising that they do not have the financial resources to bid alone, have formed alliances or unions to secure Olympic coverage. Other, smaller networks who do not have the funds to join the bidding game, do not even bother to try. This tends to limit the field of Olympic television networks to the larger, more traditional broadcast companies and continues and strengthens the hegemonic Olympic broadcasts suggested in Herman and Chomsky's Propaganda model.

When networks from smaller or poorer regions are successful in gaining television rights to the Games they may often have financial and human resource limitations. These affect the means by which they can customise their broadcasts to suit their particular audience. They may not be able to afford to supplement the host feed, or indeed even be able to send personnel to cover the Games, once again resulting in a mainstream homogenised broadcast.

While these and other constraints are a direct consequence of IOC policy there is also a concurrent realisation within the Olympic movement that the continued success of the Olympic movement is dependent on its ability to reach the widest possible audience. Consequently, for the Sydney 2000 Games, the IOC chose the EBU as the European rights holder, despite the fact that Rupert Murdoch's Sky Channel had bid at a higher price. The rationale for the decision was that the EBU could reach a larger audience, as Sky Channel is a subscription network, while the EBU is a free to air broadcaster.

A new trend has developed in the television rights bidding. Networks are now adopting a strategy of offering to purchase the rights for a package of Olympic Games, without even knowing where all of these will be held. Leading this new strategy was the US broadcaster, NBC, which in August 1995, contracted to pay $US 1.25 billion for the US rights to the 2000 Summer Games in Sydney and the 2002 Winter Games in Salt Lake City. NBC renegotiated this contract only three months later when it offered $US3.55 billion for these Games plus the Summer Games of

2004 and 2008 and the Winter Games of 2006, a total of five Olympics. Networks from other countries, for example Australia, have also adopted this packaged approach to secure ongoing Olympic rights into the 21st century.

Host Broadcasters

The task of broadcasting the Games has become far more complex since television began its Olympic association. Both a cause and a consequence of the growth of the Olympics has been an increasing number of networks broadcasting the Games, and the use of ever developing sophisticated technology. Until 1988, the Olympic broadcaster from the host country reached an agreement with the IOC to provide coverage to all the international rights holders (Spa *et al.*, 1995: 21). The Seoul Olympics began a new phase in Olympic broadcasting when a television and radio organisation linked to the OCOG assumed the role of host broadcaster. For the 2000 Olympics the host broadcaster will be the Sydney Olympic Broadcasting Organisation (SOBO). It is anticipated that the SOBO will broadcast pictures to 180 rights holders for these Games.

Feeds from approximately 40 venues will be sent to the International Broadcast Centre at Homebush, where commentary and voice overs will be added by rights holders who may also supplement this coverage with their own cameras. It is estimated that there will be:

- 3200 live hours of coverage
- 290 events
- 700 cameras
- 400 video tape machines
- 50 television Outside Broadcast Units
- 180 broadcaster organisations
- 10,000 accredited broadcast personnel
- 25 billion cumulative world wide audience
- 3200 SOBO professional staff. (SOBO, 1998)

The number of media personnel covering the Olympics has grown in correlation with the increasing importance of television as the most effective medium to disseminate the Games to the world. From Barcelona onwards the total number of accredited press at the Games has exceeded the number of athletes, which is somewhat ironic given television's technical ability to reach larger audiences. Spa *et al.* see this growth of press personnel as a result of several factors:

> .. the continued development of the media industry worldwide; the increased technical complexity (and thus personnel needed) to broadcast the Games; the desire of broadcasters to customise the output of their distinct audience needs; and, of course, the allure for any professional of being where the action is. (Spa *et al.*, 1995: 39)

Other major players in the broadcast of the Games include the National Olympic Committees (NOCs) and the International Sports Federations. At times these two bodies have acted on behalf of athletes when broadcasters have sought to initiate changes at the Games that would be advantageous to their broadcasts and perhaps not as beneficial to the athletes. For example, networks believed that the sport of fencing would be more televisual if face masks were redesigned and the traditional white outfits were changed to colour. In Seoul, US broadcasters had requested that the timing of events be altered to capitalise on their prime time audience (Spa *et al.*, 1995),

These requests highlight the pressures brought to bear by an interest group, whose presence is not essential for the staging of the Games, but vital to its preeminence in the world of sport and necessary for the economic survival of the Olympic Movement in its current form.

The Internet

While television has become the most widespread medium by which people access the Olympic Games' information and results, other forms of communications technology are playing an increasingly important role. At the forefront of this diversification is the Internet.

There are now approximately 70,000 Olympic related pages on the World Wide Web (Toohey and Warning, 1998). Many of these sites were developed for the 1996 Atlanta Games, including home pages set up by the IOC, the Atlanta Committee for the Olympic Games (ACOG) and IBM, the official sponsors of information technology for the Games. IBM claimed that its 1996 Games web-site would be the 'largest ever, with 20,000 images and pages by the end of the Games. .. There were 70 people working on the server .. preparing it to handle a load of one million hits per hour' (Stone, 1996: 42).

The official ACOG home-page was accessed 187 million times during the period of the Games. The home-page of the Nagano Olympics Organising Committee (NAOC) exceeded this number in the first six days of the 1998 Winter Games, recording 222 million hits between February 7 and 12 and an estimated 600 million hits from 1.5 million people by the end the Games. From these figures the IOC predicted that, 'the Internet will be a major force in the 2000 Olympics' (Moore, 1998: 3).

The IOC is concerned about the increasing fusion between television and the Internet and any subsequent effects that an increasing net presence may have on its broadcast rights. 'With TV rights bringing in almost half the Games operating revenue, the IOC fears the Internet could undermine its whole economic structure' (Moore, 1998: 3). As a result they are forbidding moving pictures to be shown on the Internet for the 2000 Games. While restricting this Internet option the IOC and SOCOG are looking at other possibilities of using this medium to their advantage. One suggestion is that a pool of principal organisations involved in the Games, such as SOCOG, international sponsors, IBM (the technology provider), NBC (the US television rights holder) combine their Olympic home-pages into a comprehensive 'super' site, rather than a collection of individual ones. Michael Payne, the IOC's Marketing Manager acknowledges that while the Internet may be a threat to television revenue it is not devoid of potential to be an important origin of capital. He noted that 'it's a great asset for promotion. .. and there are revenue-generating aspects of it down the road' (*Sydney Morning Herald*, 15 May, 1988: 14).

As well as providing Olympic results and information the net provides another, more interactive format. Discussion, interest and news groups permit subscribers to communicate with other fans on sports-related topics. One such newsgroup is *rec.sport.olympics*, which caters for those interested in the Olympic Games. Its readership in July, 1996 was estimated to be 16 000, with an average of 12 messages a day being posted. A study by Toohey and Warning (1998) specifically analysed its content over the month of July 1996, the month in which the Atlanta Games began. For the period of analysis all postings were recorded. The most prolific thread (i.e. series of correspondences) was one which began from a posting that expressed an opinion that the Chinese contingent was being treated unfairly by the media - 'Then why are Chinese athletics (sic) continuously being ridiculed, being hound (sic) *after. I will tell you why. It is racially motivated hate to cause distraction and frustration and you know how damaging that can be for top rank athletics* (sic)'. This thread contained 347 postings, representing approximately 1.3% of all *rec.sport.olympics* postings during the period. The thread was then chosen for an in-depth analysis to identify and trace the discussion that this topic generated.

Posters with opposing viewpoints were often dismissed and vilified by 'flaming' (abusive criticism of the previous poster's comments), often with a personal attack on the poster's character. For example *'Oh, you just pulled this one out of your ass? I understand.. Typical!'* and, *'... yours is the sort of nonsensical excuse with which cheaters face themselves in the mirror in the first place'* (Toohey and Warning, 1998: 10).

The thread developed into a series of sub-topics all related to the original posting. These threads and their relative weights are listed in Table 7.3.

Newsgroups make this type of behaviour expedient, as correspondents are physically separated. Also, posters can remain anonymous by adopting pseudonyms and concealing their actual Internet addresses. The controversy of the topic being discussed is also related to the incidence of flaming. Interestingly, the percentage of flames in this study was significantly higher than the results of the author's content analyses of two fitness related newsgroups (Toohey and Warning, 1998).

There were few, if any, examples of posters changing their original positions regarding the question of guilt of the Chinese swimmers on the basis of arguments presented by other correspondents. The ethical, philosophical and national divides that were evident at the beginning of the survey period intensified over the month studied, despite the chance to communicate and exchange ideas.

The dynamics displayed by the posters on rec.sport.olympics epitomises the passion that the Olympics evoke in many people. It also reflects the inevitability that the nexus between politics (which underpinned many of the posters' viewpoints) and the Games is enduring, with little likelihood of diminishing. It may be that the Internet actually exacerbates such political discord, rather than mollifying it. As the net becomes increasingly a part of the Olympic media, then this possibility will amplify and be beyond the jurisdiction of the existing media moguls. The term 'Olympic flame' has now taken on a whole new meaning.

Table 7.3. The development of the thread.

Topic	No. of Postings	%
Professionalism	15	4.3
Performance	15	4.3
Racism	46	13.3
Media	55	15.9
Gymnastics	16	4.6
Politics	13	3.7
Table tennis	10	2.9
Drugs	101	29.1
Drugs in swimming	32	9.2
Netiquette	33	9.5
Other	11	3.2
Total	347	100.0

Source: Toohey and Warning, 1998.

With the ever increasing media coverage of the Olympic Games and its subsequent availability to more of the world's population, firstly through the advent of satellite television and now more interactively through the Internet, the Games have now become a potent mechanism for individuals with no affiliation to the Olympics whatsoever to draw attention to issues which may also be essentially unrelated to the Olympic Movement, but vital to themselves.

Rec.sport.olympics is beyond the control of the IOC, however the effects of this and similar discussion groups may impact significantly on the Olympics in the future. The final word on the possibility on constructive international dialogue through rec.sport.olympics comes from one of the participants who conducted his own survey of the thread:

After reading postings, there is a survey of the quality of the discussions I made:
1) 'Everybody is a racist to everybody';
2) 'I am not living in a racist country';
3) 'Doping is OK because other have done it';
4) 'It is not doping because it is not in the rules';
5) 'I am a fidel citizen, so the others are wrong';

6) 'You are a fidel citizen so you are wrong';
7) 'My country's human rights report card is better than yours';
8) 'My father is stronger than yours';
9) etc...(sic) (Toohey and Warning, 1998: 12).

Radio

While radio has played a significant role in the development of twentieth century sport generally, its influence on the Olympic Games has been far less consequential.

> The four year intervals of the Olympiad did not coincide with radio's great technical improvements. Radio and the Olympic Games did not synchronize. When radio broadcasting had finally achieved a technical level at which it could provide live accounts of the Games, television was already making its appearance. (Beezley, cited in McCoy, 1997: 20)

Radio began its public broadcasts on a notable scale in the early 1920s, so that the 1924 Paris Games were the first Olympics whereby large scale radio broadcasts were technically feasible. Despite this, these Games and also the following Olympics, held in Amsterdam in 1928, received scant radio coverage in the major English speaking countries. Possible explanations for this lack of interest could be that, at this point in history, it would have been difficult to broadcast live outside the host country, as there were no international regulations or conformity regarding the allocation of wavelengths to radio stations. Additionally, transoceanic transmissions were yet to be perfected (McCoy, 1997).

The next Olympics, the 1932 Games, in Los Angeles, theoretically opened a window of opportunity for radio broadcasters to reach the large and influential American audience. Yet, even as this window opened, it was promptly snapped shut and the shutters boarded by Games organisers and their influential film producing neighbours in Hollywood. Both of these powerful groups believed that radio broadcasts of sporting events were counterproductive to their most profitable revenue source - the spectators. They argued that radio had the potential to keep their paying customers at home, glued to their crystal sets, rather than placing their 'bums on seats' either at Olympic events or at the movie houses. Consequently, the radio coverage of these Games was limited to short summaries of results, broadcast late at night, after the prime time programmes. The notion of seeking sponsorship and air time advertising during Olympic broadcasts was obviously not the economic force that it has become at the end of the twentieth century.

The following Olympic Games, held in Berlin in 1936, provided a greatly improved radio service.

> With renowned German efficiency, technicians created an elaborate short wave system which reached 40 countries during the Games. However the German Olympic Organizing Committee also issued guidelines for radio commentators

and newspaper journalists, *General Rules and Regulations for the Printed Press and Radio*, which directed announcers and reporters to restrict their comments to Olympic events and travel appreciation, with no mention of the political, and especially religious issues in Germany. (McCoy, 1997: 23)

Ironically, at these Games, as Olympic radio coverage was reaching its zenith, its ultimate media competitor, television, was launching its Olympic association. World politics, in the form of the Second World War, was also destined to play a pivotal role in radio's decline as the broadcast medium of choice for the Olympic Games. During the hiatus between these and the next Games, not celebrated until 1948, because of the world wide hostilities, commercial and government television broadcasts had begun in many countries. Nonetheless, radio still provided the major source of media coverage in London in 1948, when the host broadcaster, the BBC, provided commentary in 40 languages. While this was an improved service it was not always appreciated. For example, Australians were disappointed in the British broadcaster's lack of coverage of their nation's athletes. Consequently they sent their own commentator to the next Games, held in Helsinki in 1952.

These Games, and those following, held in Melbourne, flagged the last two Games where radio coverage outperformed its visual rival. Since this time, while there has been a radio presence at the Games, it has become a poor cousin to television. 'The pageantry, spectacle and athletic contests make the Olympics a visual event- ideal for the age of television. The timing of technological advances and world hostilities meant that radio never quite became the medium of the Olympic Games' (McCoy, 1997: 25).

Film

To date there have been over 100 motion pictures made about the Olympic Games in a number of genres, the most popular form being the documentary.

There is no known extant film of the 1896 Athens Games, however, since that time, we have visual recordings of films taken at each Games. The first feature length film about the Olympic Games was based on the 1924 Paris Summer Games and was produced by the Rapid Film Company.

Leni Reifenstahl's account of the 1936 Berlin Olympics, *Olympia*, commissioned by the ruling Nazi government, is considered by many to be the most consequential sporting film ever made. The final version, 225 minutes long, was divided into two parts; the *Festival of the Nations* and the *Festival of Beauty*. While this film's purpose was to highlight Nazi efficiency and Aryan supremacy at the Games, it has also been recognised and revered as an 'art' film and, remarkably, this appeal has endured to the present. For its time it was also inventive in its techniques.

Riefenstahl used more than 150 borrowed military troops to shoot 1.4 million feet of film. She also introduced a number of innovative cinematographic notions to highlight the dramatic impact of her work. She mounted cameras on rails to follow the sprints, placed them on horses to cover the equestrian events and installed them in tethered balloons in an attempt to shoot overhead views. To film swimming and diving events, photographers would jump into the water with a camera to follow the action. (Crawford, 1996: 406)

Other Olympic documentaries, while not as consequential, have also received a degree of critical acclaim. Director Kon Ichiwaka's *Tokyo Olympiad*, David Wolper's *Visions of 8* (based on the 1972 Munich Games) and Bud Greenspan's *16 Days of Glory* series stand out as making significant contributions to the popular acceptance of such 'infotainment' style films.

Less successful in the public arena have been the majority of those feature movies which use the Olympics as a theme in their storyline. Arguably, the one great exception to this was the 1992 Academy Award winner for best picture, *Chariots of Fire*. Set in Cambridge University, England and later in Paris, at the 1924 Olympic Games, it follows the fortunes of two British athletes, one Jewish (Harold Abrahams) and one a Scottish Congregationalist (Eric Liddell). The film 'to a great extent recreated the flavour and substance of the lifestyles, the ethos of Cambridge, the aristocratic administration of British Track and Field and the events of the 1924 Olympics' (Crawford, 1996: 406). It also highlighted religious and racial relationships within sport and the Olympic Games and the class-based English society of that period.

The majority of this genre of Olympic films have been neither commercial or critical successes. There is an certain irony in this, considering the successes of the television broadcasts of the Games which have deliberately deviated from pure sports coverage to create a storyline. This formula, of transforming the Olympics from a sporting event to a story, complete with actors, has been highly workable on the small screen. Yet films which base their storylines around the Olympic Games and its sporting aspects appear, literally and figuratively, to 'lose the plot'.

Reminiscent of the early days of film, when it was used to record the images of the Games and then shown to a paying audience, a new variation on this approach was used to record the 1998 Nagano Winter Games. The IOC licensed a production of a 70mm- IMAX, or Large Format Film, which premiered in November, 1998. With the working title of *Olympic Glory,* the film was co-produced by EMC Films and Frank Marshall and Kathleen Kennedy, two Hollywood producers whose past film credits include *E.T., Jurassic Park* and *The Color Purple*. It was directed by Keith Merrill, an Oscar winning documentary maker. The script was written by the Australian author, Tom Keneally (IOC, 1998b).

Conclusion

Historically, television rights have provided the IOC with a large percentage of its revenue and have been primarily responsible for the growth of the Olympic Movement. Although recently this percentage has diminished (from 95% in 1980 to under 50% currently), the actual amount received by the IOC from this source has increased greatly. Agreements totalling more than US$5.1 billion have been arranged between the IOC and television broadcasters since June 1995. From 2004 Olympic Organising Committees will receive a smaller share of these profits, down from 60% to 49%.

Perhaps content is not the most fruitful nor indeed the most appropriate source to tap when trying to decode Olympic media meanings. It is important to acknowledge that audiences are not entirely passive. It may be that it is their input, influenced by cues external to the Olympics, that provide the conclusive, multi-faceted and ultimate meanings to Olympic messages.

Like many other aspects of the Games its media relationship has room to improve, to search for democratisation, equality and the values the Olympics espouses. While 'faster, higher, stronger' may apply to the strength of transmission signals emanating from the venues it has at times malfunctioned in terms of the quality of the message originating about the Games.

Chapter eight:

Drugs in the Olympics: You Show Me Yours and I'll Show You Mine

> Doping is cheating. Doping is akin to death. Death physiologically by profoundly altering, sometimes irreversibly, normal processes through unjustified manipulations. Death physically, as certain tragic cases in recent years have shown. But also death spiritually and intellectually, by agreeing to cheat and conceal one's capabilities, by recognising one's incapacity or unwillingness to accept one's self, or to transcend one's limits. And finally death morally, by excluding oneself de facto from the rules of conduct required by all human society. (Samaranch, 1996a)

Introduction

There is written evidence that athletes have ingested performance enhancing substances since the time of the Ancient Greeks. Wrestlers were known to have eaten ten pounds of meat per day in the belief that it would increase their strength. Long distance runners of the same era credited sesame seeds with the ability to increase their endurance (Goldman and Klatz, 1992). Over 2000 years later athletes are still seeking a chemical advantage over their rivals.

The word 'doping' is a derivative of the Dutch word 'dop'. It first appeared in an English dictionary in 1889, where it was described as a narcotic opium mixture used in horse racing (Goldman and Klatz, 1992). Last century, in 1865, Dutch canal swimmers were reported to be using performance enhancing drugs. In the next decade so too were six-day cyclists. Their coaches were giving them a mixture of heroin and cocaine. The first reported death of a cyclist from using this concoction was recorded in 1886. 'Drug taking in sports cropped up repeatedly through the end of the nineteenth century... the Belgians were said to be taking sugar tablets soaked in ether, the French to be taking caffeine tablets, the British to be breathing oxygen and taking cocaine, heroin, strychnine and brandy' (Goldman and Klatz, 1992: 30).

Since then a number of concoctions have been trialed by athletes with varying success. While some of these potions, for example the mixture of brandy and strychnine, may have been of questionable performance value, especially when compared to their detrimental physiological effects, their psychological benefits may have resulted in improved performances.

Today, many of the performance enhancing substances used in sport are undetectable using the testing methods chosen by authorities. With the commercial and political pressures on athletes to succeed, the impulses of young, talented sportsmen and women to take drugs which will give them a competitive edge should not be dismissed as inconsequential. The temptation to cheat goes against the core of Olympic philosophy, as espoused by its leaders, The IOC have stated:

> Doping contravenes the ethics of both sport and medical science. Doping consists of:
> - the administration of substances belonging to the prohibited classes of pharmacological agents; and/or
> - the use of various prohibited methods. (IOC, 1996:4)

However, the Olympic Movement wishes to eradicate or even control the problem, it will need to be proactive in its attempts to eradicate drug use. To be effective, the IOC's doping policy would need to involve more than imposing short term punishments for offenders. A systematic, world-wide, out-of-season testing policy, combined with an intensive education programme for all NOCs to implement in their own country, is well within the current financial resources of the IOC. Because of the national prestige and financial success that comes from an Olympic victory the Olympic Movement is inexorably linked to the problem of drug use in sport, so too the Olympic Family is inevitably looked to for at least part of the solution.

Arguments For and Against Drug Use in Sport

There are cogent arguments both for and against drug use in sport. Their adherents can present each case eloquently and often quite rationally, so it is primarily an individual's own value system that will decide whether or not that person believes that performance enhancing drugs should be allowed in sport. It is a question that athletes today have to answer, although in the past, some Eastern bloc athletes and others had little say or indeed knowledge, about the drugs they were given by their own officials and team doctors. It is still a current dilemma, in the 1990s, as it is acknowledged that during this decade various Chinese swimmers have been given steroids routinely by their coaches. Some of these coaches had previously been employed in East Germany before moving to China when the East German sport system was dismantled, as a result of German reunification. It would be naive to assume that these are the only athletes currently being doped with the connivance of sport authorities, despite media interpretations of drug free sporting environments in Western nations (Magdalinski, 1998).

There are also opportunities for athletes to taint their opponent's victories by insinuating they are using performance enhancing substances, even with no concrete proof on which to base their allegations. The Irish swimmer Michelle Smith (de Bruin) was one such athlete whose victories at the Atlanta Games were tarnished by such denouncements even before the end of the Games' swimming programme. In this case however it appears that her detractors' suspicions may have been correct, as she has since been banned from competition for tainting a urine sample with alcohol, a charge she is currently contesting.

Those who argue that Olympic athletes should be able to use drugs to enhance their performances cite the following reasons.

1.   Drug taking could be monitored by doctors, so that athletes would not be taking excessive amounts of drugs. This may prevent many of the deaths or adverse side effects suffered by drug takers who have followed a 'more is better' policy. Additionally, doctors could instruct athletes regarding which drugs should never be taken and the black market trading in inferior quality drugs could be eliminated.

2.   It would create a level playing field in drug use. If all athletes had access to drugs then the Olympics would become a fairer competition. This is not to say that drug taking would be mandatory, but rather it would become a matter of open choice instead of a clandestine practice, widespread as it is. The unknown edge given to today's drug cheats would thus be eliminated, or at least acknowledged. Current practice suggests that athletes' drug use is higher in counties where doping is systemic or in the richer nations where athletes can more readily afford it.

3.   Sporting records would continue to be broken as performance enhancing substances were further refined. This would create greater excitement for spectators and continue to make sport a lucrative market for television audiences.

Those who argue against the practice of doping do so primarily for the following reasons.

1.   The use of performance enhancing drugs is contrary to the essence of sport and the philosophy of the Olympics, which places its emphasis on fair and equal competition.

2.   If doping was accepted then some athletes would still seek to gain an unfair advantage by adopting a 'more is better' policy. Checking whether or not agreed to levels of drug usage were being adhered to would be difficult to monitor.

3.   Some countries may be unable to afford the ever escalating price of sophisticated drugs. Thus, wealthier nations would be more likely to be able to participate in such a programme.

4.   Some athletes are coerced into using drugs or given them without their knowledge. This is clearly unprincipled, dehumanising and potentially

damaging to athletes, both physiologically and psychologically. Out
drug testing can uncover these practices and prevent them beco
widespread.
5.   The medical profession still does not know the long term affects of many drugs.
Even if drug use was monitored athletes might still suffer deleterious effects
from their use.

History of Drug Use in the Olympics

Athletes have been seeking a competitive advantage over their rivals in many ways
since competition is sport began. Ancient sources recount many instances of
cheating, perpetuated through a variety of forms. Ancient Greek writers, when
discussing their sporting contests, noted that equipment was tampered with, Olympic
judges were bribed and some athletes consumed mushrooms as psychogenic aids.
Thus, drug use in sport is not a twentieth century phenomenon. It is however, now
more scientifically advanced and more diverse in its forms than in ancient times.

Goldman and Klatz point out that drug use 'has been documented in all of the
sports in which weight, speed, nerves and endurance are factors' (1992: 30). The first
serious case of doping in the Olympics was recorded in 1904, when the American
marathon runner, Thomas Hicks, collapsed after ingesting a mixture of brandy and
strychnine, the drug of choice for endurance athletes of that era. Alcohol, in a variety
of forms, combined with strychnine, was at that time the most common sports
cocktail. Other drugs used to improve athletic accomplishment included caffeine,
heroin and cocaine, until the last became available only by prescription. In the 1930s
amphetamines began to replace strychnine as the most common performance
enhancer.

The 1950s, the era of the Cold War, saw the introduction of perhaps the most
devastating drug known to Olympic sport. In the Soviet Union, in an effort to
facilitate increases in the strength and power of their athletes, officials and medical
personnel gave many of their athletes injections of testosterone. This appeared to give
athletes who took it an advantage, and the Soviet Olympic medal tallies increased. To
combat this unwelcome competition, some US athletes introduced a medical counter-
measure, and began using steroids.

In the same period a number of athletes collapsed at the Games, as a direct
result of their drug use. In the 1952 Winter Olympics, held in Oslo, Norway, several
speed skaters overdosed on amphetamines and needed medical attention. In 1960, at
the Rome Olympic Games, Knud Jensen, a Danish cyclist, achieved notoriety when
he became the first Olympic athlete to die of a drug overdose during competition.

As doping became more scientific, more widely practised and its negative
effects more widely acknowledged, pressure began to mount against its use in sport.
In 1963, the Council of Europe established a Committee on Drugs, however its
success was minimal, as it could not even reach a consensus as to what constituted
'doping'. This problem of semantics has resurfaced over the years. Recently, 1998

became a watershed year in the ongoing issue, when IOC President Samaranch bought into the debate on what should constitute the agreed definition.

The year 1967 provided a tragic watershed in the fight against doping. The televised death of cyclist Tommy Smith in the Tour de France, as a result of an amphetamine overdose, spurred the IOC into action. An IOC committee reached consensus on a definition of doping and drew up a list of banned substances. The 1968 Mexico City Games marked the beginning of drug testing in the Games. However, it was not until 1974, that the IOC declared steroid use illegal. Since that time drug use and drug testing at the Olympic Games have been controversial aspects of the Games. Suggestions that the IOC and/or some OCOGs have suppressed positive results have been rife, especially in relation to the 1980 and 1984 Games (Jennings, 1996).

In 1980 no athletes tested positive, a drop of 11 from the Montréal Games and 11 less than the following Games, held in Los Angeles. At these Games there was the suggestion that there were many more positive results, but the list of potential offenders was allegedly stolen from the hotel room safe of the Head of the IOC Medical Commission, Prince Alexandre de Merode ('Drug cheats stay ahead of the game', 1996).

The most infamous case of drug use at the Olympics occurred in 1968 when the 100 metres champion, Ben Johnson, of Canada, became the 39th athlete to be disqualified from Olympic competition since testing began in 1968. His ignominious exit from Seoul, broadcast live throughout the world, was not an image that the IOC, or Johnson's sponsors, wanted to replicate. Yet, a point was made. The IOC was prepared to expel the most famous of its athletes. On this occasion there was no cover up.

Since this time an ever expanding range of drugs has been discovered in tests. There is the suggestion, because of the low number of positive results in Atlanta (only five - the same number as in Barcelona) that, rather than drug use being curtailed, 'competitors who want to cheat their way to glory are becoming more and more sophisticated about what drugs they take and when' ('Drug cheats stay ahead of the game', 1996).

Unless the IOC takes the lead that its preeminent position dictates then the accusations of its detractors, such as Andrew Jennings, that it does not want to clean up an epidemic that affects many of its stars, sound credible. Jennings (1996: 248) argues that the IOC's inactivity is motivated primarily by financial reasons and pressure placed on it by the International Federations. He believes that sponsorship deals would be curtailed if the public realised that many of their heroes' performances were drug enhanced. If this is indeed the case then the ideals of Olympism, so proudly espoused by the IOC, are being compromised by those individuals who should be living examples of its potential.

Figure 8.1. Ben Johnson wins the 100 metres at the Seoul, 1988 Olympics, ahead of Carl Lewis and Lynford Christie.

The IOC Medical Commission

In 1967 the IOC and the International Cycling Union became the first sports organisations to establish medical commissions (British Olympic Association, n.d.:1). The IOC Medical Commission's first and only President is the IOC member in Belgium, Prince Alexandre de Merode. Its current structure is:

1 Chairman
1 Vice-Chairman
5 other members (current) of the IOC
1 representative of each current Organising Committee (OCOG)
1 representative of the International Sports Federations (Summer Games)
1 representative of the International Sports Federations (Winter Games)
1 representative of the Olympic athletes.

The Commission also has a number of sub-commissions. In 1988 there were sub-commissions for:

- Doping and the biochemistry of sport
- Biomechanics and physiology of sport
- Sports medicine and coordination with the National Olympic Committees
- Out-of-competition testing.

The IOC Medical Commission has the responsibility for drug testing at the Olympic Games. All competitors are required to abide by the IOC medical code, which, in relation to drugs: prohibits doping; establishes the classes of prohibited substances and testing procedures; and determines sanctions (IOC, 1996).

Categories of IOC Prohibited Substances

The list of IOC banned substances is forever changing. As scientists and chemists invent new, more powerful performance enhancing drugs these are added to the total. Currently, in 1988 the banned substances are listed in Appendix 8.1.

Anabolic Steroids
Anabolic steroids were originally developed in the 1930s to assist cancer patients and victims of starvation for hormonal disorders and repair of muscle tissue. They are derived from the male hormone testosterone. Laura and White (1991) suggest that the Nazis may have been the first to pioneer their non-medical use, when they were issued to soldiers during World War II, in order to make them more aggressive and also to facilitate their recuperation after injury. After the introduction of drug testing at the Olympics use of steroids by athletes increased, as they were initially more difficult to detect than amphetamines. Since 1974 the IOC has tested their presence by gas chromatography

They have a number of negative side effects, which have been widely documented. These include: liver cancer and other liver ailments, For males there may be a reduction in testicular size, decrease in sperm production and loss of libido. Women may be masculinised by the drug in a number of ways, including; increase in facial hair, lowering of the voice and enlargement of the clitoris.

The IOC Medical Commission has defined that a testosterone ratio in urine in greater than 6:1 equates with an offence under its ruling (Bilder, n.d.), unless there is proof that a larger ratio is the result of a physiological or pathological condition. In 1999 the American runner, Dennis Reynolds used this as a defence for his positive result. He claimed that he had sex four times the night before his sample was taken and drunk four bottles of beer, resulting in a natural increase in his hormone levels.

Human Growth Hormone
Human growth hormone (hGH) was originally designed and developed to combat dwarfism and other growth deficiencies in children. Derived from the urine of pregnant women the drug stimulates muscular development by facilitating the production of the male hormone, testosterone (Laura and White, 1991). While the increased testosterone levels can increase an adult's size (by elongating the long bones) and strength it may have a number of debilitating side effects such as 'diabetes, hepatitis, and acromegaly, a disorder of the pituitary associated with enlarged hands and feet, thickened lips and tongue, and facial distortions, including a jutting lower jaw' (Laura and White, 1991:8).

As athletes use hGH to increase their size and strength its consumption is primarily located in sports and events which require these attributes. Track and field athletes are one example. Interestingly, because of its source, when male users are drug tested they will return a positive result for pregnancy.

Blood Doping

Drug cheats are always trying to stay one step ahead of the testers. To date many of them have been quite successful, switching to a new substance once a test has been developed to combat the use of a particular drug. For example, once the IOC had developed a test to detect steroids then some athletes began injecting testosterone (Laura and White, 1991).

Another performance enhancing option, developed in the 1970s was blood doping. This technique involves blood being extracted from an athlete, preserved by freezing and then injected back into the athlete before competition, thus increasing the athlete's oxygen capacity by up to 20% (Laura and White, 1991).

While it has never been proven definitively, it was widely rumoured that Lasse Viren, winner of the 5000 metres and 10,000 metres at the 1976 Montreal Olympic Games utilised this technique as did the 1984 US cycling team.

Blood doping was officially banned in 1985 and a test developed to detect its use. However a result of this ability to detect users a new substance, a recombinant human growth hormone, erythropoietin (EPO), was introduced to the drug users' arsenal.

Erythropoietin

Erythropoietin, known as EPO, is a recombinant human protein that dramatically increases aerobic capacity. It achieves this as it is naturally occurring hormone that stimulates the production of red blood cells that transport oxygen around the body. Thus it served a similar function to blood doping. In its natural form it is a colourless hormone produced by the kidneys which stimulates bone marrow to produce new red blood cells (Vamvakaris, 1997). When it first became available in 1988 its intended clientele were kidney patients and individuals suffering from chronic anaemia. Artificial EPO was developed to assist these individuals to obtain normal EPO levels.

The use of EPO is banned by the IOC. It is believed to be widely used in sport and give a significant advantage to athletes in endurance sports, such as road cycling, cross-country skiing and distance running. 'With one injection, or a series of injections, an automatic improvement in the stimulation of oxygen rich blood cells is generated. It replaces weeks of altitude training and makes blood doping seem cumbersome' (Vamakaris, 1997: 36).

In 1997 professional cycling introduced blood testing to combat the growing catastrophe of cyclists' deaths caused by the use of EPO. The tests are not definitive in proving that an athlete has taken EPO, however if an athlete's blood registers a haematocrit haemoglobin level higher than 50% they are suspended in the interests of their health. This is regarded as a 'health test' rather than a 'drug test'. The challenge for the testers is to be able to distinguish the artificial addition from an athlete's natural production of the hormone. The IOC has not been involved in these tests, however, it allowed the International Ski Federation to conduct these tests during the Nagano Olympics.

Research using both urine and blood samples is currently being undertaken in a number of countries including Sweden, Norway, Italy, France, Canada and England to find a reliable test for EPO. It is understood that some of the research is progressing well, and there may be a test for EPO by 2000.

The Australian Institute of Sport has also announced that it has developed a screening device for detecting synthetic EPO using blood samples. While there is further research to be done on this screening method, and the test would still require a yet to be developed confirmation test, it provides hope that this drug too will be eliminated from use by athletes who seek to gain an unfair advantage over their rivals.

Bromantan

Five athletes were caught using this substance at the 1996 Atlanta Games. Originally used by the Soviet Army as a stimulant its effects are said to be similar to Mesocarb, a motor stimulant. Its properties are similar to amphetamines and thus designed to increase mental and/or physical performances ('Two medal winners thrown out of Olympics for drug violations', 1996).

Athletes' Obligations

All athletes who currently compete in the Olympics are subject to the IOC Eligibility code. Included in this body of law is the ruling that all competitors must abide by the IOC's medical code, which prohibits doping. It includes listings of the classes of IOC prohibited drugs, obliges competitors to submit to required drug testing and provides sanctions for those caught cheating.

In collaboration with the International Federations, the IOC Medical Commission establishes the rules for collecting, sealing and testing of athlete's samples. Tests may only be carried out at laboratories that it accredits. The IOC has standardised, annual accreditation practices for the laboratories that it endorses to test urine samples under its auspices. Currently, there are only 20 laboratories worldwide that are accredited by the IOC.

From the first test, carried out at the 1968 Winter Games, until 1992, only urine samples were taken. This changed, when, at the XVII Winter Olympics at Lillehammer athletes in the Nordic ski events were require to submit to blood tests as well (IOC, 1996).

Gas chromatography, in combination with mass spectrometry (GS/MS), is the most common method of analysing urine samples. 'The only procedure not involving GS/MS is for the corticoids, where high performance, liquid chromatography (HPLC) is used in conjunction with a mass spectrometer and particle beam interface. HPLC is also used as part of the testing procedure for diuretics' (Bilder, n.d.: 3).

The majority of the tests conducted for testing of drugs used by athletes during the Olympics are qualitative, rather than quantitative - that is, if any traces of the drug are found in both urine samples, the athlete is considered to be guilty (Bilder, n.d.). Exceptions to this are the test for testosterone (which is a naturally occurring hormone) and caffeine. In these cases it is the level of the substance present in the athlete's urine which determines whether or not the athlete is deemed to have cheated.

At the Olympic Games all medal winners and a random number of other competitors in all events are required to undergo drug testing. Athletes are required to provide a urine sample, while observed by a doping control official of the same sex. These samples are divided into two jars in the presence of the athlete being tested. These containers are then labelled the 'A' and 'B' samples. Samples are then taken to the examining laboratories by security couriers, where each label is coded, so that the testing chemists have no knowledge of which athletes have provided the samples.

All 'B' samples are stored at the laboratory in secured refrigerators so they cannot be tampered with. These samples are only used if the corresponding 'A' sample tests positive. If a 'B' sample needs to be tested, then it is analysed by a 'different chemist and within a set time limit, in the presence of the athlete and a representative of the athlete and also a representative of the relevant sport's organising authority' (Binder, n.d.: 3).

Results are considered to be conclusive only when both 'A' and 'B' samples test positive, or an athlete waives the right to have their second sample analysed. If an athlete tests positive during the Games, or refuses to be tested, then he or she is disqualified from their event/s by the IOC Executive Board, with advice from the IOC Medical Commission, and suspended for two years from the testing of the second sample. Lesser penalties are handed out for offenses in certain categories of drugs, for example, pseudo-ephedrine and caffeine, when the penalty is less severe (three months). If athletes are caught during out-of-competition testing then the penalties are the same. Athletes who infringe a second time, either during the Games or in out-of-season testing, are disqualified from Olympic competition for life. When an athlete who tests positive is a competitor in a team sport then the athlete's team must forfeit and can no longer compete at that Games (IOC, 1996).

East Germany and Drug Use

In the 1960s, the relatively small country of East Germany - the German Democratic Republic - began experimenting with the use of drugs to enhance sporting performances on a systemic level. The aim of the programme was to improve their teams' sporting performances and through this the country's international prestige. Inherent in the search for prestige was the desire to demonstrate the superiority of their Communist system of government over that of their democratic West German rivals (Geitner, 1997).

Steroids were used extensively with female athletes, especially in events where strength and power was required. The swimming team, aided by such drugs, achieved a supremacy over their rivals, previously unheard of in that sport. It was at the 1972 Olympic Games, ironically held in Munich, in West Germany, that the East German women first dominated the Olympic programme. One year later, in 1973, at the first World Championship, East German women won ten of the 14 events, setting eight world records in the process.

At the Montréal Olympics of 1976, their mastery of the women's swimming competition continued, their women winning 11 of 13 events. However, the first rumblings about their drug use were beginning to surface. As with later cases, the accusers themselves faced counter charges of being poor losers. Most prominent in the accusations was the American, Shirley Babashoff, who won four silver medals (Jeffreys, 1998).

The East German women continued to reign in the pool. Between 1976 and the opening of the Berlin wall in 1989, they won 28 Olympic Gold medals. Confirmation that drugs were administered to athletes was established after the reunification of Germany when the records of the East German secret police, the Stasi, were uncovered. These files indicated that over 2000 athletes, some as young as 14, were, systematically and scientifically monitored, so that they passed drug testing during competition (Geitner, 1977).

One of these athletes, Renate Vogel, described her medical regime as follows:

The blue pills started after the 1972 Olympics in Munich. .. In the 1973 season we began to get injections also. We were given two injections per week when we were in training camp. No one was sure which shots were the steroids because we were also pumped full of vitamins B, C and D. In the beginning I didn't really think anything of it. You know, when you are around other athletes like yourself, you don't notice the difference in body size. There were very few people on the team who thought about it or really cared. They were of the opinion that the main thing was to swim quickly, and it didn't matter how. I started to notice the effect of the steroids when my clothes didn't fit any more. This was the beginning of 1973. In retrospect I can see that I had really broad shoulders. I went from a size 40 to 44 or larger. My period hardly ever came. (Shriver, in Barnes, 1997: 138)

Those athletes who refused to take drugs were punished by exclusion from teams and a loss of their special athlete privileges. Perhaps, in retrospect, these athletes were the lucky ones, as many of their counterparts on steroids were given extremely high dosages, which later translated into health problems (Barnes, 1997). The Stasi controlled the whole process and euphemistically termed it as 'supporting means' (Geitner, 1997). Their programme apparently began as early as 1971 and their involvement was thorough, extending throughout the production, development, testing and doping phases at the Institute of Research into Physical Culture and Sport (Barnes, 1997).

In the last couple of years some of the East German coaches who were involved in the doping process have been prosecuted. However it is unlikely that all those involved will be caught, and, for those athletes who died, or who are permanently affected by steroids, their punishment will not bring back their health. The political greed of the East German authorities and their wish to best their rivals resulted in one of the most devastating episodes in Olympic history.

Chinese Athletes and Drug Use

At the 1988 Olympic Games the Chinese women's swimming team won three medals. During the next ten years they continued to improve dramatically, so that at the 1994 World Championships in Rome their women won 12 of the 16 events.

Following the revelations of the East German doping programme being made public a number of coaches from Australia and the US expressed concerns that the Chinese, were achieving their success, with the aid of doping by six East German scientists who had moved to China after the German unification.

The year before, in August 1993, many believed that Chinese authorities, eager to secure the 2000 Olympics for Beijing, had kept their swimmers away from the Pan Pacific Swimming Championships, because of the possibility of positive drug tests and any subsequent backlash against Beijing's bid.

Chinese female track and field athletes had also been breaking some records, in keeping with their swimming countrywomen. In August, their athletes had won six of nine possible medals at the World Championships held in Rome. More world records tumbled at the Chinese national championships, held in Beijing. The athletes' coach, Ma Jungren denied that his athletes were cheats, insisting that it was scientific methods, endurance training (including running a marathon every day and a unique, but unpalatable diet that included 'rare worms, caterpillar fungus, dog meat and tortoise blood' (Barnes, 1997:59).

Despite these incredible improvements IOC President, Juan Antonio Samaranch, supported the Chinese, declaring that Chinese sport was clean (Jennings, 1996). Stringer, believed that the reasons for his support were clear. 'Samaranch was widely known to have favoured Beijing's bid for the 2000 Games - not the least because Chinese support was influential in delivering a block of votes vital in maintaining his own power base within the IOC' (Stringer, 1995:27).

Events were to prove Samaranch's faith in the Chinese misplaced. During the 1994 Asian Games, held in Hiroshima, the Chinese team was surprised when they were unexpectedly tested on arrival. The resulting positive tests for five women and six men (seven of them for steroid use) confirmed the suspicions of many in the swimming world (Jennings, 1996).

As a consequence of these results the other Pan Pacific swimming nations did not invite the Chinese to their 1995 championships, held in Atlanta (Jeffrey, 1997). Chinese sports authorities, concerned about their credibility, issued a statement denying that doping was systematic. World swimming authorities seemed loathe to pursue the matter, insisting there was no proof of state sponsored doping, despite the fact that Chinese athletes had tested positive 20 times since 1991 ('Early alerts on Beijing blooms were ignored', 1998). The IOC issued a statement that read: 'the IOC is very pleased to note the clear and very firm position expressed by China's sporting authorities.... They have clearly informed the IOC of their intentions to seek out and sanction the true culprits' (Stringer, 1995:27).

No Chinese athletes tested positive at the 1996 Atlanta Games, despite the rumours about their drug usage. Their performances were, however, below expectations and it appeared that their claims to have cleaned up their own house were founded. However, 18 months later at the 1998 Swimming World Championships in Perth, Australia, the problem resurfaced, when, in a furor matched only by Ben Johnson's 1998 bust, four Chinese swimmers tested positive to the banned diuretic, triamterene. The substance is believed to be used by athletes to flush the body of anabolic steroids. In an unexpected move swimming's ruling body, FINA, had ordered that all competitors in the championships be tested on their arrival in Perth, days before the event began. This was a move identical to the one that had caught the Chinese swimmers in 1994. Earlier, before the Chinese arrived in Perth, another controversy erupted when one of their swimmers en route to the championships, had been apprehended by customs agents at Sydney with a large supply of human growth hormone in her suitcase.

These two episodes added credence to the assertion by some that the Chinese doping problem was not confined to individuals. Both hGH and steroids, it was argued, were beyond the means of poor athletes (Moore and Magnay, 1998). IOC President Samaranch now appeared to have turned his back on the Chinese, stating that it would be difficult for China to win selection for staging the 2008 Games. 'They have the right to pursue a bid, but it is up to the IOC members to decide what is acceptable. I think that they would be in trouble', he said. 'I think it's very clear many would not be in favour' ('Send them home', 1998: 4).

Once again the Chinese authorities denied any involvement in the drug taking by their athletes. Shi Tianshu, the leader of the Chinese delegation at the world championships deflected responsibility to the swimmers claiming: 'it is individuals, definitely individuals' ('Send them home', 1998: 4). As the four swimmers caught for diuretic use all came from the same Shanghai club it seemed that this claim was, at the very least, ill informed.

Despite world wide condemnation of the Chinese and calls for their expulsion from the championships FINA took no further action, claiming that it was not in their power to do so. While under its rules it could expel a team if it recorded four tests for steroids in 12 months, the athletes had, in fact, tested positive only for a diuretic. This was a technicality as the purpose of the diuretic was clearly to flush steroids from the body. Sydney's Olympic Organising Committee, SOCOG, put a positive spin on the Perth scandal, contending that the 2000 Games would be cleaner as a result of the drug takers being detected (Jeffrey, 1997). Others took a different perspective, noting that drug taking in sport was a world wide phenomenon, not limited to China, and that in order to prevent its further acceptance the Chinese should be expelled from the 2000 Olympic Games. They noted that Russian swimmers had also tested positive for steroids in December 1997.

Their opponents claimed that such a position lacked credibility, for, as Jeffery pointed out, 28 of the 58 swimmers caught for drug taking since testing was introduced were Chinese and all of these were in the last decade. Her view, which is hard to counter, also claimed that systematic doping has far more devastating consequences than isolated instances (Jeffrey, 1997).

The 1998 Tour de France and its Implications for the Olympic Movement

The 1998 Tour de France became known colloquially in journalistic circles as the Tour de Farce because of the revelations of widespread use of EPO by the cyclists. As the race progressed and more competitors and even whole teams were disqualified it became apparent that the use of performance enhancing substances was accepted within this particular sporting fraternity. Public reaction ranged from approbation to censure. From the crowds that lined the route, even as the scandal progressed, it was evident that many spectators were more interested in seeing the race rather than investigating or questioning the ethical implications of doping by athletes.

The press was not as forgiving and many journalists called for an overhaul of the existing light sanctions for offenders and the ethos that allowed and contributed to the scandal. Others, of course, took the opposite view. As a result the topic of drug use in sport received a high profile in the media and many expert opinions and commentaries were sought. One such example was the viewpoint of the IOC President, Juan Antonio Samaranch.

In an interview with the Madrid newspaper *El Mundo* in July 1998, he was quoted as saying:

> Doping is any product which, first damages the health of the sportsman and, second, artificially increases his performance. If it produces only this second condition, for me that's not doping. If it produces the first it is.... The current list of [banned] products must be drastically reduced. Anything that doesn't act against the athlete's health, for me that's not doping. (quoted in Blair, 1998:63).

In the same article Samaranch is quoted as suggesting that the IOC needed to reduce its list of banned substances. This position appeared to be going against the hard line stance that the IOC had claimed it was taking against drug use in sport. Samaranch's interview was greeted with astonishment from many sports administrators. In Australia, site of the 2000 games the Federal Minister for Sport, Andrew Thompson, in typically Australian fashion, announced that he was 'gobsmacked' by the apparent change in direction from sports' most powerful administrator.

The previous year when Ross Rebagliata, the winner of the snow board event at the Nagano Olympics had tested positively for marijuana (a result he maintained was the result of passive smoking), Samaranch had formed a working group with the IOC to formulate a policy on the drug. At this time he had declared that he would seek a ban on all recreational drugs (Blair, 1998).

As a result of the media backlash from Samaranch's statements and a subsequent clarification of his statements to appease the growing chorus of adverse public and governmental reaction to his comments, the IOC President called for a world conference on doping in sport. The conference was held in Lausanne, in February 1999, and was attended by over 600 delegates.

The conference had four themes: protecting the athletes: legal and political aspects; prevention, ethics, education and communication; and financial considerations (Evans, 1999). It was hoped that the delegates would vote to ensure that sanctions for drug cheats would be applied uniformly by all international sporting federations. This outcome did not eventuate, due to the combined power of the sports of cycling, tennis and soccer, which sought and received exemptions from a compulsory two year minimum ban as penalty for first time doping offenders.

The conference voted that the final decision on sanctions applied to offenders was to be the prerogative of each international sporting federation (IF). This determination was not acceptable to some delegates. 'The British Sport Minister, Tony Banks, speaking on behalf of the European Union nations, declared that they had rejected the sanctions plan. 'It is both minimalist and permissive and it undermines the proposed two year ban" (Magnay and Korporaal, 1999). The IOC adopted a different perspective to the outcome, defending the varied sanctions on legal grounds, by arguing that this approach would result in fewer legal challenges by athletes in civil courts.

The IOC has recently come under increasing pressure from a number of the more powerful international sporting federations to accede to their differing agendas on a number of issues. The IFs are also calling for the IOC to hand over a larger percentage of profits from television and sponsorship income. The threat underlying their demands has been the withdrawal of their sports from the Games, thus decreasing the Olympic's attraction to the media. This particular instance of three IFs gaining their objective was a powerful example of the growing leverage of the IFs and the relative weakening of the IOC's authority.

The other set back for the IOC during the conference occurred when government and sporting delegates voted that the new world wide anti-doping authority would not be managed exclusively be the IOC (Stevens, 1999). It appears that the most likely scenario is that the proposed agency will be run by a cooperative of the IOC and a number of governmental agencies.

The conference's adoptions were passed by a show of applause, rather than a customary show of hands and were published in the IOC's *Highlights of the Week's Olympic News* as the 'Lausanne Declaration of Doping in Sport'. In this document the conference outcomes were listed as follows:

Education and preventative campaigns will be intensified, focusing on youth and athletes and their entourage....
The Olympic Movement's Anti-Doping Code is accepted as the basis for the fight against doping....

The minimum required sanction for major doping substances or prohibited methods shall be a suspension of the athlete from all competition for a period of two years, for a first offense. However, based on specific, exceptional circumstances to be evaluated in the first instance by the competent IF bodies, there may be a provision for a possible modification of the two year sanction.... An independent International Anti-Doping Agency shall be established so as to fully operational for the Games of the XXVII Olympiad.... The Olympic Movement commits to allocate a capital of US $25 million to the Agency.... The IOC, the IFs and the NOCs will maintain their respective... responsibility to apply doping rules in accordance with their own procedures.... Consequently, decisions handed down in the first instance will be under the exclusive responsibility of the IFs, the NOCs or, during the Olympic Games, the IOC.... The collaboration in the fight against doping between sports organisations and public authorities shall be reinforced. (IOC, 1999a: 1-2)

Summary

Athletes have been seeking a competitive advantage over their rivals in a number of ways, both legal and illegal, since sport began. Ancient sources recount many instances of cheating, perpetuated through a variety of forms. For example, the Greeks note that equipment was tampered with and judges bribed at the ancient Olympic Games. Other athletes ingested potions in order to better their performances. Thus, drug use should not be thought of as merely a malaise of twentieth century sport. It is, however, now undoubtedly more scientifically advanced and more diverse in its forms than in ancient times.

It is both gullible and arrogant to suppose that drug use by athletes only occurs in countries other than one's own. For example, in Australia, which is one of the world leaders in drug testing in sport, positive results are still being recorded on a regular basis, as evidenced in Table 8.1.

Table 8.1. Drug tests in sport in Australia, 1991-1997.

Year	Refusals	Total positive
1991-92	7	40
1992-93	21	53
1993-94	5	38
1994-95	9	34
1995-96	7	34
1996-97	4	35

Source: www.ausport.gov.au/asda/trends.html (p. 3).

The current use of drugs to enhance performance in the Olympic Games should not be seen as an isolated problem. Of course, because of the consequences of success in today's sport, seeking an advantage over one's competition is what athletes require in order to secure and maintain sponsorship, fame and prize money. Drug use in sport is also symptomatic of a larger problem of drug use in today's world, where we are conditioned to use drugs as the most expedient prophylactic solutions, rather than seeking to analyse the root cause of our medical or social problems

Although legislation, through banning of offenders, has the potential to lessen the problem of drug use in the Olympic Games, it is only a partial solution. A more complete approach would also involve the use of more educative initiatives as well. Part of the learning process of those involved with sport must be to recognise the linkages between drug use in society and drug use in the Olympic Games. The latter is a product of the former.

Appendix 8.1: The IOC Medical Commission list of banned substances.

Stimulants	Narcotics	Beta-blockers	Anabolic agents / Beta 2 agonists	Diuretics	Masking agents	Peptide hormones
amineptine	ethylmorphine	acebutolol	boldenone	acetazolamide	epitestosterone	hCG
amfepramone	hydrocodone	alprenol	clenbuterol	bendroflurmethiazide	probenecid	hGH
amphetamine	morphine	atenolol	clostebol	bumetanide		erythropoietin
caffeine	pentazocine	betaxolol	danazol	canrenone		CTH
cathine	pethidine	bisoprolol	dehydrochlormethyl	chlortalidone		
cocaine	propoxyphene	bunolol	dihydrotestosterone	furosemide		
cropropamide		metoprolol	drostanolone	hydrochlorothiazide		
crotethamide		oxprenobol	fluoxymesterone	indapamide		
ephedrine		propranolol	formebolone	spironolactone		
etamivan		sotalol	mesterolone	triamterene		
etilamphetamine			metadienone			
etilefrine			metenolone			
fencamfamine			methandriol			
fenetylline			methyltestosterone			
fenfluramine			nandrolone			
heptaminol			norethandrolone			
methylendioxyampheta-			oxandrolone			
mine			oxymesterone			
mefenorex			oxymestholone			
norphenfluramine			stanozolol			
parahydroxyamphet-			testosterone			
amine			trembolone			
pemoline						
phendimetrazine						
phentermine						
phenylephedrine						
phenylpropanolamine						
pholedrine						
prolintanepropylhexe-						
drine						
pseudoephedrine						
salbutamol						
strychnine						
mephentermine						
mesocarb						
methamphetamine						
methoxyphenamine						
methylephedrine						
methylphenidate						
nikethamide						

Source: IOC President: The IOC Medical Commission and the Fight Against Doping, http://www.olympic.org/medical/eddop.htm

Chapter nine:

Women and the Olympic Games

> Unattractive girls are comparatively good sports. Pretty girls are not. The ugly ducklings, having taken to sport as an escape and to compensate for whatever it is they lack, sex appeal, charm, ready-made beauty, they usually are too grateful to be up there in the championship flight to resent losing so much. .. There is no girl living who can manage to look anything but awful during the process of some strenuous game. .. If there is anything more aesthetically more depressing than the fatigue-distorted face of a girl runner at the finish line, I have never seen it. .. No matter how good they are, they can never be good enough, quite, to matter. (Gallico, 1940: 242-244)

Women and Sport

Societies establish, fashion and perpetuate behaviours and expectations that inform and constrain us in most facets of our life. In sport, as in many other activities, one of the key differences between the acceptance of male and female participation relates to societal perceptions of gender and its subsequent determination of appropriate roles and behaviours based on these expectations. Dimensions of gender are culturally constructed disparities between males and females that are grounded in the praxis of power and associated with concepts of 'femininity' and 'masculinity'. Thus, gender is central to the examination of the attitudes and behaviours to sport, including participation of athletes in the Olympic Games.

Orthodox stereotypes of male athletes stress their possession and application of strength, muscularity, aggression and power, characteristics which accentuate their masculinity On the other hand the athletic female is often faced with the expectation of conforming to society's definition of what constitutes 'womanly' and thus more passive behaviour. Consequently, the physical and psychological attributes which contribute to a female athlete's sporting success may conflict with society's sanctioned notions of femininity. If a woman wants to achieve excellence in a sport which involves strength and the development of a muscular body, or participate in a traditionally male sport, she risks exclusion from society's definition of 'normal'. Censure may be evidenced in various forms, for example labels questioning her sexuality. The backlash against women who do not conform to idealised feminine images is, of course, not confined to the sporting arena, it is found across many walks of life.

Historically sport has been the embodiment of hegemonic masculinity, an avenue by which males can demonstrate their superiority over females. To participate in sport is often an empowering experience for males, it has been less so for females. This is not to say that sport has been universally positive for males and disadvantageous for females. Indeed, writers such as Messner and Sabo (1990) assert that sport can also be problematic for those males who participate in sports which fall outside the bounds of its traditional masculine persona, while others, for example, Henderson (1994), note that sport can be a site of resistance for women.

Generally however females have had less opportunities than males to develop positive selfhood through physical activity. This is even further accentuated for females of certain social and cultural backgrounds where the dichotomy between masculinity and femininity is greatest and participation by women in many sports is considered to be inappropriate. The sport gender divide may be even further perpetuated by women's traditional roles in relation to their family and domestic duties, which leave them little time to pursue sport for leisure purposes.

Gendered differences in sport are not confined to the field but are also evident in administration, coaching and management. Males dominate all of these realms. The works of McKay (1992), Cameron (1995), Theberge (1988, 1991), Bryson (1987,1990) and Hall *et al.* (1990) have highlighted the comparatively small number of women in leadership positions in sports administration and coaching. This male domination of sports participation, management, administration and decision-making has put women in a position of continually being required to justify and fight for their right to equal access to facilities, funds, programmes and leadership opportunities.

Research

The major focus of many studies on gender and sport has been based on differences or otherness between males and females, debate centring on whether these dissimilarities are biologically determined or socially constructed. This philosophy of disparity has allowed its proponents to ground their arguments in a conviction of inferiority which has then been employed to justify the maintenance of male domination of sporting spaces and places.

It is because of the relative strength and speed of most males compared to most females that sense definitions of women in sport are often gauged in terms of their otherness from males. 'The salient point of this socially constructed... differentiation is that through these historical definitions women are perceived not only as 'other than' but as 'less than' men (Kane and Parks, 1992: 50). However, other writers (e.g. Hall, 1996) caution against the application of gender roles as the foundation for the analysis of women's sport because this nullifies the influences of other powerful determinants such as ethnicity, class and age.

Other research on gender issues in sport has examined sport's ideological and systemic inequities. For example, works by Bryson (1987), Stoddart (1994) and McKay (1991) highlighted discriminatory practices which prevent many females from attaining equal access and equity on the sporting field. Bryson (1990) suggested that the popular sports for boys and men have constructed and reconstructed male dominance by equating maleness with skills and attributes prized in our society, such as aggressiveness, power and strength.

In more recent years, however, much of the research in this area has moved beyond considerations of relative opportunities and participation to a deliberation of the cultural meanings and significance that we attach to participation in physical activity. This research is seeking to examine the power of sport in the construct of ideology (Theberge, 1991). Sport has been accepted to be a particularly dynamic site for the construction and affirmation of gender identity, however it is now also contended to be a site where gender expectations may become contested.

The search for gender equality at the Olympics is based on a liberal feminist perspective. Its defining characteristic has been predicated on examining and analysing discrimination, socialisation, equality of opportunity and the rights of women. It is considered to be an optimistic approach to gender issues, with links to liberal democratic principles. This theoretical basis has been applied to and driven analyses of sport as the subject of academic study since the 1960s. Scraton (1992: 7) notes that 'women have developed theoretical frameworks around their practice, claiming that theory can inform practice just as practice must be the cornerstone of theory'.

These theoretical underpinnings have allowed scholars to push the barriers of inquiry beyond only thinking in terms of women's Olympic participation rates and associated issues into a broader understanding of gender relations in society. Recent analyses question the male domination of sport, its institutional bases, values and practices, calling for sports' revaluation to better cater for all its constituents (Kew, 1997).

Women in the Olympic Games

The story of women's participation in the Olympics is one of 'struggle and diversity-power and control were fought over, not just between men and women, but between different groups of women' (Hargreaves, 1994: 10). It is over-simplistic to generalise all the historical factors influencing women's Olympic participation as a number of the barriers to equal participation are culturally, economically and politically specific (Hargreaves, 1994). Throughout the era of women's participation it is evident that the Olympics, as with other sporting events, has become a site where society's values, meanings and ideologies can be disputed.

At the modern Olympics' genesis, at the end of the nineteenth century, power relations based on gender were transferred to athletes' participation outcomes, and women, in the Olympic arena, as in life, came off second best. Even after World War I, when the openings created for women in the workplace transferred to greater freedom in many spheres of their lives, the perceptions of the masculinising effects of sport still remained dominant and acted as a deterrent to equality of access and opportunity (Birrell and Cole, 1994). The modesty, dignity and morality of female athletes, highly valued as the culturally appropriate behaviour for women, was policed by both sexes, but remained the responsibility of women. This too had an effect on determining which Olympic sports were deemed seemly for women and defined the behavioural and dress standards for female athletes who chose, or were allowed, to participate. It is interesting to note that the long standing role of the chaperone for female Olympic athletes did not have a male equivalent.

According to Hargreaves (1994), there have been three phases of women's participation in the modern Olympic Games. The first, from 1896 until 1928 was a period of exclusion of women and efforts on the part of some of them to resist this dismissal. Hargreaves describes the years 1928-1952 as the second epoch, a time of consolidation and struggles for women in the Olympics, where their events were confined to those that met the criteria of acceptability. The last phase in her classification, dating from 1952, until the present, she defines as the period of challenge to masculine hegemony. This span was triggered by the entry of the Soviet bloc into the Games and the resulting influence of their political medal agenda, wherein it was immaterial to their national governments whether their nation's medals were won by male or female athletes. The statistical pattern of women's participation in the Games is summarised in Tables 9.1 and 9.2.

The founder of the modern Games, Baron Pierre de Coubertin, had opposed women's participation in the early years of the Games (Hargreaves, 1994; Welsh and Costa, 1994). In his plans for the Games revival he had envisaged they be the preserve of amateur male athletes. This exclusivity was short lived.

At the 1900 Paris Olympic Games Charlotte Cooper became the first female modern Olympic victor, when she won the Ladies singles in tennis. She beat Helene Prevost of France 6-1, 6-4 in the final. Cooper was also half of the victorious Mixed Doubles combination. There were 1318 men and 19 women at these Games. Tennis had been introduced to the Olympics in 1900, largely because it was a sport played by women of the upper classes (Blue, 1988). It was females from privileged backgrounds that had the necessary access to the money and time needed to enable their participation in socially acceptable sports. The women at these Olympic Games came from five countries and participated in three events in two sports. Since that time women's participation in the Olympics has grown to the extent that 3626 athletes competed in 108 events in 21 sports at Atlanta in 1996. This represented 40% of athletes at these Games (IOC, 1998). Yet, parity is far less than this in other aspects of the Olympic Movement, for example, in terms of female membership of the International Olympic Committee and the total of sports and events open to women competitors compared to their male counterparts.

Table 9.1. Women's participation in the Summer Olympic Games.

Year	Sports	Events	NOCs sending female athletes	Female participants	Total participants
			Number of:		
1896	0	0	0	0	311
1900	2	3	5	19	1330
1904	1	2	1	6	687
1908	2	3	4	36	2035
1912	2	6	11	57	2574
1920	2	6	13	77	2607
1924	3	11	20	136	3092
1928	4	14	25	290	3014
1932	3	14	18	127	1408
1936	4	15	26	328	4066
1948	5	19	33	385	4099
1952	6	251	41	518	4925
1956	6	26	39	384	3342
1960	6	29	45	610	5348
1964	7	33	53	683	5140
1968	7	39	54	781	5531
1972	8	43	65	1058	7830
1976	11	49	66	1247	6189
1980	12	50	54	1125	5512
1984	14	62	94	1567	7078
1988	17	86	117	2186	9421
1992	19	98	136	2708	10,563
1996	21	108	169	3626	10,744

Source: IOC Department of International Cooperation, 1998.

Ironically, what little women's participation existed in the early Games was the result of the IOC's laissez-faire attitude to the Games' organisation. Female athletes participated in 1900 and 1904 without the IOC's official consent. Only eight women participated in the St Louis Games of 1904. All of them were archers from the US and there have since been doubts expressed as to whether or not their events were even classified as official Olympic competitions (Simri, 1977). Women's participation in the 1908 Games was more formalised (Hargreaves, 1994). At this point the IOC lacked the necessary organisational skills or infrastructure to control the Games' programmes. This was the responsibility of the Paris and St. Louis Games organising committees, which allowed inclusion in their programmes of the socially acceptable sports of tennis in 1900 and archery, classified as an exhibition event, in 1904 (Welsh and Costa, 1994).

Table 9.2. Women's participation in the Winter Olympic Games.

No.	Year	Location	Number of competitors:		
			Male	*Female*	*Total*
I	1924	Chamonix, France	16	5	294
II	1928	St. Moritz, Switzerland	25	6	393
III	1932	Lake Placid, USA	17	5	307
IV	1936	Garmich-Partenkirchen, Germany	28	6	756
	1940	Not celebrated	-	-	-
	1944	Not celebrated	-	-	-
V	1948	St. Moritz, Switzerland	28	6	713
VI	1952	Oslo, Norway	30	5	732
VII	1956	Cortina, Italy	32	5	819
VIII	1960	Squaw Valley, USA	30	5	648
IX	1964	Innsbruck, Austria	36	7	933
X	1968	Grenoble, France	37	7	1293
XI	1972	Sapporo, Japan	35	7	1145
XII	1976	Innsbruck, Austria	37	7	1231
XIII	1980	Lake Placid, USA	38	7	1283
XIV	1984	Sarajevo, Yugoslavia	49	7	1410
XV	1988	Calgary, Canada	57	7	1423
XVI	1992	Albertville, France	64	7	1801
XVII	1994	Lillehammer, Norway	67	7	1737
XVIII	1998	Nagano, Japan	80	7	3000
XIX	2002	Salt Lake City	80	7	-

Sources: Wallechinsky (1992), IOC (1998), USOC (1999).

Determined to bring order to the chaos caused by conflicting opinions on women's participation the Olympic Organising Committee for the 1908 Games in London admitted women's events of exhibition gymnastics and aquatics (Welsh and Costa, 1994). These 1908 Olympics were a watershed for a number of reasons, one of which was that the first event open to both sexes, in the sport of sailing was introduced. Other sports in which there were female competitors at these Games included tennis, archery and figure-skating (which was later shifted to the Winter programme) (Phillips, 1992).

By 1912 the International Federations that had included women's events in the Games were having a observable effect in improving their constituents' status in achieving recognition in sport. The International Swimming Federation, in particular, provides a strong example of this. At the Stockholm Games 41 of the 55 female competitors were swimmers, the remaining 14 competed in the tennis competition. Fanny Durak of Australia was the first female Olympic swimming champion. She won the 100 metres freestyle in 1 minute and 22.2 seconds, a time identical to that of Alfred Hajos of Hungary, the Games' first male winner of the same event at the 1896 Games.

Phillips (1990) notes that the task for women in the Olympic movement, as in the wider world of sport, at this time was twofold; to avoid exclusion and to create a meaningful presence. For example, in 1920 de Coubertin suggested that the 1924 Games should have no female competitors. The IOC rejected this proposal, however he was unrepentant and later, in 1925, at the Olympic Congress in Prague, he claimed that female participation in the Games was illegal (Simri, 1977). The most notable outcome of early resistance by feminist sporting to this attitude on the part of sporting officials resulted in the creation of the Federation Sportive Feminine Internationale (FSFI), under the leadership of Alice Milliat.

This group organised a separate female sporting contest, the first 'Women's Olympics', held in 1922 in Monte Carlo, with 300 competitors (Blue, 1988). Subsequent to their success and IOC's objections to the use of the word 'Olympic' in their title the event was renamed and the FSFI staged the Women's World Games in 1926, 1930 and 1934, following the four-year cycle of the Olympics, but in half way point between them. However, it would be unrealistic and simplistic to portray these gains as being universally accepted by all women. There were many women who were against the new sporting patterns of female participants, which now, more closely mirrored that of males. These opponents believed that a new model for women's sport should be adopted, based on cooperation, rather than the competitive model that events such as the Olympic Games exemplified.

It was the success and accomplishment of the 'Women's World Games' that forced the hand of the male dominated IOC into allowing more events for women onto the Olympic programme. Yet admittance for female track and field athletes to the Games was problematic. Indeed, the IOC held a conference in 1925 to examine the 'issue' of sport and women. Hargreaves (1994: 213) notes that its 'medical report was a reaffirmation of the popular nineteenth century theory of constitutional overstrain... urging caution about the type and amount of exercise... with a scientific justification limiting women's participation in track and field athletics during the following years'.

In 1928 track and field competitions in the 100 metres, the high jump, discus, 400 metres hurdles and 800 metres were added to the women's schedule at the Olympic Games to placate the FSFI. Unfortunately several competitors appeared to be distressed at the finish of the 800 metres. This supposed collapse of the women, attributed to tackling a distance in excess of their physiological limits, became a defining point in Olympic history for a number of reasons. Initially the IOC used it as a justification of its previous stance to severely limit women's participation and consequently women were only allowed to compete at shorter distances in track events for about four decades. Some of the strength-related field events were also expunged from the programme. More recently feminist scholars have chosen the 1928 800 metres as the exemplar of the oppression of female athletes in the Games.

Count Baillet-Latour had followed de Coubertin as President of the IOC and also continued his predecessor's line of philosophical opposition to female Olympians in certain sports. In 1930 he suggested to the Olympic Congress, held in Berlin, that women should only be allowed to compete in 'aesthetic events'. His list of acceptable sports included skating, tennis, gymnastics and swimming. This wish to downsize female's participation was inversely proportional to the plans to increase the number of sports for men. Such opposition has continued throughout the twentieth century in many forms.

In 1936 attempts to include females competitors in the equestrian events and hockey competitions were rejected (Simri, 1977). In 1984 when Gabrielle Andersen-Schiess' attempts to finish the marathon were broadcast throughout the world the press was still questioning the endurance ability of females, despite the fact that she had recovered less than two hours later. 'Marty Liquori, the television analyst, was not impressed with her courage, repeatedly saying: 'Someone should take charge and stop her. .. Someone should walk out there and take responsibility and grab her' (Birrell and Theberge, 1994: 354). The notion of the female athlete as a frail individual has been an enduring feature of the Olympic saga.

Women in Administration

While it is evident that Olympic female athletes are growing in numbers and in percentages of athletes competing the Games the same cannot be said about their administrative counterparts. It was not until 1981 that the first women were admitted to the IOC. To date there have been 12 women elected (see Table 9.3). While there has been a mind set change within the IOC to be more inclusive of women, some critics (Jennings, 1996; Sheil, 1998) believe that the changes are too slow and are only tokenistic. Be that as it may, the change has lately been in the right direction and is being implemented through a number of initiatives. For example, in December 1995, the IOC President Samaranch established a Women and Sport Working Group whose purpose was to provide advice to the Executive Board and himself on issues related to females and the Olympics. As with all IOC working groups it is only an advisory body.

In July 1996 the IOC adopted the following proposals:

1. The NOCs should immediately establish as a goal to be achieved by 31 December 2000 that at least 10% of all the offices in all their decision-making structures (in particular all legislative or executive agencies) be held by women and that such percentage reach 20% by 31 December 2005.
2. The International Federations, the National Federations and the sports organizations belonging to the Olympic Movement should also immediately establish as a goal to be achieved by 31 December 2000 that at least 10% of all positions in all their decision-making structures... be held by women and that such percentage reach 20% by 31 December 2005. ..

Table 9.3. Female IOC members (June 1998).

Name	Country
Ms Pirjo Haggman*	Finland
Ms Flor Isava Fonseca	Venezuela
HSH Princess Nora of Liechtenstein	Liechtenstein
Ms. Anita L DeFrantz	USA
HRH the Princess Royal	Great Britain
Ms Carol Anne Letheren	Canada
Ms Vera Caslavska	Czech Republic
Ms Gunilla Lindberg	Sweden
Ms Shengrong Lu	China
HRH the Infanta Dona Pilar de Borbon	Spain
Ms Irena Szewinska	Poland

Source: IOC Dept. of International Cooperation, 1998. * Since resigned.

3.   The Olympic Charter be amended to take into account the need to keep equality for men and women' (IOC Department of International Cooperation, 1998: 22).

The Media and Women in the Olympic Games

The media are major contributors to sport's hegemonic discourse, which values male sport more highly than female sport. One of the outcomes of this alliance is that studies investigating relationships between women's sport and the media have found a consistency of findings: that female sport is grossly under-represented in newspaper, radio and television coverage (Fasting and Tangen, 1983; Australian Sports Commission and Office of the Status of Women, 1985; Wilson, 1990; Theberge, 1991; Ferkins, 1992; Stoddart, 1994; Phillips, 1997). While results of some of these studies indicate that there has been an increase in female coverage, it would be difficult to interpret any of the results as truly addressing a situation which is seen by many as discriminatory (Phillips, 1997). Thus, it is manifest that this research has had little, if any, impact on reducing existing inequities or changing the sentiments of those who determine what is seen, heard, or read in the media.

As a result of the symbiotic relationship which has developed over time between the mass media and sport, the mass media have now become one of the key benefactors and key beneficiaries of institutionalised sport and, as such, have become a forceful site for constructing gender discourse and fashioning hegemony. As Daddario (1994: 276) notes, 'This is particularly the case for the Olympic Games which offer long-term profitability for the networks, with many hours of potential commercial revenue.' The Olympic Games, as portrayed by the media, may thus provide consensual views of female's athletic abilities, views which carry over into other spheres of women's lives.

The increase in the percentage of Olympic athletes who are female has not always been assisted by their media representations. The press have not always willingly helped in seeking equality for them. In 1928, *for example,* 'Fed up' in *The Bulletin* wrote: 'after the 800 metres race at the Olympiad, knocked out and hysterical females were floundering all over the place. Competition in such events can serve no useful or aesthetic purpose in feminine existence' (Phillips, 1992:36). This was neither the first nor the last such scathing viewpoint of women's athletic ability.

The sports media, in particular, have constructed narrative and visual messages texts and sub-texts which emphasise physical differences between men and women and consequently have contributed to the construction of a gender hierarchy, based on traditional notions of masculine strength and feminine frailty. While males are often portrayed in a manner that accentuates their athletic abilities, females are presented, at times, in terms which define their femininity and/or body image, rather than their athleticism. Consequently, these portrayals often depict women's perform-ances as being inferior to men's. The Olympic Games broadcasts are important in these constructs because of their status as the pinnacle of athletic achievement. They are considered by many people to present and define a consensual view of women's athletic abilities that is carried over into other spheres of their lives. Yet from Olympic television broadcasts Higgs and Weiller (1994: 245) believe, 'there is reason to worry about audience sensemaking about the athletic abilities and limitations of men and women'.

Apart from general principles of equity these results are disturbing because of the media's pervasive influence on society. One of the most common reasons girls have cited as an incentive for becoming active in sport and selecting a particular discipline is the influence of role models (House of Representatives Standing Committee, 1991: 10). Yet girls and women have a paucity of female sports heroes to model themselves on, not because females are not participating and succeeding in sport, but rather because their achievements have largely been ignored by the media. Ignoring female sport in turn sends the message to many sections of the community that women's sport is unimportant, trivial and unworthy of attention. This then serves to reinforce and legitimise the patriarchal male sport model as hegemonic (Toohey, 1997).

When asked why they persist in showing mainly male sports and continue to ignore women's sport the media continue to justify their position based on questionable logic, for example, that women's sport is dull and lacks excitement, viewers are uninterested in it, and it is generally not newsworthy ('Women, sport and the media', 1988: 6). However, an Australian case-study of the Summer Olympic Games has shown that the public is attracted to televised female sport, if given the opportunity to watch it (Toohey, 1997).

A survey conducted during the 1988 Seoul Olympic Games indicated that 90% of respondents watched it on television at least once and 44% daily. Swimming, gymnastics and diving were the three sports which respondents most enjoyed. Television coverage of these three sports provided fairly equal coverage of male and female competition, indicating that viewers enjoy watching female sport, if given a chance ('Task of sending the news home', 1988; Toohey, 1997). Total televisio coverage of women's events during the 1988 Olympics equalled 33% of sports coverage, significantly higher than during regular programming (Toohey, 1997).

These results are not unique. A similar survey of Australians during the 1992 Barcelona Olympics produced comparable results and attitudes. Some 98% of respondents watched the television coverage of the Games. Swimming, gymnastics, rowing and track and field were the most watched sports with swimming, gymnastics, and track events being the three most popular sports (Sweeney and Associates, 1992). These events included almost equal numbers of male and female athletes, and there was greater than equal television air-time devoted to women's events compared to men's. It is quite realistic to suggest that, if the women's events were not good television, viewers would have changed channels. Television rankings indicated that they did not, so they must have enjoyed the coverage (Toohey, 1997).

While certain links can be identified between viewers' nationalistic sentiments and their programme preferences, data did not indicate that this was relevant for these broadcasts. Success does however influence television directors' and programmers' selection of which sports to broadcast. For example, in 1988 when the Australian women's hockey team won the gold medal it received 424.4 minutes of coverage. The 1992 team was less successful and this resulted in less air time. While the success rate of Australia's female athletes partly explains their Olympic television exposure, it is not the complete answer, for Australian women are also successful in other international sporting events, yet these do not receive air time on commercial television. Thus, while connections can be deduced between nationalism and sporting success and television network decisions to provide increased coverage of women's sport during the period of the Olympics, these factors are not always related to audiences' initial views on the female sports they most enjoy watching - that is, audiences can be 'created' by the provision of appropriate coverage. This implies that arguments for continuing under-representation of women's sport, based on lack of the excitement factor and viewer interest are clearly fallacious (Toohey, 1997).

At the Seoul Summer Olympics in 1988 there were 151 men's events, 72 women's events, and 14 mixed. The Australian team comprised 193 male competitors and 73 female (27.4%). In 1992 there were 272 members of the Australian team, of which 108 (37.0%) were female. This is greater than the Olympic average of 29% for the 169 competing teams at the Games. Women could compete in 38% of the 257 events in the 26 different sports (*Australian Olympian*, 1993). In the 1988 study, female athletes received 33% of the air-time given to their male counterparts. In 1992, events for women received 30% (270[1] minutes) of the total of 908 minutes of sports shown during the time surveyed. These percentages far exceed those found in the previous surveys of regular programming practices.

As previously noted, during the 1988 broadcasts viewers indicated that swimming, gymnastics, diving and track and field were by far the most popular sports ('Task of sending the news home', 1988). Time devoted to swimming was 249 minutes for women (48.6%) and 263 minutes for men. Gymnastics coverage was 338

---

[1] Times are rounded to the nearest minute.

minutes, 21 seconds for men and 287 minutes for women (46.0%). Men's diving received 219 minutes and women's diving 123 minutes (36.2%). Track and field broadcasts showed 731 minutes of male events and 587 minutes of women's events (44.5%). Thus female events received a significant amount of the time (44%) allotted to these sports (Toohey, 1997).

During 1992 viewers indicated that the four most popular sports shown during the Olympic broadcasts in descending order were swimming, gymnastics, track and field, and rowing. During the 'Highlights' programmes surveyed, swimming received a total of 167 minutes, of which men's events accounted for 90 minutes and women's events 76 minutes (45.3%). Gymnastics coverage lasted 35 minutes, of which women received 13 minutes (37.8%) and men's 21 minutes. Track and field broadcasts were of a longer duration, 197 minutes, of which 101 minutes were devoted to women's events (51.3%) and 98 to men's events. Rowing coverage was 34 minutes, of which women's events received 14 minutes (43.2%). Once again, as in 1988, the proportion of female sports coverage in these four sports categories, at a 44% on average, was higher than the 30% recorded for the Olympic Games coverage as a whole and far higher than for non-Olympic sports programming (Toohey, 1997).

A study investigating Australian newspapers during the 1992 Olympics also indicated that women's sport received greater coverage than at other times. Hall analysed three major metropolitan daily newspapers, one in New South Wales, one in Victoria, and one in Western Australia. The New South Wales paper (*Sun-Herald*) allocated 31% of the total Olympic coverage to females, the Melbourne paper (*The Age*) 30% and the *West Australian*, 27% (Embrey *et al.*, 1992: 11), well above the 4.2% average found in the Stoddart (1994) study referred to above.

The findings of these two Olympic broadcasting content analysis studies indicate that the 'female deficit model' (which indicates that women's sport is judged by comparing it to men's and consequently often considered to be lacking speed and strength and thus excitement) is not all-pervasive. This may indicate that the key to breaking existing patterns of sports programming lies through promotion of female sport at major events. While this is not an answer in itself, it could be a legitimate starting point to reduce the inequities in sports broadcasting that currently exist (Toohey, 1997).

It needs to be acknowledged however that increasing media coverage does not necessarily guarantee equality. Some researches conducting content analyses have shown that women's sport reporting can trivialize, marginalise and at times demean females (McKay, 1991; Duncan *et al.*, 1994: 80). An increase in this type of portrayal may indeed be counterproductive in establishing women's sport as an activity worthy of increased exposure in a manner consistent with that afforded the male equivalent. For example, American research examining the media's qualitative portrayal of female athletes in the 1992 Winter Olympics concluded that, while women were being represented in physically challenging events that advanced women's equality in terms of participation in these sports (e.g., the luge and the biathlon), paradoxically media portrayals did not always emphasise athletic performances traits. An examination of the corresponding Summer Games broadcasts showed that the women's gymnastics was framed by an emotion-charged narrative focusing on athletes' personal lives, their youth and attractiveness and their diminutive stature (Daddario, 1994).

Different descriptors were used for women engaged in masculine sports and those involved in feminine ones. While the strength of the former was cited, it is the beauty of the latter that was accentuated. There were examples of the press fashioning their own views about female athletes in both these Olympic broadcasts. Examples of marginalisation practices included in these Olympic telecasts included: condescending descriptors; the use of compensatory rhetoric; the construction of female athletes according to an adolescent ideal; and the presentation of female athletes as driven by cooperation rather than competition (Daddario, 1994: 275). Daddario's rhetorical analysis concluded that 'the sports media reinforce a masculine sports hegemony through strategies of marginalisation' (1994: 275). Even though women are shown to be competing in sports that require strength, speed and endurance, the narration may give only qualified support or negate the athleticism of the competitors through a media logic which seeks to appeal to viewers, especially women by creating human interest story lines, via the narrative approach to Olympic broadcasts.

Eleanor Holm Jarrett: A Case Study of A Female Olympic Athlete

Despite growing evidence about female's physical ability and their sporting capabilities, society's collective assumptions of their frailty have formed the ideology in which the Olympics is placed. In the past the Olympic power brokers themselves have helped define and institutionalise this construction which has served to reinforce their power, restricting, confining and subordinating female athletes. Yet, it would also be limiting to assume that all females have conformed to their expected roles. Those women that have contested the stereotypes have had to battle powerful ideologies, they have resisted the logic of male supremacy. Acknowledging that these social barriers exist, and may be even more effectual than beliefs about biological differences, relocates analysis of female participation in sport from its immediate and obvious site. It allows discourse to be placed in the wider context of the power structures in society and examine how we are socialised by and through them. One such woman who battled the stereotypic image of femininity, compliance and the Olympic power barons was Eleanor Holm Jarrett.

Eleanor Holm Jarrett was selected as a member of the 1936 US Olympic team to compete as a backstroke swimmer. Her subsequent dismissal from the team has been suggested by some to have been either the result of an overprotective attitude towards female athletes or a case of double standards, although others suggest that these sentiments are open to question (Leigh, 1974). Regardless of the reason, her lack of traditional training methods was the overt reason for her expulsion from the US team.

This was to be her third Olympic Games. She had competed in Amsterdam in 1928, winning a bronze medal in the 100 metres backstroke. In 1932, in Los Angeles, she won the gold medal in the same event. She had won the US National Championship in this event 12 times, the first time when she was only 13 years old.

Between the 1932 Games and the 1936 Games, she had set records in every backstroke event swum by women. In addition to her swimming prowess she was extremely attractive and by the age of 16 she had been offered a job in the Ziegfeld Follies in New York. She refused this offer, but not the one she received from Warner Brothers Studios in Hollywood. This contract guaranteed her $US500 per week and acting lessons from Josephine Dillon, the first wife of Clarke Gable (Mandell, 1971).

Figure 9.1. Eleanor Holm Jarrett.

Because of these Hollywood connections, the first questioning of her amateur status occurred. Obviously, a portion of her attraction to the movie studios was her aquatic skills and pressure was applied by the studios to induce her to appear in the water on screen. While she had no qualms about pool side publicity shots, the strict amateur rules would forbid this and so Eleanor temporarily abandoned acting.

Despite this sacrifice she encountered opposition from the Amateur Athletic Union (AAU) concerning her amateur status and, more importantly, her questionable standing was brought to the attention of the American bastion of amateurism, Avery Brundage, who had acquired an almost monopolistic hold on leadership positions within American amateur sport (Gibson, 1976).

Amateurism had been an integral component since the Olympic revival and Brundage embraced this belief fervently, adopting amore rigid stance than even de Coubertin. Holm Jarrett's amateur 'purity' came under close scrutiny from Brundage. Gibson provides this philosophy as the *raison d'être* for subsequent events. In a letter to John T. Taylor, dated May 21, 1934, Brundage stated:

The advertisement of Eleanor Holm Jarrett in the *Gantes Swimming News*... in my opinion eliminates her from amateur competition. This is the same sort of offence for which proceedings were instituted against Babe Didrickson. I am surprised to see this advertisement because apparently Miss Holm has been very careful to protect her amateur standing. Her appearance in moving pictures is only allowed so long as she does not appear in any role that has connection with sports or games or athletic events, provided that in the advertisements there is no reference to her athletic prowess. If there have been any violations of this understanding she will be eliminated from amateur competition. (Brundage in Gibson, 1976: 94-95)

During December 1934, when the AAU met in Miami, Florida, the question of Mrs Holm Jarrett's amateur status was raised. Mrs Holm Jarrett competed in amateur swimming under the jurisdiction of the metropolitan association of New York which had already examined her case and had found no cause for concern. The charges initiated against Mrs Holm Jarrett at the AAU convention were initiated by the central association of Chicago, an interesting development as this was hardly a geographic area in which Holm Jarrett would be likely to have much contact, but more understandable when it is considered that this was the centre of 'Brundage territory'. The focus of the charges was the use of her picture and endorsement in an advertisement for a swimming suit, as alluded to in Brundage's letter (*New York Times*, 8 December, 1934: 20). Following its investigation the AAU decided that Holm Jarrett had not contravened her amateur status and she was allowed to continue her swimming 'career'.

The trials for the US swimming team for the 1936 Olympic Games were held at Astoria, Long Island, New York. Holm Jarrett won the 100 metres backstroke final in spite of the fact that she had been 'partying' with her husband, the band leader, Art Jarrett, the night before (*New York Times*, 25 July, 1936). This was a typical training regime for her. When she boasted of training on caviar and champagne these claims were not unfounded. According Holm Jarrett, they had done her no harm in the past and she saw no reason to modify her behaviour when selected for the 1936 team.

As mentioned in Chapter 4, the US participation in the 1936 Games was fraught with problems, principally centring on the Nazi doctrine of anti-semitism. These problems did not dissipate once the US had committed itself to competing. The public, which was the principal source of funding, was reticent to contribute, so that, ten days before the team was due to depart, it was still some $US150,000 short of its target. A last minute drive raised $US75,000 and notwithstanding the threat of constant cutbacks a full contingent of athletes and officials set sail on the SS Manhattan, when she departed for Europe on 15 July.

Each athlete had been issued with the *American Committee Handbook*, containing information pertinent to competitors, a congratulatory note from Brundage and a list of rules and regulations. After reading the handbook the athlete was required to sign a certificate accepting its conditions. Portions of this document are germane to subsequent events because of the sections dealing with training methods and the expected demeanour of athletes. For example, in the document it stated 'it is understood, of course, that all members of the American Olympic team refrain from smoking and the use of intoxicating drinks and other forms of dissipation while in training' and 'I agree to maintain strict training during the voyage and until my competition in Berlin is completed' (Rubien, 1936: 53). Holm Jarrett, as did all other members of the team signed the certificate, thus agreeing to abide by its conditions.

One day out of port Brundage, on behalf of all officials, lifted the ban on alcohol and cigarettes, leaving the degree of indulgence to the discretion of the individual athlete. In lieu of total abstinence the athletes were placed on their honour to maintain their fitness. However, by July 18, the first reports of athletes carousing reached the ears of officials. No athletes were singled out for disciplinary action and team managers were to be responsible for enforcing a stricter ban. Relations between some of the swimming officials and Holm Jarrett had been strained before the sea voyage.

Press reports for the next few days gave no more information of behaviour problems. Apparently, even the 10 p.m. curfew was lifted on one occasion. In the *Los Angeles Times* (23 July, 1936: 7) Brundage was quoted as saying:

> The fact that we were dealing with high-strung athletes who had emerged from an extended series of strenuous tryout [sic] contributed to our problem. However, on being placed on their honour, they responded magnificently, maintaining a high standard of conduct and trained conscientiously under obvious shipboard handicaps.

The following day the papers carried a contrary communication: 'Mrs Jarrett has been dropped from the American team for violation of training rules and her entry into the Olympic Games has been cancelled' (*New York Times*, 24 July: 21). This was the first occasion that an American athlete had been dismissed from a US team en route to the Games.

The decision to dismiss Holm Jarrett was made at an American Olympic Committee meeting. Testimony regarding her indiscretions was furnished by: Ada Sacket; Herbert Holm, the Manager of the Women's Swimming team; Herbert Lawson, the team physician; and the ship's doctor. The accused was not invited to attend. Press reports suggested that her discharge was triggered by an on-board party she attended on 17 July, escorted by the writer, Charles MacArthur, husband of the actress Helen Hayes. The straw that broke the camel's back however, was that on her way back to her cabin after another party on 24 July, she bumped into Mrs Sackett while in a less-than-sober state. Immediately after this incident the team's executive called a meeting and voted unanimously to dismiss her (*Los Angeles Times*: 25 July, 1936: 13, 15).

Eleanor's demeanor had not endeared her to officials. Initially, she had complained to them about inequities in accommodation. Officials were travelling first class and athletes in third class cabins. Later she had boasted of impunity from team rules. The *Los Angeles Times* (25 July, 1936: 25) reported that: 'Prior to last Saturday's warning Mrs Holm Jarrett had declared she liked to imbibe and enjoy the relaxation of party life and intended to do so regardless of what officials may think. Waving her hand to all listeners she declared: 'This is the way I'm accustomed to train and I don't see why I should change now'. She had also boasted that officials wouldn't dare to put a champion off the team. When she found news to the contrary her attitude change. She became contrite, declaring 'I'm on the spot now, I feel like jumping overboard but will train and not touch another drop if I'm given another chance' (*Los Angeles Times*, 25 July 1936: 25).

Such declarations were not enough to sway the committee, even when she insisted that she was not a lone transgressor and that other team members were as guilty as she. Meanwhile, team athletes and coaches rallied to her defence. From a total of 330 athletes, 220, including all the women's swimming team, signed a petition requesting clemency. Some coaches spoke in favour of her reinstatement. One athlete was quoted as saying: 'She deserves punishment for misbehaviour but many of us feel she's being made the goat for other less conspicuous offenders against disciplinary orders and training rules' (*New York Times*, 25 July, 1936: 7).

In America, too, the incident created much controversy. 'Dink' Templeton, the Stanford University Track coach declared:

> The Olympic Committee, as had been its wont, dared the young lady with threats and Eleanor is not a gal to take a dare. It is unfortunate that a true reflection of the difference between the committee and the athletes, who are looked on as prize livestock and taken to Europe to be exhibited for the benefit of the august American Olympic Committee, had to be brought to light in this manner. .. But it will probably be patched up and should be a means of closer understanding between the two classes of free tourists, one of which earns its way, while the other holds the whip hand. (*New York Times*, 25 July, 1936: 7)

Art Jarrett, Eleanor's husband, thought that it would be a good idea to give all the swimmers champagne, in the hope that they would win some races. Not everyone, however, was so sympathetic. One of the strongest anti-Jarrett comments came from Lawrence Robertson, head coach of the Olympic Team. He was quoted in the *New York Times* (25 July, 1936: 7) as saying 'The Greeks had the right idea over 2,000 years ago when all women were barred'.

Eleanor was given the opportunity to present her case to a subcommittee. This group abided by the previous decision, meaning there was now no further avenue for recourse. The AOC requested the return of her uniform and booked a return passage for her on to the US on the 'Brennan'. Eleanor, however, had no intention of being dismissed so easily.

Once her name had been officially withdrawn from the 100 metres backstroke event, Eleanor's attitude reverted to attacking the AOC. She issued a 700 word statement condemning its actions. In this document she insisted that there was no general rule against drinking, the bars in the athletes' section of the ship were open daily and on one occasion did not close until after midnight (*Los Angeles Times*, 26 July 1936: 1). Brundage's response was brusque. He was so offended by the article that he suggested that the AAU (of which he was President) might consider rescinding Holm Jarrett's amateur status, although he did not specify the ground on which this dismissal would be based.

As she could no longer compete Eleanor accepted the offer of the International News Service to cover the Games as a reporter. Even in this role she attracted attention, especially at the Opening Ceremony as the *New York Times* reported in a style that reinforced the notion of the fragile female (3 August 1936: 19):

> She came bravely to this initial pageant, a little figure in a rose costume and a picture hat and she sat in the front row to do her job, She was courageous, in a sense, and for a while she chatted gaily, taking notes meanwhile, and all went well until the flag passed and behind it came the serried ranks of American women competitors. ... That was too much and she was missing. Her colleagues found her sobbing her heart out in a far corner of the press room.

Apart from this temporary breakdown Eleanor's high spirits and public appearances were not curtailed. The *New York Times* on 29 July reports her meeting with former Crown Prince, Frederick Willhelm and being escorted through the Netherlands Palace. True to form Eleanor was anything but retiring, complimenting the Prince on his handsome features, suggesting that he would be an asset to the movie industry in Hollywood and that Americans would go crazy over him if he should ever grace their shores with his presence.

While Eleanor was charming Europe her relations with Brundage were becoming more strained. Brundage utilised his power to disqualify Eleanor from amateur competition in Europe, invoking his authority as head of the AAU. In essence this action was purely of punitive nature as Eleanor had no intention of competing in Europe. Its effectiveness lay in demonstrating the power of those athletes who questioned authority. Eleanor took this further disqualification in true form, commenting:

> He may have the power to suspend me in Europe ... but this is the first time I knew he could just point a finger at a person and say; 'Now you're a professional'. 'I call this adding insult to injury. ... I do not see how he can do it without giving my case some kind of hearing. If they start barring everyone who takes a drink, they won't have any amateurs left'. (*New York Times*, 9 August, 1936: V2)

Even though her competitive time as a swimmer was now finished, the situation was not entirely detrimental. The brouhaha had created a deluge of publicity, much of it in Holm Jarrett's favour. Publicity is the staff of life to a celebrity and so it appeared in Eleanor's case. On her return from Germany she set out on a vaudeville tour throughout the US accompanied by her husband. This signalled the beginning of her rise as an entertainer. The following year she discarded both her singing career and her husband and acquired a new one of each. She married Billy Rose (previously the husband of Fanny Brice) and joined his 'Aquacade'. Not only was she the star of this show but she also returned to Hollywood, playing the role of Jane in a 1938 version of *Tarzan of the Apes* movie which featured Glen Morris (winner of the 1936 Olympic decathlon) as Tarzan (Mandell, 1971).

The AOC purged Eleanor's name from its 1936 *Official Report*. Even its photograph of the Women's Swimming team is minus her visage. The only direct mention of her occurs on page 279, when it is noted that Eleanor Holm Jarrett of the Women's Swimming Association of New York, won the 100 metres backstroke at the finals of the Women's Swimming Trials. Brundage circuitously mentions her dismissal in the 'Report of the President' (p.33) but does not refer to her by name. He insinuated that the whole incident was blown out of all proportion by those who wished to discredit the Olympic Committee because of decision to attend the Games in spite of the exclusion of Jews from the host nation's team.

What was the prime reason for Eleanor Holm Jarrett's dismissal? Obviously she disobeyed the rules of the AOC, but her instant dismissal, without an opportunity to plea her cause, defies the boundaries of due process. Avery Brundage had tried to dismiss Holm Jarrett through the proper channels in 1934 and failed. On the S.S. Manhattan he had a second opportunity and this time he succeeded. Female athletes of this period were far more rigidly bound by what society considered to be acceptable codes of feminine behaviour than today's woman. Would Holm Jarrett have been dismissed for the same offence had she been male? Should she have been dismissed from amateur status by the lone decree of Brundage is another vexed question. She would have automatically forfeited her amateur status when she performed with the Aquacade, and, in hindsight, as the next two Olympics were cancelled this action meant little, except perhaps to Eleanor.

Although 1936 has long passed, a form of poetic justice has been met. Avery Brundage's character has been shown to be less than honourable and in conflict with the ideals he espoused and censured others for not adhering to. In a 1980 *Sports Illustrated* article he was described as a lecherous adulterer, while Eleanor Holm Jarrett received far more positive recognition by being inducted into the Women's Sports Foundation Hall of Fame (Johnson, 1980). These two seemingly unconnected events occurred within two months of each other.

The double standard of moral and social behaviour condoned by the sports establishment of the 1930s and illustrated by the Holm Jarrett saga provides a strong case study to illustrate one aspect of the inequities and ordeals that have been experienced by some female Olympic athletes.

Sex Testing

The idea of male's athletic supremacy has resulted in one of the most controversial tests in sport, that being 'sex testing'. Hargreaves (1994: 222) notes that 'the femininity control test, which is obligatory for all female Olympic competitors ... is the most potent symbol of the concern to prove that there is an absolute distinction between the sexes'.

Before the test's introduction to the Olympic Games in 1968, the same Games that a woman first lit the flame in the Olympic cauldron, only a few men had been caught posing as female Olympic competitors. Not all of these had been deliberate attempts to gain an advantage. Some of those uncovered had gender ambiguities that even they were unaware of.

Blue gives examples of some of the most commonly known examples of such athletes who were exposed to the world as having gender irregularities.

> In 1938 a German high jumper was found to be a hermaphrodite, with both male and female organs. Two Frenchwomen on the relay team which won silver at the 1946 European championships were later found to be living as men, but whether they had pretended to be women or were now pretending to be men was not completely certain. A skier who had failed the chromosome test... had her male sex organs hidden inside her body since birth. In 1980, the elderly Mrs Stella Olsen, a Polish American, who had been the 1932 Olympic 100 metre sprint champion as Stanislawa Waldrewicz, was killed as an innocent bystander in a robbery and it was discovered that she had male sex organs. (Blue, 1988: 160)

In the 1936 Olympics Waldrewicz, who competed for Poland but was known in the US where she lived as Stella Walsh, was beaten by Helen Stephens, who represented the USA. Paul Gallico, writing in his usual uncomplimentary manner towards female athletes and sports administrators, described what occurred after the 100 metres women's final.

> Miss Helen Stephens, a big rangy schoolgirl from Mississippi, out-galloped all the best women sprinters ... including Poland's favorite Stella Walsh. The Poles ... immediately accused Miss Stephens of being Mr Stephens.
>
> The American Athletic Union ... revealed solemnly that before being permitted to board the boat to uphold the honour of the USA as a member of its Olympic team the Olympic Committee had had La Stephens frisked for sex and checked her as being hundred per cent female. With no thought whatsoever for the feelings of the young lady in question these findings were triumphantly if ungallantly aired in the press. (Gallico, 1940: 233)

In a similar invasion of privacy, in 1966, when sex testing was first introduced by the International Amateur Athletic Federation at the European Track and Field Championships at Budapest, all of the 243 female entrants were required to appear nude before a panel of doctors. 'The 'nude parades' were humiliating as physicians searched for the absence of a vaginal opening or an enlarged clitoris or testicles' (Canavan, 1997: 16). This practice of physical inspections continued. Later, Mary Peters, the British Gold medalist in the Pentathlon at the 1972 Munich Games, described the procedure as 'the most crude and degrading experience I have ever known in my life' (Jennings, 1996: 214).

Because of the growing resentment against this physical examination it was replaced by a chromosome test, the Buccal Smear Test. The test involved taking a scraping of buccal mucosa from the inside of the woman's mouth. The sample was then subject to microscopic examination. This evaluative technique led to a new set of problems as it provided a new criterion to determine eligibility as a female competitor. Not everyone believed that its definition of 'female' was correct. Eva Klobukowsa, from Poland, became the first candidate to fail this new test. It was found that Klubukowska possessed a Y chromosome in addition to the XX combination that was determined to be the only standard for being classified as a 'woman'. Consequently she was banned from further female sporting competition, even though it was thought that her genetic makeup provided her with no physical advantage (Blue, 1988).

In 1992 at the Barcelona Olympic Games the Buccal Smear Test was replaced by a polymerase chain reaction (PCR) form of testing (Jennings, 1996). These present tests are far less invasive than the early measures of testing, however arguments for or against their use continue. On one side are those who believe that they provide the genetic 'level playing field', by only including competitors in female only designated competitions who are genetically 46 XX. On the other side of the coin are those who argue that there are female athletes now excluded from Olympic competitions for minor genetic irregularities which do not endow them with any additional physical advantage.

At the close of the twentieth century, with a greater tolerance in many Westernised societies for individuals who have either changed their gender or who choose to live as the opposite gender, it is only a matter of time before the IOC's rulings are contested in the judicial system. In Australia and the US cases have been brought before the courts challenging such rulings in domestic sporting competitions. Like so many other issues relevant to the Olympic Movement there is no easy answer and, whatever the ruling, those who are not on the winning side will feel aggrieved. Because so many cultures are represented at the Games then determination of one's sex may continue to be based purely on standardised and restrictive genetic terms, rather than taking cases on an individual basis.

Sydney 2000

The Sydney 2000 Olympic Games will have greater access for female competitors than any previous Olympic Games in terms of events and number of days of competition. There will be 118 women's events in the Sydney 2000 Olympic Games compared to 97 in Atlanta, an increase of 21 events for women. Women will be contestants in all but three sports on the Olympic programme (boxing, baseball and wrestling), but at the same time will compete exclusively in softball and the disciplines of rhythmic gymnastics and synchronised swimming. This increase has occurred in three ways. First by the introduction of two new Olympic sports (taekwondo and triathlon), both of which have women's events. Second by a sport (women's water polo) increasing the number of its events for women and, last, where sports have reduced the number of men's events and have concurrently introduced a women's programme - for example modern pentathlon has included a women's event for the first time and has accordingly reduced the number of male athletes competing from 32 to 16 and weightlifting has included women on the programme for the first time and reduced men's events from ten to eight.

Conclusion

Historically one of the most controlling arguments used to oppose women's participation in sport is that men are physically superior to women in performance measures (Figler and Whitaker, 1995). Yet, 'from an anatomical and physiological standpoint, males and females are more alike than different .. other than the obvious differences in reproductive organs' (Figler and Whitaker, 1995: 301). The differences between women and men in terms of physical performances are relatively minor and the gap is closing. During the twentieth century women's athletic performances have improved more than males (Simri, 1977). It is also arguable that such measurable differences in athletic performance may have social expectations and opportunities as their basis, rather than biological variance (Figler and Whitaker, 1995). In sport, even today, it appears that norms and standards are still based on male performance, consequently females' sporting achievements are judged in terms of their otherness. As a result they are generally perceived to be inferior or less than that of their male counterparts. This viewpoint of sex-based differentiation has become accepted as biologically natural, rather than socially constructed and culturally reproduced. Yet research has 'raised serious doubts, if not refuted, the commonly held and taken-for-granted assumptions concerning physical/physiological sex differences' (Scraton, 1992: 8).

Through sex-role socialisation we learn to behave in ways that are expected of us as either males and females. One aspect of this is that boys tend to be channelled into instrumental activities such as sport. Sport, in Western societies, is considered to be a highly instrumental activity, inconsistent with notions of feminine behaviour which is based on the attributes of dependence, passivity and physical and emotional weakness.

Arguments that female athletes are physically unsuited to intense physical training or sport competition have been shown to be invalid. There is no conclusive evidence that competitive sport is any more dangerous for females than males (Figler and Whitaker, 1995). Some conditions, such as menstrual irregularities (for example amenorrhoea) have been associated with strenuous physical activity, although these symptoms are considered to be reversible (Figler and Whitaker, 1995). Women have yet to achieve their Olympic potential, despite the fact that the IOC has now acknowledged it has to adopt a more active role in redressing the gender-based inequalities in the Olympic Movement that have existed for over 100 years. As part of this process, the IOC has created performance goals in this area - a move that is relatively recent and still not universally acknowledged as being necessary or advisable. As with other aspects of the Games, this historical inequality is not unique to the Olympic Movement. Gendered disparity has been part and parcel of sport throughout its history and has been based on two main assumptions; that women are physically inferior to men and that it is unbecoming for them to indulge in certain activities, many Olympic sports being included on the list of inappropriate pastimes.

Chapter ten:

Case-Studies

> The Olympic Games requires a tremendous investment of human, financial and physical resources from the communities which stage them. They challenge (or distract) the best talents available for the better part of a decade and well beyond the terms of most governments. They play a decisive role in the character and progress of a region's economic development. ... At the level of ideology they illuminate competitive notions of public good. Not surprisingly bidding for and staging a public festival on this scale can be a highly charged political exercise, requiring the consummate skills of negotiation and consensus building from those in leadership. (Kidd, 1992a: 154)

Introduction

Every Olympic Games can be seen as a learning experience, for host cities and nations, for the Olympic Movement and for sport at large. The Games are such a large-scale event that they also have repercussions beyond sport, contributing to the development of contemporary world culture and affecting international politics. What then can be learned from the experience of individual Olympic Games? In the earlier chapters of the book the focus has been on particular dimensions of the Olympic phenomenon, such as politics, economics, media, drugs, gender. Here we examine individual Games in the round.

Each Olympiad tends to generate more research and commentary than its predecessors. Consequently there is generally more written material available on later Games - more data, more evaluation, more comment and analysis - than on earlier Games. The main case-studies presented here therefore focus on the last two Summer Games - Barcelona and Atlanta - and look forward to Sydney 2000. Appendix 10.1 provides a brief overview of the Games of the modern era, with guides to the literature on individual Games.

Barcelona 1992

Introduction

What was unique about the Games of the 25th Modern Olympiad, held in Barcelona in the region of Catalonia, Spain in July 1992? The initial notable feature is the choice of Barcelona at all. Why? Because Catalonia is the home of the President of the IOC, Juan Antonio Samaranch - and the city where he spent much of his professional administrative life, prior to taking up the IOC presidency in 1980. It was in Barcelona and Catalonia that Samaranch served in various administrative roles under Spain's Franco régime, although precisely how close he was to the régime and just how prominent, is a matter of some dispute (Jennings, 1996: 28-33). The City of Barcelona bid for the 1992 Games in competition with, among others, Paris. The latter was seen by many as the front runner and Jennings (1996: 127) suggests that Barcelona would not have been awarded the Games if Albertville had not, somewhat surprisingly, won the Winter Olympics for 1992, thus making a second French venue in 1992 impossible (it was only from 1994 that the Winter Games were switched to run two years after the Summer Olympics). As can be seen from Table 10.1, Paris still commanded considerable support, but Barcelona won majority support in the third round of voting.

Table 10.1. IOC voting for the 1992 Games.

City	Round 1	Round 2	Round 3
Barcelona	29	37	47
Paris	19	20	23
Belgrade	13	11	10
Brisbane	11	9	8
Birmingham	8	8	-
Amsterdam	5	-	-

Source: Cuyàs (1992) p. 316.

This examination of the 1992 Barcelona Games considers in turn the philosophy of the Games, their organisation and their economic dimensions. To understand the significance of the Olympic Games to Barcelona and the surrounding region of Catalonia, it is appropriate to consider the historical background, which we do first, drawing on Brunet (1993).

History

Barcelona is an industrial Mediterranean port in north-eastern Spain, with a population of 1.6 million, in an urban built-up area with a population of some 3.0 million. It is the capital of Catalonia, a region which has its own language and national identity and ethnic links with people over the border in France, similar to the situation of the Basque region in northern Spain. Following rapid industrialisation in the nineteenth century, Barcelona found a place on the world stage when it hosted international 'universal exhibitions' in 1888 and 1929. During the Civil War of 1936-39, the Barcelona area saw some of the most bitter resistance to the Fascist forces of General Franco, whose régime subsequently ruled Spain from 1939 to 1975. During much of the Franco era Barcelona and the surrounding region experienced economic depression and physical neglect.

An interesting footnote in political history is that, in 1936, Barcelona was to be have been host to an alternative 'Popular Olympic Games' organised by Socialists and Communists in opposition to the 'Hitler Games' in Berlin, and one of a series of Workers' Olympics held in the first half of the century (see chapter 4). The day before the games were due to start a military uprising, inspired by Franco, took place in Barcelona and the Spanish Civil War had begun. The 6000 athletes and estimated 20,000 visitors were forced to return home (Riordan, 1984; Pujadas and Santacana, 1992).

With the return of democracy in 1977, Catalonia, along with other regions of Spain, acquired an autonomous regional government, dominated by right-wing nationalistic parties, while the city of Barcelona was governed by left-wing coalitions. The 1980s was a period in which Spain sought to 're-enter' Europe, politically and economically, after the years of relative isolation under Franco. The year 1992 was an important watershed in this process:

> For the central government, the Barcelona Olympic Games were a piece within the overall group of events of the '1992 project'. They were not only in coincidence with the Seville Universal Exposition and the Madrid European Cultural Capital, but in a wider sense, the will of the central government was to show the world how Spanish society had modernized and transformed, and aspired to play an important role in the heart of the European Community. (Botella, 1995: 141)

Organisation
As is required by the IOC for all Olympic Games, the organisation of the Barcelona Games was vested in an Organising Committee, the 1992 Barcelona Olympic Organising Committee (COOB'92), with involvement of the Barcelona City Council, the Government of Catalonia, the Government of Spain and the Spanish Olympic Committee. The Mayor of Barcelona was President of COOB'92. Public works were carried out by a specially established public corporation, Barcelona Holding Olympic, S.A. (HOLSA), owned jointly by the Spanish Government and Barcelona City Council.

Philosophy
A number of contributors to the volume of essays published after the Barcelona Games, and entitled *The Keys to Success* (de Moragas and Botella, 1995), agree that

the most significant feature of the Barcelona Games was the role they played in the economic, physical and political regeneration of the city. As one of the contributors put it:

> The Barcelona Games will only with difficulty be known as a technological event, in spite of having outdone the levels of quality and complexity of all previous editions. Nor will they be recalled as a commercial success, in spite of the fact that the economic management was considerably more brilliant than in Los Angeles. Nor will they take on a significant political meaning, even though they coincided with historical changes in Eastern Europe, making them the most universal Games in history. .. everyone would agree .. that the true success of the Barcelona Games lay in the transformation the city underwent. (Millet i Serra, 1995: 189)

What was the nature of this transformation? Following the neglect of the Franco years, hosting the Olympic Games was seen as much more than a sporting event for the city: it was an opportunity to catch up on decades of lost economic opportunity.

> The mobilization of energy generated by hosting the games was to serve the development of the city. In this way, the Olympic Games would act as a catalyst and provide an excuse to bring about *urban change* that would improve the *quality of life* and the *attractiveness* of Barcelona. (Brunet, 1993: 11)

This 'urban project' involved a number of major tasks, namely to: '.. open the city to the sea, supply it with basic transportation infrastructures, turn the old port into a place for public use, modernise the commercial port and the airport' (Abad, 1995: 13). The project was conceived in a unique way. Rather than seeking to concentrate Olympic facilities as much as possible, as has been done in other host cities, the decision was made to distribute the facilities in four 'Olympic Parks' around the city, one of which involved the redevelopment and opening up of the ocean frontage to create the athletes' village. In addition some facilities were decentralised to other cities in the region. The urban project also involved the construction of a system of ring-roads to link the Olympic Parks (Millet i Serra, 1995: 193). Thus the Olympics provided the impetus for a massive change to the urban infrastructure of the city.

This 'catalyst syndrome', which involves host cities using the occasion of the Olympic Games as a catalyst for developing, or redeveloping, urban infrastructure way beyond the immediate needs of the Games, is not unusual, although in Barcelona it was seen in extreme form. The syndrome particularly relates to transport developments, such as the building of freeways, rail systems and airports. Such developments cannot be economically justified on the basis of a single two week or month-long event, even an event as large as the Olympic Games, but, since the developments would undoubtedly facilitate the smooth running of the Games, the latter provides the deadline for their completion. Often these are projects which have been 'on the drawing board' for many years but, because of lack of funds or political or technical disagreements, they have not been proceeded with. The hosting of the Games focuses the attention of politicians and things get done which would otherwise not get done, or would be delayed. As one member of COOB'92 put it, in referring to the planning task for the Games: ' .. what mattered eleven years ahead of time was to determine the dominating idea that would allow us to do in five or six years what had not been done in fifty, with the risk of taking another fifty if the opportunity was not taken' (Abad, 1995: 12).

Figure 10.1. Barcelona, 1992: Opening ceremony.

While the syndrome is largely a public sector phenomenon, driven by politicians, it can also be seen in the private sector - for example in the timing of the building of hotels. However, while sentiment may play a part in such commercial decisions, more hard-nosed, rational factors are also likely to come into play - for example the calculation that a period of high occupancy for a hotel during the few weeks before, during and after the Games, would be a good start to the business, which would also benefit from the enhanced image of the host city, resulting in increased tourism and business traffic after the Games.

In smaller cities and smaller countries the scale of the undertaking to host the Olympic Games is daunting, and is viewed as a public test of the capabilities of city or country in the eyes of the world. Abad (1995: 12) recalled three years after the Games that '..little more than five years ago few people thought that success was possible'. In the lead-up to the Games, '.. the question of our image before the world was still pending: to 'come across well', to overcome the fear of universal ridicule'. In the event, the success of the Games, according to Abad, left a '.. moral legacy, the affirmation that we as a country could and knew how to do things well' (Abad, 1995: 12).

This qualitative dimension is related to an issue raised in chapter 4, namely the question of political and community support for the Games. Abad, as a member of COOB'92, is of course not impartial, but he expressed the political imperative as follows:

> Citizens, being undoubtedly those most directly affected, could not, did not want to, nor had to remain ignorant or distant. They had to be informed, of course. Yet beyond this, they could not remain passive but had to be active partners, giving support to the organization with their participative attitude, both demanding and impatient. This great challenge, that of confidence - laid over skepticism if you wish - won out in the end. Only when the citizens had made the project fully their own did it acquire the category of 'untouchable', so that nobody, neither political parties nor administrations nor people in general could allow it to be denaturalized or pushed to one side. (Abad, 1995: 16)

Economic Aspects

The gross cost to COOB'92 of running the Barcelona Games was some US$1.3 billion, made up as shown in Figure 10.2 and Table 10.2. After the cost of facilities, it can be seen that the second largest item is 'Services to the Olympic Family' - consisting primarily of provision of accommodation, subsistence and transportation for athletes (10,200), members of National Olympic Committees, International Federations and trainers (3400), judges and umpires (2400), media personnel (5800), guests of the Organising Committee (2700) and sponsors and their guests (9200).

The costs were approximately balanced by income generated, as shown in Figure 10.3 and Table 10.2. This shows the dominance of sponsorship and television rights, as discussed in chapter 6. But in the case of Barcelona the significance of lottery income and the comparatively small contribution of government grants are also notable. The latter is explained by the existence of the lottery, but also by the fact that government expenditure was largely on infrastructure investments.

As shown in Table 10.3, these investments amounted to some US$6.3 billion, or almost five times the running costs of the Games. Approximately 40% of this expenditure was on transport schemes and 36% on development of the Olympic facility precincts. Private sector investment, particularly on hotels, accounted for one third of the total.

Is this pattern of expenditure typical of the Olympic Games? Brunet (1993: 69) compares investment expenditure in Barcelona with that in the previous four Olympic Games and shows that, while expenditure in Barcelona was considerably higher than in Seoul, Los Angeles and Montréal, it was lower than in Tokyo in 1964. As discussed in chapter 6, the extent to which this type of expenditure should be counted as 'Olympic Games costs' is debatable.

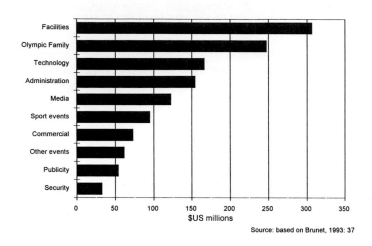

Source: based on Brunet, 1993: 37

Figure 10.2. Barcelona Games: Organising Committee expenditure.

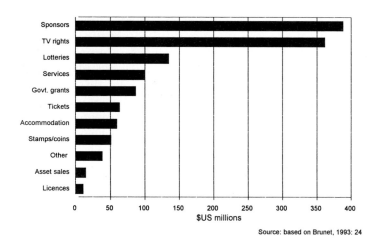

Source: based on Brunet, 1993: 24

Figure 10.3. Barcelona Games: Organising Committee income.

Table 10.2. Barcelona Games: Organising Committee budget.

Expenditure	US$ million*
Facilities and surroundings	305.8
Services to the Olympic Family	246.8
Technology	165.3
Support/administration	152.8
Media services	121.7
Sport event organisation	93.6
Commercial management/ticketing	71.2
Ceremonies and cultural events	60.3
Publicity/promotion	52.9
Security	31.3
Total	1301.6
Income	
Sponsors	387.7
Television rights	361.1
Lotteries	134.3
Services	99.9
Government grants etc.	86.3
Tickets	63.0
Accommodation	59.1
Stamps/coins	50.2
Other	38.1
Sale of assets	14.0
Licenses	10.2
Total	1303.9

* Converted from pesetas at 150 to US$ (1999 exchange rate).
Source: based on Brunet, 1993: 24, 37.

Table 10.3. Barcelona Games: investments 1986-1993.

	US$ millions
Roads/airport	2521.7
Olympic areas (Poblenou, Montjuïc, Vall d'Hebron, Diagonal area, Port Vell)	2250.3
Cultural, health etc. facilities	141.5
Improvement of hotel facilities	799.2
Olympic satellite villages	466.1
Other sporting infrastructure	198.7
Total	6377.5

* Converted from pesetas at 150 to US$ (1999 exchange rate).
Source: based on Brunet, 1993: 43.

Brunet (1993) conducted a detailed assessment of the economic impact of the Games on Barcelona. Total expenditure on the Games, including all investment expenditure, the expenditure of COOB'92 and expenditure by visitors, was US$7.8 billion. After multiplier analysis (see chapter 6), this produces an estimated 'global economic impact' of US$20.7 billion, which results in an additional annual average of 59,000 full-time equivalent jobs over the period 1986 to 1992 (Brunet, 1993: 119). However, to treat this as a net effect of the Games assumes that none of the investment expenditure would not have taken place but for the Games. While, as discussed above, the 'catalyst' effect may cause public bodies to undertake investment which would not otherwise have been undertaken, it is likely that at least *some* of the Barcelona infrastructure investments - for example on some roads or hotels - would have taken place without the Games, so the economic impact of this portion of the expenditure should not be attributed to the Games. Thus the size of the economic impact of the Games would seem to have been exaggerated in this case.

A further issue in assessing the economic impact of the Games is the question of just how the investments are funded. Some of the funding came from international sources (TV rights, sponsors, visitor expenditure) and some from the national and regional governments and can therefore be considered a net gain for the city.

Investment by the city government, if funded by loans, eventually has to be repaid; if funded from current taxes, then the money represents taxpayers' funds which, if not used for these investments, would have been spent on something else. Thus, while it is true to say that the levels of expenditure and jobs indicated are attributable to the Games, it should not be assumed that they represent, in total, a net gain for the city.

In the case of Barcelona, however, the 'catalyst' effect is considered highly significant. Brunet summarises the effect as follows:

> This legacy is summarized in the urban transformation of Barcelona and the changes in the economic structure (greater capitalization, greater tertiary activity, greater internationalization, greater attractiveness, greater central focus, greater productivity, and greater competitiveness). The permanent additional employment that was a product of the greater collective capital and the private investments prompted by the Olympic Games and, in short, the greater capacity of the economic fabric, was calculated in this study to be 20,000 individuals. (Brunet, 1993: 119)

Economic impact studies of 'hallmark' events generally refer to the stimulus which the event is expected to give to tourism, not just during the Games, but for a number of years after. This appears to have been borne out in the case of Barcelona, with the number of visitors to the city increasing from less than two million in 1990 to more than three million in 1996, and the number of participants in congresses increasing from around 100,000 to over 200,000 in the same period (De Lange, 1998: 132-133), although it must always be borne in mind that such increases might possibly have come about even without the Games.

Sporting Impact

As noted in chapter 4, one of the aims of the Olympic Movement is the promotion of sport participation by the community in general. Truñó (1995), a member of COOB'92 and a member of Barcelona City Council, provides some evidence on the impact of the Games on sport participation in Barcelona. Initially, he points out that new sporting facilities provided for the Olympics were a lasting legacy for sport in the city. But of course facilities can become 'white elephants', if not appropriately managed. A new system, referred to as 'concerned management', was introduced to operate many of the new facilities, involving contracting of management to local private organisations.

> One of the keys to the successful functioning of the city's new sports facilities was precisely this management model, which made it possible for local administration to close the gap between itself and the average citizen by means of sport organisations which were in touch with the day-to-day reality of sporting activity and which were well-known in their respective neighbour-hoods. (Truñó, 1995: 51)

The large 'flagship' facilities were managed by a new body, *Barcelona Promoció* (Barcelona Promotion). This and the private contract organisations provided a total of 450 new jobs in facility and event management and maintenance.

Truñó quotes survey evidence indicating that the proportion of the population participating in sporting activity at least once a week rose from 36% in 1983, to 47% in 1989 and 51% in 1995 and he notes that 300,000 people belong to the city's 1200 sports clubs. A school programme, 'Campus Olympia', involving school use of the Olympic facilities, was launched in 1993, attracting 1750 participants, rising to 6500 participants in 1995 (Truñó, 1995: 56).

Conclusion

There is a wide consensus that the 1992 Olympic Games were a success. The success was not related particularly to events in the sporting arenas, although the Games produced their fair share of sporting drama and new records. Rather, the success appears to have been related to the interaction of city, culture, event and people. John MacAloon expresses it as follows:

> A preliminary review of Olympic media coverage .. shows a striking agreement that the city of Barcelona itself was the star of the Games. .. In a sense, Barcelona upstaged the Olympics, though in another sense the Olympic created the 'Barcelona'. .. The nightly flows of people on the Ramblas, and the fact that the sociability of evening extended so quickly and deeply in to the wee morning hours, attracted participation and special social rapport from persons in whose home environments pleasures are taken indoors and 'the streets are rolled up' at midnight. .. For many visitors, this code of seeing and being seen brought the people and the material city of Barcelona into a common expression of

spectacle logic. .. This public meeting of guest and host populations .. was unprecedented in my experience of summer Olympic games. I believe it is what will be remembered about Barcelona for those who were there, long after the outcomes of this or that competition or the grandiose entertainments of the opening ceremonies have been forgotten. (MacAloon, 1995: 182-183)

Other aspects of the success story were the stimulus given to the economic regeneration of Barcelona, as discussed above, and the boost to Catalan nationalism, a feature which MacAloon asserts, was, to outsiders, a private 'conversation' between Catalonia, Spain and the rest of Europe.

Atlanta 1996

Introduction
Atlanta, Georgia, in the southern United States, has a population of 400,000, with a further 2.5 million in the surrounding urban area. Famous around the world as the site of the Reverend Martin Luther King's assassination and the headquarters of Coca Cola, it was one of 14 American cities which, in 1987, sought the United States Olympic Committee's endorsement as the United States candidate city for the 1996 Olympic Games. When it entered the international bidding competition in 1988, it faced five other cities: Athens, Belgrade, Manchester, Melbourne and Toronto. Being the centenary Games of the modern era, Athens was the popular favourite. Further, many believed that just 12 years after the Los Angeles Games was too soon for another American city to host the Games. However, as shown in Table 10.4, in the five-round sequence of IOC votes at its January 1990 meeting in Tokyo, Belgrade and Manchester were eliminated in the early rounds, and Melbourne's and Toronto's votes swung behind Atlanta in the last two rounds, giving it a decisive win over Athens. While it is always claimed that cities win on the basis of their bid and the facilities they offer for the athletes and spectators, the fact that the city hosts the headquarters of Coca Cola, the Olympics' most consistent and generous sponsor, is thought by some to have been influential in the choice of Atlanta (Jennings, 1996: 133-134).

Table 10.4. IOC voting for the 1996 Games.

City	Round 1	Round 2	Round 3	Round 4	Round 5
Atlanta	19	20	26	34	51
Athens	23	23	26	30	35
Toronto	14	17	18	22	-
Melbourne	12	21	16	-	-
Manchester	11	5	-	-	-
Belgrade	7	-	-	-	-

Source: Watkins, 1997: 14.

The Atlanta bid was initiated by Atlanta lawyer, Billy Payne, who established the Georgia Amateur Athletic Foundation for the purpose, and later became the high profile President and Chief Executive Officer of the Atlanta Committee for the Olympic Games (ACOG). In the enthusiastic words of the official report of the Games:

> One man's vision to bring the Olympic Games to his city inspired thousands to participate in something beyond themselves, to demonstrate their human grace and offer their innate kindness to the world. Buoyed by their tenacity and their faith, this man's dream grew and the power of his dream united a community, a city, a state, a nation, and ultimately a world in sharing an experience so uplifting to the human spirit that for a span of time all peoples were united. (Watkins, 1997: 6)

Philosophy
The Atlanta Games were an entirely private sector phenomenon, without the usual financial under-writing by government. In fact, the constitution of the state of Georgia precluded it from taking on a number of the obligations normally required by the IOC and neither did the Atlanta city council take on these obligations, although it was supportive and involved. The obligations were taken on by a specially created body, the Metropolitan Atlanta Olympic Games Authority (MAOGA), which in turn passed them on to the ACOG itself (Watkins, 1997: 18). Continuing the practice initiated in Los Angeles, the 'spirit' of the Games was seen by many observers as highly commercial, with the activities of sponsors very much to the fore.

The substantial urban infrastructure programme seen in Barcelona and other Olympic cities in the past was not a feature of Atlanta, a modern city with a modern, albeit road-based, transport system and one of the world's busiest airports. While major new facilities were built for the Games, use was made of the local university campus, so that Olympic facilities, including the athletes' village, had post-Games university usage.

Economic Aspects
Because of differences in accounting practices, it is difficult to compare the finances of different Olympic Games in any precise way. Nevertheless, broad patterns are apparent. As shown in Figure 10.4 and Table 10.5, while total expenditure of the Atlanta Committee for the Olympic Games (ACOG) was, at US$1720 million, some US$400 million higher than that of COOB'92, there was no additional infrastructure budget, which had amounted to US$6.3 billion in Barcelona.

As with Barcelona, broadcasting rights and sponsorship (here referred to as 'joint ventures' and TOP III) provide two thirds of all income of the Organising Committee (see Figure 10.5 and Table 10.5). But there is a major difference in the remaining third, with Atlanta generating over US$400 million in ticket sales, compared with Barcelona's mere US$60 million. Atlanta did not have Barcelona's access to lotteries or government grants to make up the balance.

Humphreys and Plummer (1992, 1993) estimated that the net economic impact of the Games on the economy of the state of Georgia would be over US$5 billion, generating some 77,000 jobs, over the period 1991-1997. They also note the legacy of almost US$600 million worth of sporting and other facilities, largely paid for from Olympic revenues.

Table 10.5. Atlanta Committee for the Olympic Games: budget.

Expenditure	US$ million
Administration	218.0
Olympic programmes and physical legacy	68.0
Marketing/PR	44.0
Ceremonies	27.0
Transportation/logistics	133.0
Security/accreditation	35.0
Technology	219.0
Sport event management	91.0
Other services	57.0
Ticketing	35.0
Merchandising	18.0
Host broadcasting	141.0
Olympic village	110.0
Facilities	494.0
Reserves	32.0
Total	1721.0
Income	
Broadcast rights	568.3
Joint venture	426.4
TOP III	81.2
Ticket sales	425.2
Merchandising	31.9
Other	188.0
Total	1721.0

Source: Watkins, 1997: 222.

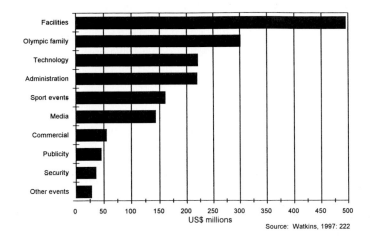

Figure 10.4. Atlanta Committee for the Olympic Games: expenditure[1].

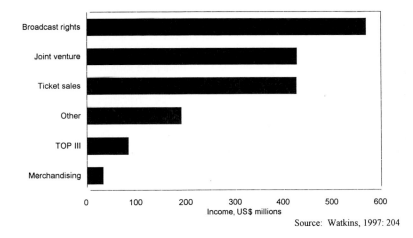

Figure 10.5. Atlanta Committee for the Olympic Games: income.

Events

In addition to the high level of commercialisation, Atlanta will also be remembered for three unfortunate phenomena: the bomb in 'Olympic Park' , the problems with the computerised results system and the alleged transport chaos.

---

[1] Using same categories as in Figure 10.2.

Reports suggested at the time that coordination of security might be a problem at the Atlanta Games because of the large number of agencies involved, including municipal, state and federal bodies. In the middle of the Games period, on day 9, a bomb was detonated in Olympic Park, a down-town area created as the focus of activity for Olympic spectators and residents. Two people were killed and many injured. It is still not clear who was responsible.

Despite having one of the busiest and most sophisticated airports in the world (De Lange, 1998: 141) Atlanta received a great deal of negative media coverage because of defects in its transport system. Such complaints are not uncommon at Olympic Games, when taxi and bus drivers who are not familiar with the local area are drafted in to cope with the burst of demand, but the problems seemed to be greater than usual in Atlanta, with complaints of long delays and poor coordination.

The Atlanta Games received further bad publicity when the computerised results system provided by IBM as part of its sponsorship commitment, malfunctioned in the early days of the Games.

The organisers' problems were exacerbated by inadequate facilities provided for the media (Gratton, 1999), who broadcast stories not only on the sporting events but also on their own experiences. Up to 10,000 accredited media representatives, attend an Olympic Games for whom extensive services must be provided, including accommodation, transport and appropriate communication technology. When something goes wrong, the story has worldwide coverage. In addition, as many as 5000 non-accredited journalists just 'turn up'; they are provided with few services and must generally make do with the facilities provided for the public. Without privileged access to the events and the athletes, they can be on the look out for any extraneous story which will produce headlines back home.

The result of these 'glitches' was that, in his speech at the closing ceremony, the IOC President, Juan Antonio Samaranch, failed to make the traditional declaration, that the Atlanta Games had been the 'best ever' .. they were merely 'most exceptional' (Attwood, 1996). Typical of some journalists' comments were those of Michael Cockerill, one of the *Sydney Morning Herald's* Olympic correspondents:

> Whatever the Atlanta Olympics were, they were not Barcelona. Arguably the greatest Games of the modern era were followed by arguably the worst Games of the modern era - the only argument being just how bad Atlanta was. The sincerity and hospitality of the Georgians notwithstanding, these Games were fundamentally flawed from the outset. No amount of effort could disguise the obvious fact that Atlanta is not a particularly nice city. Nice people, yes. Nice place, no. .. The Atlanta Olympics have been the ultimate hard-sell. The International Olympic Committee, to its eternal discredit, sold out for money. And it got burnt. It is true the sporting competition has been memorable, and the crowds have been the largest in Olympic history. But only in America is bigger always viewed as better. Many others prefer a more human scale. And the scale applied most in Atlanta was the one that measured profit and loss,

television ratings, and advertising income. These were the Private Enterprise Games. But they cost. (Cockerill, 1996)

Sydney 2000

Introduction
Sydney, with a population approaching four million, and renowned for its spectacular harbour and unique Opera House, is the largest city in Australia and the capital of the state of New South Wales. The British founded the city in 1788 as a colonial convict settlement, displacing the indigenous population, whose descendants now form only a small proportion of the population. The city has grown rapidly, particularly in the twentieth century, being host to waves of immigration from first Britain, then southern Europe, and more recently Asia. It is a 'new world' city with a high-rise central business district surrounded by seemingly endless single-storeyed residential suburbs stretching inland for 40 kilometres. Sydney has a long-standing tradition of mostly friendly rivalry with Melbourne, the capital of the state of Victoria and Australia's second largest city. Melbourne, was host to the 1956 Olympic Games and is arguably the sporting heart of the nation, but was an unsuccessful bidder for the 1996 Games, having beaten Sydney to become the Australian candidate.

On September 24, 1993, amid much euphoria, the City of Sydney was awarded the right to host the Games of the 27th Modern Olympiad in the year 2000. Sydney won the bid by a narrow margin in competition with Beijing, Manchester, Berlin and Istanbul. Table 10.6 shows the results of the four rounds of IOC voting which resulted in Sydney's selection.

Table 10.6. IOC voting for the 2000 Games.

City	Round 1	Round 2	Round 3	Round 4
Sydney	30	30	37	45
Beijing	32	37	40	43
Manchester	11	13	11	-
Berlin	9	9	-	-
Istanbul	7	-	-	-

Source: IOC web-site (29.4.99): http://www.olympic.org/facts_e/citydoc_e/

The strengths of Sydney's bid for the year 2000 Games were, reportedly, its claim to be the 'athletes' Games', reflected in the concentration of most of the sports in two locations (Homebush Bay and Darling Harbour), and the housing of all the athletes in one village adjacent to the main site. Other factors believed to have been influential in the decision of the IOC were the fact that many of the needed sports facilities were already in existence, the apparent strong support from the community,

Australia's long and consistent record of participation in the modern Olympic Games (Australia claims to be one of only two countries - the other being Greece - to have been represented at every one of the modern Olympic Games) and the environmental components of the bid.

The bid was organised by the Sydney Olympic 2000 Bid Ltd (SOBL), technically a private company, but with high profile public figures among its board membership. SOBL had raised its $20 million (US$12m)[2] budget largely from private sector sponsors and a $5 million federal government grant. The bid was nevertheless underwritten by the New South Wales state government, which would be responsible for building many of the facilities. The bid document (SOBL, 1993) included a budget for the running of the Games which showed a total cost of $1.7 billion, off-set by income primarily from television rights, sponsorship and ticket sales, to produce a small surplus of $15 million, later revised downwards to $6 million.

Such is the scale of the modern Olympic Games that even the bid process is a major undertaking. In Sydney's case, the story of the bid is available in book form in *The Bid: How Australia Won the 2000 Games*, written by Rod McGeoch, the CEO of SOBL, and journalist Glenda Korporaal (McGeoch and Korporaal, 1994). The notable feature of the saga is the assiduous lobbying of IOC members to gain their votes, a long-standing practice which has been subject to much criticism (e.g. Booth and Tatz, 1994) and has led to the current difficulties faced by the IOC over the whole bidding process.

Critics

During the period up to the announcement of its success there were few local critics of Sydney's bid, leading to some questioning of the independence of the media, especially given that leading media executives were members of the bid committee (Bacon, 1993). The most high profile and consistent critic was Max Walsh of the *Sydney Morning Herald*, who produced a series of articles criticising the financial basis of the bid (Walsh, 1992, 1993a-c). It is claimed that critical articles by freelance journalist Mikael Kjaerbye, published in September 1993 in *Reportage*, the newsletter of the Australian Centre for Independent Journalism (Hendy and Kjaerbye, 1993; Kjaerbye, 1993; Salleh and Kjaerbye, 1993a, b), had been rejected by a number of newspapers. Whether this lack of criticism was as a result of an organised media/government conspiracy or a spontaneous and uncoordinated desire on all sides not to jeopardise the bid by providing competing cities with critical ammunition, criticism of the idea of holding the Games in Sydney was muted (Lenskyj, 1997). No pressure groups emerged to oppose the bid as happened, for example, in Berlin and Toronto.

Following the success of the bid, however, criticisms and concerns emerged on three fronts: financial, social and environmental.

---

[2]   Subsequent dollar sums in the chapter are in Australian dollars, unless otherwise indicated.

Figure 10.6. Public celebration in Sydney, September 1993, on news that the city had been awarded the 2000 Games.

Financial Critics

Financial criticism of the Sydney proposals had, in fact, been put forward by Max Walsh from as early as 1992 and continued throughout 1993 (Walsh, 1992, 1993a-c). In October 1993 he was joined by Bob Walker (1993) Professor of Accounting in the University of New South Wales and a consistent critic of government financial practices. The criticisms focused on a number of issues, the main one being that there appeared to be, in effect, *two* Olympic budgets rather than one. The first, was the official 'Games' budget, while the second, which it was claimed the government was being less than open about, involved a number of major infrastructure items, which together cost some $1.5 billion.

The New South Wales government claimed that these items were quite properly separated from the main budget because they would have been incurred regardless of the success or failure of the bid; the effect of the Olympic bid was merely to bring them forward in time. In fairness to the government, the *Homebush Bay Strategy,* had been adopted by the government as early as August 1989, and included a number of the disputed items (Sydney Olympic Games Review Committee, 1990: 9-10). An information sheet produced by the responsible government agency, the Homebush Bay Development Corporation, in October 1992, stated:

> The development of Homebush Bay is proposed over a 15-20 year period and will cost the NSW Government an estimated net $667 million in today's dollars. The *Masterplan* for Homebush Bay is primarily a non-Olympic plan, however it could be expanded to accommodate facilities necessary for the Olympics. The

costs for the development are therefore purely non-Olympic based and will be required over an extended development period up to 2010. Overall, the development costs will be $807 million and will be offset against an expected $140 million income derived through property asset sales. Government has already committed $300 million for the construction of the Sydney Aquatic and Athletics Centre and associated infrastructure which are due for completion in 1994. (Homebush Bay Dev. Corp., 1992: 1)

As for the media and athlete villages, the government asserted that the funding of the villages would be undertaken by private developers, for subsequent sale as private dwellings. Critics questioned whether the Sydney housing market would be able to absorb the several thousand units involved, and therefore whether the villages would be attractive to private developers. In the event, private developers took on the project and decided to solve the market glut problem by providing many of the housing units in temporary, demountable form.

Other financial criticisms put forward by Walsh and Walker included the following:

- the Games budget erroneously counted the sale of a public asset (the Royal Agricultural Society showground site) and government grants as income - the critics were vindicated here;
- the possibility that the facilities inherited from the Games could become a financial liability rather than an asset had not been considered - this remains to be seen but, since major facilities have been developed by the private sector, this is not directly the government's or Games organisers' problem;
- because of its high profile, political rather than economic factors would govern the planning of the event, resulting in an inevitable cost blow-out - here the critics have been partially vindicated (see below);
- interest payments on capital were ignored - this is a matter of opinion, since government expenditure has been funded from current income rather than borrowing;
- additional capital spending by the New South Wales government on the scale envisaged would need to be financed by savings or deferral of expenditure from elsewhere, such as education and health - here the critics have been largely vindicated (NSW Audit Office, 1998: 60-61);
- the anticipated size of television fee income and corporate sponsorship indicated in the Games budget were questioned - here the critics were proved wrong: actual broadcasting fee income was higher than anticipated, although the flow of sponsorship income is being affected by the IOC bribery scandal;
- the economic benefits from the Games were being promoted as some sort of panacea for Australia's economic problems when, in fact, when related to GDP and overseas earnings, the impact was quite small - critics have been vindicated here; the amount of unrealistic promotion of the benefits of the Games by

government has been limited, although media coverage sometimes gives a contrary impression.

Social Impact
In addition to purely financial considerations, there were concerns that the Games could have adverse social impacts on the community, through disruption to such services as housing and transport and the diversion of resources from existing social programmes (Hall and Hodges, 1996). A two-part social impact report was produced by the state Office on Social Policy setting out a framework for the conduct of such a study (Johnston, 1993) and making proposals for the establishment of a process for dealing with potentially adverse social impacts before, during and after the Games (Deakin, 1993). The factors considered in the report were: housing and accommodation; transport; employment and training; economic and pricing issues; health and the environment; social and community services; security and human rights; recreational issues; cultural issues; population change; and sub-population issues. Of these issues, the one taken most seriously has been housing, with fears that demand for short-term rentals before and during the Games would raise rents and tempt landlords to evict long-term, low-rent tenants. A report prepared for the housing charity, Shelter, confirmed this danger (Cox *et al.*, 1994).

The 'Green Games'
In the context of the IOC's emerging concern for the environment (see chapter 4) the environmental, 'Green Games', emphasis of the Sydney bid was seen as an important ingredient in its success. The environmental organisation Greenpeace was directly involved in the bid, which included an environmentally innovative design for the athletes' village and an explicit set of *Environmental Guidelines* (SOBL, 1993c). The Homebush site itself was faced with severe environmental problems, due to decades of use by industry and as a dumping ground for domestic and industrial waste. It had never been a secret that the Homebush site required massive expenditure for decontamination, although the bid budget underestimated the cost by a substantial margin.

However, apart from the issue of costs, questions arose over a number of environmental issues. Doubts were expressed as to whether the site could be adequately decontaminated at all and whether the best procedures were being used (Beder, 1993). The feasibility of ferry access to the site was queried, since the bay would require dredging, and would cause disturbance to toxic wastes in the river bed (Salleh and Kjaerbye 1993b; Whittaker, 1993) - in fact, although funds were set aside for the task, at the time of writing, the bay has still not been decontaminated, although, in reality, ferry access was never considered a realistic proposition for the bulk of visitors to the Olympic site. Doubts were expressed as to whether the 'green' features of the athletes' village would survive seven years of government, developer and architects' inputs (Whittaker, 1993) and whether the green guidelines for the whole event had enough 'teeth' (Salleh and Kjaerbye, 1993a).

The environmental performance of the 'Green Games' has been subject to considerable public scrutiny. In 1995, a coalition of Australian environmental groups, with government funding support, formed Green Games Watch 2000 Inc. to monitor the environmental performance of Sydney 2000 developments. The organisation has produced a series of reports and newsletters drawing attention to Olympic agencies' environmental failings (Green Games Watch 2000 Inc., 1999). A 1998 conference on the subject aired a number of criticisms of the 'Green Games' efforts (Cashman and Hughes, 1998) and, while a number of environmental 'firsts' have been achieved, the question of whether the overall performance of the Sydney 2000 Olympics will fully merit the accolade 'Green Games' remains to be seen (Lenskyj, 1998a, b; Prasad, 1999).

Organisation

In accordance with IOC rules, the organising of the Games was entrusted to the Sydney Organising Committee for the Olympic Games (SOCOG), a body constituted by Act of the New South Wales Parliament, with membership appointed by the New South Wales government, the City of Sydney and the Australian Olympic Committee. In its early days SOCOG experienced a number of changes in the Chair and Chief Executive Officer. While the constant changes at the helm were not accompanied by scandal or bad blood, they were certainly unsettling for the organisation. Eventually the state government Minister with responsibility for the Olympic Games, Michael Knight, took over as chair - a move criticised by many as 'politicizing' the Games, but one which at least ensured a largely trouble-free relationship with the government. A career public servant, Sandy Hollway, was eventually appointed as CEO and, at the time of writing, looks set to remain until the Games are complete.

Within SOCOG, a separate organisation, the Sydney Olympic Broadcasting Organisation (SOBO) was established to coordinate broadcasting arrangements. Much of the facility development was initially in the hands of a number of government bodies, causing a certain amount of confusion and over-lapping of responsibilities. Eventually a single body was created - the Olympic Coordination Authority (OCA) - which took over responsibility for the main site at Homebush and a number of other sites, and coordinated the state's direct involvement and the tendering process for private sector involvement. An additional body, the Olympic Roads and Traffic Authority (ORTA), was created to oversee transport arrangements. To complete the organisational arrangements, the Sydney Paralympic Organising Committee (SPOC) was established, with close links with SOCOG. The result is that the employed staff running the Paralympic Games and the Olympic Games will be much the same.

Opinion polls suggest that public support for the Sydney 2000 Games has generally been strong, but commentators have drawn attention to the 'short cuts' in planning procedures arising from the significant powers vested in the OCA and the Minister for the Olympics, which raise questions as to the extent to which the public have been consulted, involved and made aware of developments (Beder, 1993: 17;

Lenskyj, 1994; Dunn and McGuirk, 1999). While other bidding cities and host cities have seen significant opposition (Lenskyj, 1992, 1994, 1997), in Sydney criticism has been muted. The major public opposition has been to the location of the beach volleyball facilities on Bondi Beach, but at the time of writing, the extent of this opposition and its likely success in preventing the building of the temporary stadium are unclear.

Figure 10.7. Homebush Bay, Sydney, showing the Olympic stadium and Aquatic Centre and facilities for a number of other events.

Economic Dimensions

The financing of the Games has followed the pattern set in other host cities with, as the critics implied, two budgets. The first is the budget of SOCOG, concerned with the direct organisation of the Games and largely funded from television revenues, sponsorship and ticket sales. Table 10.7 shows that, while the original bid budget, as indicated above, was of the order of $1.7 billion and showed a small surplus, the version produced by the state Audit Office in 1998 showed that even the original budget had been underestimated by some $200 million, while the revised version had grown to over $2.5 billion and showed a small deficit.

The second budget, that of the OCA, was concerned with facilities and other infrastructure and is shown in Table 10.8. Again it can be seen that the original bid costs had been underestimated, in this case by some $900 million, and the revised budget was $1500 million higher, at $2.4 billion. While five years had elapsed between the original bid and the new sets of estimates, very little could be put down to inflation. The major changes were due to the inclusion of items in the budget which had previously been deliberately or fortuitously excluded.

Table 10.7. Sydney Organising Committee for the Olympic Games: budget.

Expenditure	1993 Bid Budget A$m	1998 Revision A$m
Games support	222.8	543.3
Precincts and venues	392.6	526.7
Sport	152.6	165.0
Villages	158.0	180.6
Games Services	211.1	175.0
Broadcasting	211.1	195.6
Commercial	36.0	111.6
Marketing and image	84.0	82.7
Co-ordination	-	69.8
Ceremonies	50.2	39.2
Government & ATSI	-	7.8
Command/control/communication	-	6.1
Australian Olympic Committee	60.0	75.0
Paralympics	20.2	16.7
Payments to government	273.0	285.0
IOC payments	-	11.1
Contingencies	120.8	75.8
Total	1992.4	2587.6
Income		
Sponsorship	622.1	873.7
Ticket sales	266.7	600.9
Broadcast receipts	948.0	1032.2
Consumer products	96.6	65.2
Other	-	25.0
Total	1933.4	2579.0
Surplus (-Deficit)	-59.0	-8.6

Source: Audit Office of New South Wales, 1998.

The fact that these budget changes were later made so clearly and unequivocally can be seen to be due to two factors. Firstly, between the bid and the new estimates, there had been a change of state government, from Liberal to Labor. The new government had no compunction about suggesting that the previous government had been hiding the true cost of the Olympic from the public. Secondly, the review was carried out by the New South Wales Audit Office, an organisation specifically charged with taking an independent and, if necessary, critical view of government expenditure. While the publication of the Audit Office report in late 1998 caused a flurry of headlines about the 'Olympic Budget blowout', the political fallout of these revelations was minor. The Labor government was returned with a much increased majority in the March 1999 elections.

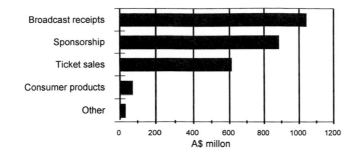

Figure 10.8. Sydney 2000: Organising Committee income.

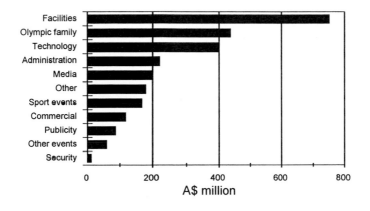

Figure 10.9. Sydney 2000 Organising Committee expenditure.

As part of the bid process consultants KPMG Peat Marwick (1993) produced, free of charge, an economic impact study in which they estimated that the economic impact of the Games on the Australian economy would be some $7.3 billion, resulting in 165,000 one-year full-time equivalent jobs (see Table 10.9). This included generated tax revenues of some $1.9 billion, a factor largely ignored in subsequent debates on the cost of the Games. Although other studies have since been conducted, of overall economic impact (NSW Treasury and the Centre for Regional Economic Analysis, 1997) and of tourism impacts (Tourism Forecasting Council, 1998), the basic approach and findings of KPMG Peat Marwick have not been challenged. It should, however, be borne in mind that the impacts of $7 billion and 165,000 jobs are spread over 13 years; since the annual GDP of Australia is some $500 billion and the labour force is more than 10 million, the impacts amount to only 0.1% of GDP in that period.

Table 10.8. Sydney 2000: Olympic Coordination Authority budget.

	Bid budget	Adjusted bid budget	OCA budget 1998
Expenditure	*A$m*	*A$m*	*A$m*
Media village	-	-	127.8
Athletes' village	-	-	72.7
Athletes' village site remediation	-	-	99.6
Other venue costs	77.8	109.8	227.1
Olympic stadium	360.4	360.4	126.3
Transport	-	267.2	422.3
Sydney Superdome	84.9	84.9	156.5
Development of showground	-	327.0	388.2
Sports hall	119.7	119.7	-
Contingency items	108.5	108.5	68.5
Services infrastructure	-	94.6	115.1
Site infrastructure	27.8	109.2	116.8
State athletic/aquatic centres	216.8	216.8	216.8
Site remediation	-	77.9	47.9
Operating costs	-	18.7	235.9
Total	995.9	1894.7	2421.5
Income			
Race days	30.8	30.8	-
Showground sale proceeds	86.4	86.4	-
Site sale	-	-	35.0
SOCOG rental fee	58.9	58.9	77.0
Federal government contribution	157.4	157.4	175.0
State government contribution	31.5	31.5	-
SOCOG construction fee	209.7	209.7	218.7
Recurrent income	-	-	73.1
Other	-	-	8.8
Interest	57.0	57.0	30.4
Total	631.7	631.7	618.0
Net OCA cost (met by NSW govt)	364.2	1263.0	1803.5
Private sector capital expenditure	1185.6	1185.6	1084.8

Source: Audit Office of NSW, 1998: 73.

It should also be noted that the KPMG Peat Marwick study was an economic impact study and not a cost-benefit analysis. The report outlines the range of issues which would need to be taken into account in a full-scale cost-benefit study, as shown in Appendix 10.1. These would include environmental and social factors as well as financial items. Prepared as an adjunct to an economic impact study, which tends to ignore non-economic factors, the KPMG Peat Marwick schema is more detailed in its listing of benefits than costs. However, it would provide a good starting point for such a study if combined with the social impact report (Office of Social Policy, 1993). Ideally such a cost-benefit analysis should be undertaken *before* a decision is made to go ahead with a project, but this rarely happens. More often cost-benefits studies are undertaken after an event, as a form of post-event evaluation, as was done with the Adelaide Grand Prix (Burns *et al.*, 1986) and the Brisbane Commonwealth Games (Lynch and Jensen, 1984). Whether such a study will be undertaken on the Sydney Games remains to be seen.

Table 10.9. Sydney 2000: economic impact 1991-2004*.

Increase in GDP by area:	*Aud$m.*
Australia	7336
New South Wales	4587
Sydney	3560
Increase in GDP by industry sector	
Manufacturing	1150
Retail trade	1238
Personal services	1133
Finance	992
Construction	373
Other	2578
Total	7336
Increase in taxation revenue 1991-2004	
Commonwealth	1934
New South Wales	376
Local Government	73
Increase in annual jobs	*No.*
Australia	156,198
New South Wales	89,504
Sydney	73,089

Source: KPMG Peat Marwick, 1993 * 'Most Likely' Scenario.

One major benefit item is missing from the KPMG Peat Marwick framework, namely the *psychic* value of the Games - the value of the enjoyment and satisfaction which many Australian, New South Wales and in particular Sydney residents might obtain from the Games, net of the displeasure and offence which some might experience. In their cost-benefit study of the Adelaide Grand Prix, Burns *et al.* (1986) found that the estimated psychic value of the event to the residents of Adelaide was the largest item on the benefit side of the equation.

Events

The lead-up to the Sydney 2000 Olympics was not without its problems. In any project lasting seven years and involving thousands of people, there are bound to be problems along the way, and the Sydney 2000 Olympics are no exception. At the time of writing, the ultimate test of the management skills of the organisers - the staging of the Games - has not taken place, so whether 'it'll be alright on the night' remains to be seen. The public problems of the Sydney 2000 Games, as discussed below, were relatively minor and were largely overshadowed by the highly publicised problems faced by the IOC in 1998/99.

The IOC Bribery Scandal. The IOC bribery and corruption scandals which arose towards the end of 1998 are discussed in more detail in chapter 11. Here, it is appropriate to draw attention to the effect of these events on the Sydney Games. While the accusations of improper behaviour mainly involved the Salt Lake City 2002 Winter Games, the impact on Sydney was notable because of the numerous accusations made against Australian IOC member and SOCOG Board member, Phil Coles. At the time the accusations were made public, SOCOG was still short of some $200 million in sponsorship money. It is widely believed that the bad publicity hampered SOCOG's effort at raising this money. Consequently, in May 1999, SOCOG announced cuts of some $75 million in expenditure.

Floating the Stadium. The main Olympic stadium, with 110,000 seats the largest ever, was built by a private sector consortium. Some government subsidy was involved, but the consortium planned to finance at least half the $600 million cost by selling membership shares in the stadium. For $10,000 investors would have shares in the company and a seat at the stadium for all events for the first 30 years of its life, including the Olympic Games. Unfortunately, the public were less than enthusiastic and fewer than half the 30,000 memberships were sold, leaving the underwriters to make up the $200 million shortfall.

The Marching Bands Fiasco. This problem resulted from the decision of the organiser of the opening ceremony, Ric Birch, to deploy, as part of the entertainment, a 2000-person marching band made up primarily of American and Japanese marchers, with only a small representation of Australians. When this fact emerged, the marching band fraternity of Australia was outraged and was supported by talk-back radio hosts and their callers and by politicians. As a result of the adverse publicity, SOCOG decided to cancel the contract with World Projects Corporation (WPC), an American company contracted to provide the marchers. Hundreds of young marching band players, who had been fund-raising in order to pay their way to Sydney, were reportedly disappointed and WPC took SOCOG to court. Eventually SOCOG reversed its decision and reinstated the contract, but with the proviso that more countries were to be represented in the band and more Australians were to be included (Moore, 1999). The whole saga was represented in the media as an example of inept bungling, just at the time when the Olympic tickets went on sale.

The Beach Volleyball Saga. This problem arose from the decision of the organisers to hold the Olympic beach volleyball competition in a specially constructed temporary stadium located on the world-famous Bondi beach. When the plans for the stadium were submitted for consideration by the local council, various local residents' groups raised objections to the scale of the structure, the amount of beach that would be commandeered and the length of time (six months) for which it would be required. For a while it appeared that the local council would oppose the facility and various alternatives, such as artificial beaches in football stadiums, were mooted. However, with some minor changes, the plans were approved and went ahead, but some local residents were still threatening to 'lie down in front of the bulldozers' rather than allow the facility to go ahead. Again, the media attention was intense, this time the Olympic organisers being portrayed as undemocratic and riding roughshod over community interests.

The Tickets Embarrassment. In October 1999, widespread disappointment among those who had been unsuccessful in the ballot for Games tickets turned to outrage when it emerged that tickets to 'sold out' prime events were still available at several times face value, to corporate and other organisations that could afford them and that, after overseas visitors, media, sponsors and the Olympic Family had been catered for, less than a third of the tickets overall, and in some prime events as few as 10%, were available for sale to the Australian public. At the time of writing, SOCOG was being investigated by the Australian Competition and Consumer Commission for misleading advertising.

Conclusion
Few doubt that the Sydney 2000 Olympic Games will prove to be a sporting success. Whether they will be a financial and environmental success is less certain. As much a political and media phenomenon as a sporting event, it will be interesting to see whether financial, environmental or sporting issues dominate the debate on the Games during the post-Games period. At the time of writing, the Games are 12 months away: tickets have gone on sale with a high level of response from the Australian public, IOC bribery scandals have largely disappeared from the newspaper headlines and a number of the Olympic facilities are being put through their paces in 'test events'. Everyone involved is looking forward to 'the greatest Olympic Games ever'.

Appendix 10.1: Items for a cost-benefit study of the Games (KPMG Peat Marwick).

BENEFITS	COSTS
Housing	
• Increased capital appreciation • Increased rate of revenue • Urban consolidation • More low-cost housing close to city • Regeneration of Homebush Bay site and improved site amenity	• Reduced housing affordability for first time buyers and low-cost rent accommodation • Urban consolidation (high density) leading to increased congestion
Transport	
• Increased utilisation of existing transport infrastructure leading to improved revenue/capital • Increased public transport leading to reduced pollution/congestion and increased accessibility	• Cost of provision
Sports facilities	
• Better distribution of facilities • Better located show grounds. • Increased range of national and international venues • Better standard and range of facilities leading to improved sporting standards • Increased recreational amenity at Penrith (rowing centre)	• Operating costs • Under-utilised facilities, i.e. potential operating losses if demand less than supply
Tourism	
• Increased international exposure of Australia and Sydney • Greater number of jobs in the tourism industry, particularly benefits for the low skilled unemployed • Increased number of tourism related services (e.g. restaurants, shops) which are also available to residents • Increased level of accommodation which thereby allows Sydney to tender for other major events, with consequent economic spin-offs	• Environmental costs from increased visitation • Short-term waste management issues associated with Olympics and sustained increased visitation • Increased congestion • Pecuniary externality of extra demand leading to increased costs imposed on locals, particularly in popular tourist areas • Potential over-supply of accommodation after Games

BENEFITS	COSTS
Technology	
• Knowledge gained from rejuvenating Homebush Bay site could be applied to other degraded sites • Increased communication infrastructure and know-how • Systems development leading to internationally marketable service • More rapid deployment of new media technologies, e.g. high density TV	• None mentioned
Human capital	
• Large scale employment associated with Games • Reduced unemployment leading to reduced social problems associated with unemployment • Technology transfer from visiting Olympic support staff, e.g. production, event staging, computing, etc. • Improved sporting prowess through increased exposure to international standard competition	• Post-Games demobilisation
Economic	
• Business development; Sydney's profile as a place to do business enhanced by Olympic exposure (overseas business people attending the Games identifying investment opportunities)	• Inflationary impact of increased tourism • Investment in Olympics 'crowd out' investment in other productive enterprises
National Identity	
• Increased national pride through increased international exposure • More awareness of Australian culture following from Olympics Cultural Programme	• None mentioned

Source: KPMG Peat Marwick, 1993.

Appendix 10.2: The Games of the modern era

This Appendix draws on a number of sources which provide accounts of a number of or all of the modern Olympic Games, including Findling and Pelle (1996), Cuyàs (1992), De Lange (1998), Gordon (1994), Guttman (1994) and the irreverent Sheil (1998) and Jennings (1996). References to literature dealing with individual Games are given separately in each entry; being confined to English-language material, this tends to be more extensive for Games hosted in English-speaking countries. Appendix 4.3 provides a listing of official Games reports.

I: 1896, Athens, Greece
The organisational aspects of these first Games of the modern era are discussed in Chapter 3. See also Mallon and Widlund (1998b), Holmes (1979) and Davenport (1996).

II: 1900, Paris, France
The Paris Games, which lasted from May to October, were appended to the Universal Paris Exposition - at de Coubertin's urging, but against the wishes of the exposition organisers. While 19 nations were represented by over 1000 competitors, by all accounts, the event did not enhance the prestige of the Olympic idea. Gordon reports:

> .. the festival set new, heroic standards of confusion. It was spread over five months and most of Paris and the surrounding countryside, and it turned out to be the kind of carnival that might well have been scripted by the Marx Brothers. Competitors waged fierce fishing contests in the Seine, indulged in ballooning and fire-fighting matches, raced underwater and through water-obstacle courses, and took rifle pot-shots at live pigeons. .. The athletic events were held in the Bois de Boulogne, where shady elm trees often got in the way of the discus and hammer, and also tended to block the timekeepers' view of the starter. (Gordon, 1994: 29)

There were disputes between competitors, accusations of cheating and confusion as to whether the event was the official Olympic Games at all, or just a sport programme of the exposition - which was perhaps not surprising since the programme was referred to as the *Concours Internationaux d'Exercises Physiques et de Sports*. Mallon (1998) refers to these and the 1904 St Louis Games as the 'Farcical Games'. See also Howell and Howell (1996).

III: 1904, Saint-Louis, USA
Despite the lessons of 1900, the Games were again incorporated into an international exposition - the St Louis World Fair. Only 12 countries were represented, by a shrunken field of under 700 competitors, of whom some 70% were from the United States. 'Even Baron de Coubertin did not attend. Neither France nor England sent a single competitor ..' (Gordon, 1994: 40).

Again the event appears to have been less than impressive, with the initial winner of the marathon being disqualified for having hitched a lift in a car for 11 miles, the eventual winner later admitting to having been dosed on strychnine sulphate, eggs and brandy, and the final events of the Games being little more than exotic sideshows of the fair (Gordon, 1994: 42). Against the wishes of the IOC, 'Anthropology days' were held, in which only non-white competitors were allowed, and which consisted of a number of traditional activities, such as spear throwing, participated in by competitors representing various indigenous groups from around the world. See also Barnett (1996) and Crawford (1991).

IV: 1908, London
Originally planned for Rome, the 1908 Games were staged in the purpose-built White City stadium, seating 68,000. The Games lasted six months, from April to October, and were generally considered to be well-organised, with over 2000 competitors for the first time. Metric measures were used as standard for the first time. Some 21 sports were involved, including ice skating and specially written rule-books were introduced for the first time and more women's events were included. But there was reportedly considerable antagonism between the British organisers and judges and some of the teams, particularly the United States.

The distance for the marathon was set at this Games, being the distance from Windsor Castle, the royal residence, west of London, to White City - 26 miles, 385 yards (42.2 km) - and has remained at that distance ever since. The actual race was, however, controversial, with the collapsing initial winner being helped over the final yards by officials, resulting in his disqualification. See also Matthews (1980) and Coates (1996).

V: 1912, Stockholm, Sweden
The 1912 Stockholm Games were well organised and notable for officially involving women's events for the first time. Electronic time-keeping and the photo-finish were used for the first time. There were 2500 competitors, including 57 women, from 26 countries. At de Coubertin's behest, competitions in music, painting and poetry, inspired by sport, were held (Ueberhorst, 1996).

VI: 1916, Cancelled
Originally planned for Berlin, these games were cancelled, due to the World War (see Durick, 1996).

VII: 1920, Antwerp, Belgium
The 1920 Games were held in Antwerp in Belgium, the country most affected by the ravages of the Great War. They were held without the support of the Belgian government, in quite spartan conditions. The defeated countries - Germany, Austria, Bulgaria, Hungary and Turkey - were excluded. The Olympic Flag was first displayed at these Games (Lucas, 1983) and the athletes' Olympic Oath was introduced (Renson, 1996).

Renson (1996) indicates that the official report of the Games (see Appendix 4.3) is inaccurate and that Mallon (1992) provides a corrected version of the athletic results. See also Lucas (1983) and Renson (1985).

VIII: 1924, Paris and Chamonix, France
The Paris Games of 1924 saw the first use of the Olympic motto 'Citius, Altius, Fortius'. The Games were broadcast via radio for the first time, and 1000 journalists were in attendance. Spectator numbers, at 625,000, were much higher than for previous Games (Welch, 1996). The question of the definition of 'amateur' arose, and it is these Games that form the background to the film *Chariots of Fire* (see also Beck, 1980 and Dyreson, 1996).

Welch (1996b) provides an account of the first Winter Games, held at Chamonix, France. This event was only recognised by the IOC retrospectively, in 1926 (Gordon, 1994: 414).

IX: 1928, Amsterdam, Netherlands and St Moritz, Switzerland
The Amsterdam Games of 1928 saw the introduction of women's track and field events (Morrow, 1992). The Olympic Flame was introduced for the first time, the flame having been brought from Olympia, but not by relay. Almost 300 women competitors (10% of the total) took part (Goldstein, 1996). Simmons (1996) provides an account of the St Moritz Winter Games.

X: 1932, Los Angeles and Lake Placid, USA
The 1932 Games were held at a time of world-wide economic depression, with unemployment rates as high as 30% in some countries. Nevertheless, the American organisers were determined to 'put on a show' for the 'first Olympics held outside Europe since the farce of St Louis in 1904' (Gordon, 1994: 134). The Coliseum, seating 100,000, and a swimming pool with 17,000 spectator seats, were constructed for the event, resulting in over a million spectators (Pieroth, 1996b). The Coliseum was used again for the 1984 Games. Innovations at these Games included the first specially constructed athletes' village (for men competitors only), teletype communications for the press, electric photo-finish timing, and individual medal ceremonies incorporating a podium as well as flags and national anthems. Foreshadowing the 1984 Games, the organisers returned a profit of US$1 million (Gordon, 1994: 135). See also Barney (1998), Lucas (1982), Pieroth (1996a) and Stump (1988). Fea (1996a) provides an account of the Lake Placid Winter Games.

XI: 1936, Berlin and Garmich-Partenkirchen, Germany
Because of the controversy arising from their links with the German Nazi regime, the Berlin Games of 1936 have been written about more than any other Olympic Games (e.g. Snyder, 1936; Spencer, 1966; Holmes, 1971; Mandell, 1971, 1978; Gotlieb, 1972; Kass, 1976; Kidd, 1980; Marvin, 1982; Guttman, 1988; Hart-Davis, 1988; Gray and Knight-Barney, 1990; Wenn, 1991, 1996; Murray, 1992a, b; Masumoto, 1993, 1994; Dyreson, 1994; Herz and Altman, 1996; Krüger, 1996; Rosenzweig,

1997). The political aspects of the Berlin Games have already discussed in some detail in chapter 5 and it is not proposed to elaborate on that discussion here.

Again, held in a massive, specially built stadium, which still stands, Berlin was the first Games to feature the torch relay from Olympia. It was also the first to be celebrated in an official film, in this case two films, shot by the controversial Leni Riefenstahl (Masumoto, 1993, 1994). The Games were televised for the first time at Berlin, albeit to a very small domestic audience. With almost 4000 competitors, it has been suggested that the Berlin Games marked a turning point from Olympic sport as a mere personal pastime for élite performers, to an activity which was taken seriously by governments and which required serious devotion and commitment to training on the part of athletes, raising again the issue of professionalism (Gordon, 1994: 156, 161). Pierre de Coubertin did not attend the Berlin Games, and died just a few weeks after their conclusion.

Stauff (1996) provides an account of the Garmisch-Partenkirchen Winter Games.

XII: 1940 and XIII: 1944, Cancelled
The 1940 Games were originally planned for Tokyo but, following the Japanese invasion of China, were later awarded to Helsinki, only to be cancelled with the outbreak of the Second World War (see Pattengale, 1996). The 1944 Games, also cancelled, had been awarded to London in 1939 (Manning, 1996). Scharenberg (1996) and Engelbrecht (1996) provide accounts of the events surrounding the cancelled Winter Games.

XIV: 1948, London, England and St Moritz, Switzerland
As with the 1920 Antwerp Games, the 1948 Games took place in a city still affected by the disruption and shortages of war (Martueci, 1988; Baker, 1994a, b). Nevertheless, the event attracted over 4000 competitors from 59 countries and, by using mostly existing facilities and being successful in selling tickets to a British public starved of international sporting events during the war years, the organisers managed to return a profit (de Lange, 1998: 61). The London Games were the first to enjoy a multi-million worldwide audience, with the BBC broadcasting commentaries in 43 languages (de Lange, 1998: 61). Thus the new Olympic stars, such as Fanny Blankers-Koen of the Netherlands, who won four gold medals, and Emil Zatopek of Czechoslovakia, who won the 10,000 metres, became household names around the world.

Simmons (1996) provides an account of the St Moritz Winter Games and MacDonald (1998) provides an account of United States involvement with ice hockey at those Games.

XV: 1952, Helsinki, Finland and Oslo, Norway
Originally planned for 1940, the Helsinki Games of 1952 attracted over 5000 competitors. They were notable for the first appearance of the Soviet Union (Jokl *et al.,* 1956; Maxwell and Howell, 1976; Hornbuckle, 1996), inaugurating the 30 year

Cold War sporting rivalry between the two Great Powers. Germany and Japan re-entered the Games. The hero of the Games was Emil Zatopek, who won three gold medals. MacDonald and Brown (1996) provide an account of the Oslo Winter Games.

XVI: 1956, Melbourne, Australia/Stockholm, Sweden and Cortina, Italy

The Games of the XVIth Olympiad were awarded to Melbourne by the IOC in 1949, but years of wrangling followed, resulting in protracted delays in building facilities, and incurring the wrath of IOC president Avery Brundage over the delays (Gordon, 1994: 200). The 1956 Melbourne Olympics, the first to be staged in the southern hemisphere, were, however, widely viewed as a great success. Referred to as the 'Friendly Games', Gordon says of them:

> When the Olympic Games moved into Melbourne .. it was as if the city had been touched by a certain magic. Nothing before or since .. has ever evoked such sheer emotional involvement from the whole community. .. there was .. a dimension that seemed almost transcendental. Certainly there was about those Games, at a time of fierce international tension, a reassuring innocence. (Gordon, 1994: 203)

Consistent with the 'friendly' theme, and prompted by a letter from an Australian schoolboy, in the closing ceremony the athletes mingled, rather than parading in separate teams, a tradition which has been maintained ever since.

Because of Australia's strict quarantine regulations, the equestrian events were held in Stockholm, Sweden. Political boycotts arose for the first time, with a number of countries withdrawing as a result of the Suez crisis. And for the first time the Soviet Union gained more medals than the USA.

Mainly as a result of the distance to Australia from the main northern hemisphere population centres (and bearing in mind that travel was by ship), the number of competitors fell to 3000.

The Melbourne Games have been the subject of a numerous studies and commentaries from academics and others (e.g. Donald and Selth, 1957; Kent and Merritt, 1986; Soldatow, 1980; Mazitelli, 1988; Woodhead, 1988; Cahill, 1989; Wenn, 1993; Gordon, 1994; Jobling, 1994, 1996; Cashman, 1995; Davison, 1997).

Hall (1996) provides an account of the Cortina Winter Games.

XVII: 1960, Rome, Italy and Squaw Valley, USA

Originally promised the Games of 1908, Rome had waited more than 50 years to host the Games, which were presented as a mixture of the ancient, with classical backdrops for a number of events, and modern, with a spectacular new 100,000-seat stadium and other modern venues (Davies, 1996). The costly facilities were partly funded by a government-run soccer lottery, but revenue from television rights were also a source of income for the first time. The IOC became concerned about the scale of the Games, and placed a limit of 7000 on the number of athletes and of 1800 on officials (de Lange, 1998: 71); in the event the number of athletes was just 5300. Despite underlying international tensions (for example, over South Africa and recognition of China) the Games took place without political disruption.

The first Paralympic Games were held in Rome following the 1960 Games. Ashwell (1996) gives an account of the Squaw Valley Winter Games.

XVIII: 1964, Tokyo, Japan and Innsbruck, Austria
Originally promised the 1940 Games, it was 24 years later that the Olympics came to Asia for the first time. Although the Games were generally free from political incident, Indonesia and North Korea were excluded over events related to the recognition of China (Alam, 1996). The Japanese invested huge sums of money in transport infrastructure and sporting facilities, raising the issue, as discussed in chapter 6, of just what categories of expenditure should be deemed 'Olympic' expenditure and which categories charged to local development.

Sporting highlights included Australian swimmer Dawn Fraser and Russian rower Vyacheslav Ivanov defending their Olympic titles for a record third time.

Kennedy (1996) gives an account of the Innsbruck Winter Games.

XIX: 1968, Mexico City, Mexico and Grenoble, France
Mexico City, is 2500 metres above sea level, making it the highest altitude location at which the Olympic Games have been held. Together with the infamous air pollution of the city, this presented problems for many athletes, but also resulted in a larger than usual number of broken records. Politically the Games were notable for two separate German teams, East and West, being involved for the first time, and for the banning of South Africa, in face of threatened boycotts by African teams over its apartheid policies. Wendl (1998) points out other unique features of these Games; they were the first:

* to be held in a 'developing country';
* to be held in Latin America;
* in which the running events took place on a synthetic surface;
* in which a female athlete lit the Olympic Flame at the opening ceremony;
* at which athletes from African countries came to the fore.

Sporting highlights included Bob Beaman's long-jump record, which remained unbroken until the 1990s, and the introduction of the 'Fosbury Flop' by American high-jumper Dick Fosbury. The Games are, however, remembered particularly for the political events which surrounded them, namely the student riots and their suppression before the Games, which reportedly resulted in the death of over 100 protesters, and the 'black power' salute of American black athletes, as discussed in chapter 5 (see Arbena, 1991, 1996; Aguilar-Darriba, 1988).

Brown and MacDonald (1996) provide an account of the Winter Games at Grenoble. Brohm (1978: 123), outlines a critical thesis that promotion of the Olympic

ies at Grenoble was linked to the French government's perceived need to promote resorts in the French Alps.

XX: 1972, Munich, Germany and Sapporo, Japan

The Olympic Games returned to Germany after a period of 36 years. The Games were notable for their costly and architecturally dramatic sporting facilities, for the seven-medal haul of American swimmer Mark Spitz and the instant fame of Russian gymnast Olga Korbut; but mostly they will be remembered for the terrorist attack on and subsequent death of Israeli athletes, as outlined in chapter 5 (see Czula, 1978; Lenk, 1976; Groussard, 1975; Guttman, 1984; Mandell, 1991; Brichford, 1996).

Brohm (1978: 126-134) uses the examples of both the Munich Olympics and the Sapporo Winter Olympics to outline the idea of a 'capitalist state-sports bloc' or a 'state monopoly capitalist bloc' - that is a close relationship between sporting organisations, government and business interests designed to promote the interests of business - in the case of Munich a wide range of business interests are involved, including those concerned with the construction of venues and infrastructure, while in Sapporo the focus is on ski equipment manufacturers. See also: Addkison and Simmons (1996) for an account of the Sapporo Games.

XXI: 1976, Montréal, Canada and Innsbruck, Austria

The 1976 Olympics were experienced and have been remembered as a kaleido-scope of contradictory narratives and outcomes. Promised as a 'modest', 'self-financing' Games, they ended up with such monumental facilities, constructed with little regard for their cost, that the Montréal Games have become a byword for gargantuan extravaganzas. (Kidd, 1996: 153)

Despite this reputation, Kidd points out that, with revenue of $430 million (including $235 millions from a special lottery) and running costs of $207 millions, the Games actually produced a surplus of $223 million. The $1.20 billion deficit arose from the extensive expenditure on city infrastructure, including transport. (See Auf der Maur, 1976; Commision Royale Enquête, 1977; Baka, 1976; Dewar, 1976; Franks, 1988; Iton, 1978, 1988; Kidd, 1992; Ludwig; 1976; Marsan, 1988; Takac, 1976; Wright, 1978).

With the growing importance of the media in paying for and bringing the Games to the world, Montréal marked the point at which researchers began turning their attention to the pattern of media coverage of the Games - see, for example, Chorbajian and Mosco (1981), MacAloon (1989), McCollum and McCollum (1981), Rabkin and Franklin (1989), Wenn (1976).

Kennedy (1996a) provides an account of the Winter Games at Innsbruck.

XXII: 1980, Moscow, USSR and Lake Placid, USA

The 1980 Moscow Olympics, held in the Soviet Union when the Cold War was still a feature of international relations, were notable for the Western boycott, led by the

United States, in protest at the Soviet invasion of Afghanistan. The boycott included the USA and Canada and Israel and some Moslem nations, but not all Western nations joined the boycott - in the case of Britain, the bulk of the Olympic team attended despite the government's call to join the boycott. Only 80 countries took part in the Games. Such overt political disruption so soon after the Munich events and the financial problems of Montréal, raised doubts about the survival of the Olympics, and Riordan (1996: 153) suggest that those in the West who resented the sporting success of Eastern bloc countries saw this as an opportunity to recast the Games as a Western event. See also, Barret (1980), Barton (1983), Booker (1981), Crossman and Lappage (1992), Deane (1985), Hazan (1982), Hulme (1988, 1990), Duncan (1986, 1990) and Real *et al.* (1989), and Fea (1996a) on the Lake Placid Winter Games.

XXIII: 1984, Los Angeles, USA and Sarajevo, Yugoslavia
In response to the USA-led boycott of the 1980 Games, the Soviet Union led a 'tit-for-tat' boycott by most of the Eastern bloc countries, claiming that anti-Soviet sentiment in the USA posed a security threat to its athletes.

Following the excesses of Montréal few cities were prepared to take on the financial risks now associated with the Olympics, so Los Angeles was awarded the 1984 with no opposition. It was the first 'private enterprise' Games, with the contract to undertake the Games being struck with a private company, rather than a city council. True to their word, the Americans, with $290 million of television revenue and extensive commercial sponsorship, produced a financial surplus of $225 million. This regenerated worldwide interest in hosting the Games and ushered in the commercialisation of the Games, as discussed in chapter 6. Economics Research Associates (1984) estimated that the economic impact of the Games on California was some $2.5 billion.

For analysis and comment on the Los Angeles games, see: Biles (1988), Chalip and Chalip (1992), De Lange (1998: 105-114), Duncan (1986), Duncan (1990), Edwards (1984), De Franz (1988), Farrell (1989), Haage and Riesinger (1988), Henry (1984), Lawrence (1986), Levitt (1990), MacAloon (1991), Network 10 (1984), Nixon (1988), Perelman (1985), Real *et al.* (1989), Reich (1986, 1989), Shanklin (1988), Simon (1988), Ueberroth (1986), Wilcox (1994), Wilson (1993, 1994, 1996).

Dunkelberger (1996) provides and account of the Sarajevo Winter Games.

XXIV: 1988, Seoul, Korea and Calgary, Canada
Seoul was an unlikely choice for the Games, given that South Korea lacked any great Olympic tradition, and given the political uncertainty of a divided country (Guttmann, 1992: 165; Palenski, 1996). In the first Games for 12 years to be unaffected by boycotts, and the last Games of the Cold War era, the Soviet Union and East Germany emerged in first and second place in the medal table. The Seoul Games were most notable for the drug scandal involving 100 metre winner Ben Johnson of Canada, who, having tested positive for anabolic steroids, was stripped of his medal, in favour of Carl Lewis of the USA (see chapter 8).

For further commentary on and analysis of the Seoul Games see Boutilier and San Giovanni (1991), Chalip (1990), De Lange (1998: 115-124), Herr (1988), Hiller (1989, 1990), Hyup (1990), Joynt *et al.* (1989), Kang (1988), Jeung *et al.* (1990), Kim (1988, 1990), Lee (1989), Mohsen and Alexandraki (1989), Mount and Leroux (1994), Pound (1994), Switzer *et al.* (1989), Tewnion (1993), Wamsley and Heine (1994) and Whitson and Macintosh (1993).

The Calgary Winter Games were notable for the major research project on public participation and awareness of the Games (Ritchie, 1990; Ritchie and Smith, 1991; Ritchie and Lyons, 1990; Haxton, 1995). See also Canadian Ministry for Fitness and Amateur Sport (1986), City of Calgary and Alberta Tourism and Small Business (1985) and Wamsley (1996).

XXV: 1992, Barcelona, Spain and Albertville France
The Barcelona Games are discussed in this chapter. Lellouche (1996) and Haag (1994) present accounts of the Albertville Winter Games.

XXVI: 1996, Atlanta, USA and 1994, Lillehammer, Norway
The Atlanta Games are discussed in this chapter.   See also Maloney (1996a). Maloney (1996b) and Mcintyre (1995) present accounts of the Lillehammer Winter Games, which started the new practice of running the Winter Games two years apart from the Summer Games.

XXVII: 2000, Sydney, Australia and 1998, Nagano, Japan
The Sydney Games are discussed in this chapter. See also Booth and Tatz (1994a, b), Cashman (1995), Cashman and Hughes (1998, 1999), Cronau (1993a, b), Hooker Research (1993), and Olympic Coordination Authority (1996). Findling (1996) presents an account of the Nagano Winter Games.

Chapter eleven:

The Future of the Olympic Games

The Olympic Games are not what Pierre de Coubertin intended them to be. They will never be simply an occasion for athletes to compete in friendly rivalry, for spectators to admire extraordinary physical performances, and for everyone involved to feel himself or herself a part of the family of man. But the Olympic Games are not the opposite either. They are not simply occasions for sexism, racism, religious fanaticism, ideological display, nationalism, commercialism and the instrumentalization of the body. Every four years, as the Olympics more nearly approach or more tragically disappoint our ideals, they provide us with a dramatic indication of who we are. Perhaps that is the best argument for their continuation. (Guttmann, 1988: 443)

Introduction

The modern Olympic Games have survived for over 100 years, but during that period their future has not always been assured. Will the Games survive for a second century, and if so, in what form? These are the questions addressed in this chapter.

When we began writing this book, in early 1997, the idea that the future of the Olympic Games might be questioned was, at least in the popular mind, unthinkable. In the aftermath of Atlanta, the Games appeared to be going from strength to strength. However, as we write this last chapter, in the early months of 1999, scandals have erupted over alleged corrupt payments to IOC members in relation to the selection of Salt Lake City for the 2002 Winter Olympics and in relation to the selection of other cities to host the Games. These events are discussed in more detail below, but it is worth bearing in mind that this is not the first time that doubts about the Games' long-term viability have been raised.

In the early years of the century the Olympic Games barely enjoyed a separate existence at all: they were mere appendages to international trade expositions (for example, in Paris, 1900, and St Louis, 1904). Of the Paris Games, even Pierre de Coubertin himself is quoted as declaring: 'It's a miracle that the Olympic movement survived that celebration' (quoted in Gordon, 1994: 29). In 1980 Lord Killanin, in handing over the presidency of the IOC to Juan Antonio Samaranch, is quoted as having said: 'Good luck. I don't think the Games will survive your presidency' (quoted in Pound and Johnson, 1999).

Financial problems threatened the continuation of the Games in the 1970s, when it was widely believed that the 1976 Montréal Olympics had virtually bankrupted the host city, to the extent that only one city - Los Angeles - was interested in bidding to host the 1984 Games. But money has not been the only threat to the Games. War caused their cancellation in 1916, 1940 and 1944 and, as we have seen, political disputes intervened in the disagreements over South Africa's involvement in the 1970s and 1980s and the Cold War boycotts in 1980 and 1984. Since 1988 in particular, highly publicised drug scandals have also raised questions about the Games' future.

The various crises faced by the Olympic Games, and the IOC's responses to them, have attracted criticism, even from the Games' most ardent proponents. In 1981, one of the most consistent academic champions of the Olympic Movement, wrote:

> .. among scholars of the Olympic Movement, an unmistakable malaise pervades its future. The universality of the play instinct, humankind's passion for competing in and watching games, plus the special attraction of the Olympic Games combine to make the immediate demise of the games unlikely. But all human institutions are inherently imperfect, and if loving care and sensible revisions are not at work, the Olympic Movement and the Olympic Games will die prematurely. (Lucas, 1988a: 427)

Numerous commentators have predicted or called for the end of the Olympic Games. For example, Marxist Jean-Marie Brohm and his colleagues wrote a number of anti-Olympic tracts in the 1970s, seeing the Games as: '.. the most extreme example of the moronic sports spectacle, the purpose of which is to hammer obedience to the bourgeois order into the heads of young people and the oppressed masses generally', and calling on '.. all workers the world over to condemn the masquerade of the Olympics ..' (1978: 168).

Also writing in the 1970s, McMurty (1973) outlined 'A case for killing the Olympics'. In the 1980s Edwards (1981) wrote of the 'Crisis in the Olympic Movement', Hoberman published *The Olympic Crisis* (1986) and Rose (1988) asked the question: 'Should the Olympic Games be abolished?'. The latter discussion considered the propositions that the Games should be abolished because they were too big, too professional, too commercial and too political, but concluded that they deserved to be abolished because they failed to live up to their own declared ideals in promoting peace and human rights. The Olympic Movement stood accused of paying only '.. obsequious respect to human dignity and to an honest yearning for the survival of the planet' (Rose, 1988: 404).

The question of the Games' survival can be discussed in terms of two related but distinct dimensions: the external environment and internal organisational issues. The external environment includes the political, social, cultural, technological and economic conditions within which the Games operate; they may not necessarily affect the Games themselves directly, but have an influence through changing relationships and economic pressures and changing values, lifestyles and patterns of consumer behaviour. Internal organisational issues relate to the nature of the Games themselves and their governance and organisation. These broad issues are discussed in turn below.

The Environment of the Games

A number of external conditions are discussed here, namely the question of war and peace, the growth of leisure, the commercialisation of sport, competition from other sporting events and communication technology.

War and Peace

With the end of the Cold War, the threat of world-wide conflict, which has forced the cancellation of the Olympic Games on three occasions this century, has been lifted. While numerous conflicts continue around the world, nuclear conflagration, which would end civilisation as we know it, now seems unlikely.

The Cold War itself threatened the Games' survival on a number of occasions. It divided the world into the West, or 'first world', led by the United States, and the Eastern bloc (or 'second world'), led by the Soviet Union. The developing countries (or 'third world') were aligned with one or other of the two sides or sought to maintain some sort of neutrality. In many ways it was a tribute to the political acumen of the leaders of the Olympic Movement that these world-wide divisions did not result in more frequent disruption of the Games than the mutual boycotts of 1980 and 1984, as described in chapter 5. One perspective on the era between 1952 (when athletes from the Soviet Union took part in the Games for the first time) to 1988 is that the intense east-west rivalry which was a feature of the Cold War, resulted in far more importance being attached to international sporting contests than might otherwise have been the case. But whether the Olympic Games actually played a role in preventing the *Cold* War from becoming *hot* - that is in promoting and maintaining world peace, as the *Olympic Charter* claims - is debatable.

The idea of international sporting events being a substitute for war - 'war without weapons' - is an intriguing one. The term 'bread and circuses', has been used to describe the practice of the ancient Roman state of supposedly pacifying the masses by providing them with free food and quasi-sporting entertainment to keep them occupied and unconcerned about serious political issues. The long-standing existence of ritualised forms of combat within and between many communities, as described by anthropologists (e.g. Cherfas and Lewin, 1980), suggests that aggression, particularly among young males, may be endemic and in need of some form of outlet. One thesis is that the Olympic Games therefore contribute to the maintenance of peace by absorbing these aggressive tendencies, as a number of science fiction films, such as *Rollerblade*, illustrate. A complementary thesis is that the survival of the Olympic Games, and of other international sporting events, is dependent on the continuation of international peace, since their role as outlets for aggression and competition is necessary *only* in the absence of war. A third thesis is that events such as the Olympic Games make war *more* likely by celebrating and stimulating nationalism and aggression.

It is not possible to test any of these theses empirically since, despite the rhetoric, the role or influence of the Olympic Games, if any, in these matters, is likely to be minor and is swamped by much more significant causes of war and peace, such as the play of national and ethnic political and economic interests. Nevertheless, the promotion of peace is a prime goal of the Olympic Movement, and is enshrined in the *Olympic Charter* (see chapter 4). From time to time, attempts are made to revive a modern version of the 'Olympic Truce' during the Games. There is, however, no evidence to suggest that, in reality, the Olympic Games have any effect on modern armed conflicts. Nevertheless, the idea that people should join together in sporting contests rather than fight each other in wars is a noble one and perhaps has an educational, if not practical, value.

The Growth of Leisure

The traditional view of the growth of leisure is that one of the consequences of economic development is that, at a certain stage, leisure time increases and leisure industries expand to serve the leisure needs of an increasingly affluent and increasingly 'leisured' population. Sport and sporting contests can be seen as part of the growing leisure industries and can therefore be expected to become increasingly important in future. This is predicated on a world which enjoys increasing prosperity and which continues to develop through *industrial* stages into *post-industrial* and possibly *post-modern* phases. In these conditions, activities previously seen as 'unproductive' become increasingly significant, in an economy where production of material goods becomes ever more automated and in a culture where ephemeral, electronically communicated events and images hold centre stage. Thus we have seen, in recent years, that the Olympic Games and other 'hallmark' events have become one of the most potent tools of 'city boosterism', which sees cities competing to host sporting events in order to achieve or maintain 'world class' status and thus secure jobs, prosperity and economic security (Syme *et al.*, 1989; Roche, 1992; Whitson and Mackintosh, 1993; Hall, 1994).

As the Panhellenic Games of Ancient Greece and the games and circuses of Ancient Rome testify, major spectator events can take place only when certain conditions prevail, including the existence of a leisured and prosperous citizenry, a peaceful environment and facilities for travel. All these conditions - together with modern communication technology - have come together in the modern era. They cannot, however, be taken for granted. The inevitability of the scenario of increasing industrial productivity continuing to deliver increased wealth and increased leisure to the mass of the population in the Western world has recently been questioned. The smooth growth path which had come to be expected for Western economies was interrupted first by the oil crises of the 1970s. These were followed by high inflation and high unemployment in the West, the rise of the 'tiger' economies of the east in the 1970s and 1980s, the disruptions caused by the adjustments of Russia and Eastern Europe following the collapse of the Berlin Wall, and the recent financial crisis in Asia. More specifically, it has been suggested that, after many decades of declining working hours and increased leisure time, those with jobs in the West - at least in the USA - are working longer rather than shorter hours and are faced with a 'time squeeze' (Schor, 1991; Zuzanek and Veal, 1999). Thus increased leisure time may not inevitably deliver ever-increasing numbers of sports participants and spectators as was expected in the past.

In fact, given the commoditised form in which the majority of people enjoy modern sporting events, large amounts of leisure time are not required undertake the necessary act of consumption. The average individual in the Western world currently spend some three hours a day watching television (Murdock, 1990: 77). If, during the fortnight of the Olympic Games, half of those viewers were to devote an hour to watching Olympic coverage, the television networks broadcasting the signal would more than recoup their outlays in advertising revenue. Thus, while increasing leisure time would help the television networks in selling the 'consumption' of sporting events via television, this is not a necessary condition for continued success. Sport merely competes - generally very successfully - with other television 'product' for the viewer's time, and the Olympic Games, as arguably the leading sport 'brand', has no difficulty in attracting a high market share. The continued success of the Olympic Games as a consumer and media 'product' is therefore not necessarily dependent on increasing leisure time. This leads naturally to the question of commercialisation.

Commercialisation of Sport
The modern era has seen the commoditisation and commercialisation of numerous activities, including sport. Sport has been transformed from an amateur activity undertaken by small, self-help groups, into a global business, bolstered by the advertising power of television and the vehicle of sponsorship. Along with this goes the development of sport as a popular cultural phenomenon, which celebrates sporting heroes alongside film stars and rock stars. This nexus between the sport event and its many related stakeholders is illustrated in Figure 6.1 in chapter 6.

The Olympic Games, as the most significant of world sporting events, are therefore at the vortex of this dynamic economic and cultural phenomenon. Thus it is no longer just athletes and sport enthusiasts who have an interest in the survival of the Games: they are joined by mass media organisations, advertisers, sponsors, venue owners and a host of professionals, such as managers, marketers, agents, trainers, coaches, physiotherapists and psychologists (and even academics and authors of books!) who depend for their livelihood on the resources flowing into what is now an industry. Of course this level of involvement on the part of non-sporting, and non-Olympic, interests could contain the seeds of destruction of the Games. The 'spirit' of Olympism is ostensibly non-materialist: the alliance between Olympism and commerce is therefore a contradictory and potentially unstable one. The question might be asked: how can all these organisations and 'hangers on' be making money out of the Games when the whole ethos of the Games is about something other than making money? As we have seen, the Olympic Games are unique in being associated with a 'movement' and a philosophy, 'Olympism', with almost religious connotations. Olympism enshrines certain ideals which, as with a religion, its custodians are sworn to uphold. Many see commercialisation in particular as undermining these ideals. How can the Games be about the 'spirit of friendly competition' and 'participation for its own sake', when such enormous rewards are available to those involved, both as athletes and as associated marketers and sponsors? The Olympics, in such circumstances, it is argued, become a vehicle for the pursuit of personal, material gain, rather than for the celebration of sport.

Looked at another way, in a capitalist world in which commerce operates on a global scale, a phenomenon as well-known as the Olympic Games clearly has market potential; the question is, who should benefit from this? The IOC has taken the view that the Olympic Movement should share in the material rewards that flow from the commercial exploitation of the Olympic 'brand'. International market research shows that, among the general public, the Olympic rings are the most widely recognised symbol in the world, beating those of Shell, McDonald's and Mercedes, and the public generally associate the Games and their symbols with positive moral values while not objecting to commercial sponsorship (Meenaghan, 1997). This translates into hundreds of millions of dollars worth of marketing potential, which the IOC has chosen to exploit rather than ignore.

The Los Angeles Games of 1984, termed the 'Hamburger Games', were the first to bring the commercial dimension to the fore and also saw the first signs of a backlash against commercialisation of the Games. Similar sentiments were expressed in relation to the highly commercialised Atlanta Games of 1996. Thus the very source of financial salvation for the Games is at the same time seen by some as a source of danger. However, while traditionalists bewail the loss of 'innocence' or 'purity' in the modern, commercial, Games - while at the same time often arguing that such innocence never really existed (Gruneau, 1984) - the evidence suggests that, for the time being at least, the general public is prepared to take its sport with increasing helpings of commercialism, in the form of advertising and sponsorship. Nevertheless, there remains a chance that the public will one day cry 'enough!' or simply lose interest, and turn away from the commercialised sporting 'product'. Sponsors and advertiser who provide the funds would simply switch their resources to whatever new phenomenon the public turn to. The chances of this happening to any significant degree seem, however, to be a remote.

A particular feature of the commercialisation of sport is the professionalisation of the athletes themselves, brought about by the increased flow of money into sport and the consequently enhanced market value of athletes. The degree of professional-isation varies from sport to sport and from country to country. Nevertheless, the value of an Olympic gold medal, in terms of subsequent appearance money and endorsement income, can amount to millions of dollars for some athletes. The principles of the Olympic Creed concerning the importance of *taking part* as opposed to *winning* (see chapter 4) are placed under a certain amount of strain when the direct and indirect financial rewards for winners are so great. In particular it is often suggested that it is the prospect of large financial rewards which tempts athletes to take proscribed performance enhancing drugs. As discussed in chapter 8, the pressures on athletes from this source are likely to increase in future rather than decrease. The potential responses of the Olympic Movement to these pressures and their likely impact on the future of the Games are discussed further below.

Finally, in considering commercial and economic factors, it should be noted that the scale of the Games, and with it their cost, increased markedly in the post-World War II era. Initially the process of decolonisation, and more recently the break-up of the Soviet Union and the growth of nationalist movements in many parts of the world, including those currently being seen in the Balkans and Indonesia, have resulted in an increase in the number of member countries in the Olympic Movement. All member countries have the right to enter a team in the Games, however small. The cost to host cities of mounting the Games has therefore increased substantially and with this has come an increased risk that they might not pay their way commercially or, if publicly funded, might place unacceptable financial burdens on host cities and governments The threat of bankruptcy dissuaded cities from offering to host the Games in the 1980s. While recent Games, particularly those which have taken place in the United States, have been run profitably, this is not guaranteed. Again, the response to the pressures to increase the scale and consequent costs of the Games is an organisational challenge for the Olympic Movement and the IOC in particular, and is discussed further below.

In the early period of the modern Olympic Games' existence, lack of money was their major problem and the main threat to their survival. In contrast, in an era of commercialisation and commoditisation, the sheer quantity of money flowing into sport, and the 'strings attached' to it, appear to present equally challenging problems.

Competition from other Sporting Events
In addition to the effects of commercialisation, a reason why the public might fail to be drawn to the Olympic Games in future is that they might find other sporting events more attractive. The preeminence of the Olympic Games may be threatened by the rise in popularity of other international sporting events. It is already the case that the soccer World Cup commands a larger television audience than the Olympics (Cashman, 1999: 5). For a number of sports, such as tennis, basketball and soccer, the Olympic Games do not represent the pinnacle of competition. Even in some 'classic' Olympic sports, such as swimming and athletics, their own world championships can be seen as at least as important to athletes. In some cases the Olympics retain a distinctive role by placing restrictions on the eligibility of competitors, for example the age restrictions on soccer players and the amateur status of boxers. Thus, increasingly, the Olympic Games retain their status as a result of

tradition, their overall 'aura' and their multi-sport nature. It is possible that these features could, time, lose their 'edge' in terms of public attraction and therefore attraction to advertisers and broadcasters.

Communication Technology

It can be argued that the current scale and status of the Olympic Games, as with other major international sporting events, is owed entirely to the developments in communication technology over the last 30 years - in particular the development of satellite television broadcasting. The ability to broadcast pictures of the event instantly, or, in edited and packaged form, within a few hours, to anywhere in the world opened up substantial advertising markets. This in turn has delivered substantial sums of money into the Olympic Movement, enabling the phenomenon to expand and develop - a seemingly virtuous circle. Will this apparently happy state of affairs continue? Subject to the public demand considerations discussed above, the answer is assuredly: yes.

Further developments in television technology are likely to continue to generate advertising and sponsorship income. Television picture quality is set to improve with the move to digital technology, further enhancing the ability of the broadcasters to deliver a 'being there' sensation for the viewer. Further enhancement of satellite capacity will facilitate the transmission of more images, complemented by high-capacity fibre-optic cable which will deliver multiple channels to subscribers' homes. Thus, in addition to the *broad*casting of the Games to mass audiences using free-to-air signals, via advertiser-sponsored media, we will see *narrow*casting to subscribers who are interested in specific aspects of the Games (Lynch *et al.*, 1996). It is possible to envisage coverage of all 28 or so of the Olympic sports being simultaneously transmitted to the home by satellite and cable - and perhaps involving the Internet. This is what the technology will offer. Whether it will actually develop into a significant feature of sport broadcasting in future depends not just on technological possibilities but also on financial and economic realities and consumer taste and willingness and ability to pay.

This Western scenario must be balanced by consideration of possible trends in the developing world. One scenario sees the developing world slipping deeper into crisis and further poverty. Alternative scenarios see massive growth in consumer markets - including sporting consumers - as economic growth takes hold. The rapid rates of growth of the Asian 'tiger' economies during the 1970s, 1980s and early 1990s and the ability of China to maintain high economic growth rates over a decade or more, demonstrates that the latter scenario is a possible one. Communications entrepreneurs such as Rupert Murdoch would not be investing in China if this were not a distinct possibility. Broadcasters already position satellites over the Indian Ocean to broadcast to India's one billion population and attract advertising revenue from international companies.

The Organisation of the Games

The modern Olympic Games, while rooted in history, have nevertheless changed dramatically in the 103 years of their existence. For some, however, change has not been fast enough or radical enough. Numerous suggestions have been made for change over the years. A number of these are reviewed and evaluated here, including: the question of a permanent site for the Games; whether the Games should be limited in scale; whether changes should be made to the sporting programme; whether criteria for admission of athletes to the Games should be modified; and the issue of the use of performance enhancing drugs. Finally, the question of the reform of the International Olympic Committee and the overall structure of the Olympic Movement is addressed.

A Permanent Site?
It has often been suggested that the Olympic Games should be staged at a permanent site rather then being moved to a new city in every Olympiad (Loder, 1997). What would be the advantages and disadvantages of such a move? These issues are discussed in turn below.

Advantages
Having a permanent site for the Olympic Games could produce a number of advantages, including: the end of the 'bid circus'; cost savings; the provision of ideal facilities and management benefits.

1. *The end of the 'bid circus'.* Elsewhere in this final chapter the question of bribery and corruption within the IOC is discussed. Most of these problems have arisen in relation to the process of deciding on the awarding of the Games to bidding cities. The use of a permanent site would remove this source of temptation. The 'bid circus' is expensive: even without the wining and dining and 'junketing' of IOC members, the development of a bid can be an expensive process, involving planning, feasibility studies and in some cases the construction of expensive facilities to demonstrate a city's commitment. A permanent site would save this time, money and effort.
2. *Cost savings.* A permanent site would produce further long-term cost-savings to the Olympic Movement in not having to subsidise the building of new facilities every four years, bearing in mind that a large proportion of the cost of mounting the Games is met from the broadcasting rights and world-wide sponsorship funds which accrue initially to the IOC. The resources which are devoted to the building of facilities could, it is argued, be devoted to the promotion of sport in other ways.
3. *The provision of ideal facilities.* At a permanent site it might be expected that ideal, 'state-of-the-art', facilities could be built. It could be claimed that the current system already provides ideal, state-of-the-art facilities, but this is not true for all facilities at all Games. The need to constantly upgrade facilities at

a permanent site could of course negate at least part of the savings noted in 2 above. It might also be countered that, whereas each new host city tends to build new state-of-the-art facilities for each Games, with a permanent site, the temptation might be to 'make do', and not to upgrade facilities for every Olympiad.

4.   *Management benefits*. With the current system, each host city must learn how to run the Games from scratch - some host cities have more experience than others in managing 'mega-events'. But the Olympic Movement takes a risk, every time it awards the Games to a new host city, that the organisation will malfunction. The most recent example of such risk becoming reality was the transport problems claimed to have been experienced at the 1996 Atlanta Games. At a permanent site there would be at least a core of permanent staff, with accumulated experience on how to run the Games. Equally, of course, such a permanent team could become complacent and staid, and deliver a less well managed event than those provided under current arrangements.

Disadvantages

Disadvantages of a permanent site include: the loss of 'reach' likely to result from not spreading the benefits of the event around the world; the problems caused by constant environmental conditions of a single site; the risk presented by host country politics; and the problem of actually choosing a permanent site. These are discussed in turn here.

1.   *Not spreading the benefits*. Not holding the event in different parts of the world would have a number of negative consequences. First, certain regions of the world might come to feel alienated from the Games - this might well be the case if the permanent site were to be located in the 'first world' - Greece has often been mentioned as a potential location for a permanent Summer Games site. Second, the legacy of superior sporting facilities which the Games leave behind in host cities around the world would be lost. Third, the 'party' which cities enjoy when they play host to the Games, and which reportedly leaves behind a legacy of goodwill for the Olympics, would be lost. While residents in the permanent host city would have a 'party' every four years, the role of the Games as a world-wide 'goodwill ambassador for sport and the Olympics' would be lost. Fourth, the learning experience which goes with hosting the Games, which can be said to benefit sport management worldwide, would no longer be spread around - the Games would be run by a permanent, albeit highly skilled and experienced, bureaucracy. Fifth, the economic stimulus which the Games bring, through construction as well as from visitors to the event, would again not be spread around but, in a more limited form, would be enjoyed only by the permanent host city. Sixth, a permanent site would fix the Games in one time-zone, with implications for television coverage and revenues. This issue is further complicated by the fact that the bulk of such funding currently comes

from US media and sponsoring companies - an investment which produces maximum returns when the Games are held in the USA.

2.   *Environmental conditions.* Sites vary in terms of such things as average humidity, temperature and altitude. A permanent site would result in just one set of environmental conditions, which would therefore always tend to favour one type of athlete. Moving the event around prevents the development of such built-in environmental discrimination.

3.   *Host country politics.* There would always be the possibility that the host country would be politically unacceptable to some participating countries. For example, for a period during the 1960s Greece was ruled by a military junta ('the colonels') which was not acceptable to much of the rest of the world. Of course such issues arise with the current system, but at least factors such as political stability and human rights records of bidding countries can be taken account of in the assessment process.

4.   *Choosing the permanent site.* Just where would the permanent site be located? Greece is a sentimental favourite for the Summer Games; within Greece the two options would be Olympia and Athens. However, Olympia does not have the necessary infrastructure (such as an international airport and the required hotels) so its provision would add considerably to the cost of establishing the permanent site. The performance of Athens in 2004, in hosting the Games for the first time since 1896, will clearly be a relevant to this discussion. There has been little discussion of possible permanent sites for the Winter Games.

Considering all of these issues, it would seem that, as a world-wide phenomenon, and despite the difficulties presented by the bidding system, the Olympic Movement will continue to see the disadvantages of a permanent site as outweighing the advantages.

The Scale of the Games

We have already noted that the increasing numbers of member countries have produced pressures to increase the scale of the Games. There are also pressures to increase the number of events, from sports not currently included and from women's events, which currently constitute only one third of the total.

The sheer size of the Games has, as noted above, increased the cost and financial risk involved in hosting them, but it has also increased the planning and logistical challenges - and the risk of organisational failure. For example, in the case of the Atlanta Games of 1996, negative press reports of transport problems at times threatened to undermine the goodwill which any host city expects to gain from hosting the Games. If the Games were to become so big that the logistical and financial problems of running them outweighed the benefits generated for host cities, their future would be in doubt.

Any reduction in the scale of the Games runs the risk of reducing their attraction to advertisers and sponsors: it is, after all, the sheer scale of the Games which is a large part of their attraction. However, as a result of the deliberations of the 1997 Centennial Olympic Congress (Mbaye, 1996) the IOC decided to limit the number of athletes in the Summer Games to 10,000 and the number of officials to 5000. This limitation is somewhat arbitrary - why not 11,000 or 12,000 athletes? And the limitation itself presents problems, since any additional event can only be introduced at the expense of an existing one or by reducing the number of participants in existing events.

For the time being these overall restrictions are seen as the solution to the problem of gigantism, but whether they stand the test of time will depend on the responses to the demands of excluded sports and women's sport organisations.

The Sporting Programme

Lucas (1992: 212) suggests, without being specific, that some sports currently included in the Olympic programme are incompatible with its ideals. Some might argue that sports which are violent in nature (for example, boxing, shooting) are incompatible with the Olympic Movement's goal of promoting peace. The irony of this argument is that the origin of the Games, in classical Greece, lie in the training of young men for combat in war. A second type of event which might be considered for exclusion are those activities which do not involve 'citius, altius, fortius' .. that is, activities which must be judged on the basis of aesthetics rather than measurable speed, height or strength. The problem with this principle is that, while it would exclude certain controversial activities such as synchronised swimming and ice dancing, it would also be in danger of excluding other, more traditional activities, such as gymnastics and diving. A third type of activity which might be considered for exclusion are those which , because of their cost, involve only a small number of élite, wealthy, participants. This applies particularly in the area of equestrian events. The latter attract those with the wealth to maintain horses or those with access to horses professionally, such as land-owners or the military. Cycling might also come into this category since the cost of modern 'high tech' bicycles can only be afforded by teams sponsored by cycle manufacturers, which are based in the wealthier countries. Thus cycling has moved closer in nature to motor sports, which have always been excluded because of their exclusive and commercial nature.

Criteria for Entry

How should participants in the Olympic Games be selected? Present selection procedures do not ensure that the 'best in the world' compete, because of the need for widespread involvement by member countries. Thus, for example, if any one country is limited to, say, three entrants in a particular event, but that country has the top six performers in that event, then the fourth, fifth and sixth best performers in the world will be excluded. Meanwhile, since any country that can meet certain minimum standards is entitled to send a team, numerous quite mediocre performers get to compete at the Olympics, while many top performers are excluded. Thus the Olympic principle of widespread participation is promoted at the expense of excellence. This is one of the reasons why, for some sports, as discussed above, their own world championships, which may operate on different principles, are seen as representing a higher standard of competition.

Performance Enhancing Drugs

As outlined in chapter 8, the Olympic Movement has assumed a leadership role in relation to the control of performance enhancing drugs in sport. The very ethos of Olympism is antithetical to the use of performance enhancing drugs. Three alternative future scenarios are outlined in chapter 8, namely: 1. continuation of the *status quo*, in which performance enhancing drugs are banned, but their use is known to be widespread as chemists and athletes keep 'one step ahead' of the enforcement system; 2. a considerable enhancement of the enforcement régime, resulting in effective elimination of proscribed drugs from the Games; and 3. abandonment of prohibition, resulting in a 'competition between chemists' rather than between athletes.

Few see the first option as viable; to make strong statements about drugs, but not to devote the necessary resources to ensure their elimination raises questions as to the integrity of the Olympic Movement, and of the IOC in particular. Any such questioning poses a threat to the continued viability of the Games from both commercial sponsors and traditional enthusiasts for the 'purity' of sport. Since the third, 'open slather', option is unthinkable given the stance of the Movement to date, the IOC has no choice, if its integrity is to be preserved, but to expand considerably the resources and measures devoted to research on drugs and testing of athletes.

Reform of the IOC

In chapter 4 we noted the undemocratic and anachronistic nature of the International Olympic Committee, and the fact that it had been subject to criticism for many years for its lack of accountability and questionable *modus operandi*. In 1998/99 these issues have been brought sharply into focus and have been subject to unprecedented public scrutiny and debate.

The year 1998 was in many ways a watershed year in international sport. It was rocked by a number of scandals, including the drug use revelations in the Tour de France, the Pakistani and Australian cricket bribery allegations and positive drug tests for high profile athletes, including Irish Olympic medal-winning swimmer Michelle de Bruin, tennis player Peter Korda and members of the Chinese national swimming team. The Olympic Games have added, in no small measure, to this year of scandal. Indeed, as a result of allegations of involvement in bribery and corruption by its own members, the IOC faced one of the most serious crises in its history. Juan Antonio Samaranch himself admitted to the gravity of the situation when he acknowledged that, 'the system is not working... we have to change the system' (quoted by Korporaal and Evans, 1999: 3).

The current crisis erupted in November 1998, when a Salt Lake City television station broke a story alleging that the city's Bid Committee had paid for an IOC member's daughter to attend the American University in Washington D.C. (Evans, 1998). Following this revelation, in December 1998, the Swiss IOC member, Marc

Hodler, announced publicly that he believed that there was 'massive corruption' in the IOC, that there were up to 25 corrupt IOC members whose votes could be bought and, reflecting the claims of Simpson and Jennings made five years earlier (1992; Jennings, 1996), that every Games for the last ten years had been tainted by such bribery (Stevens and Stewart, 1999; IOC, 1999a).

Initially Hodler was considered to be a 'whistle blower', with some axe to grind, and he received no support from his fellow IOC members. Hodler is, however, 'a very senior member of the IOC, the author .. of the so-called 'Hodler Rules' designed to limit the expenses incurred by candidate cities, as well as the President of the FIS[1] for almost 50 years' (IOC, 1999a: 4). 'Whistle blowing' from such a source could not easily be ignored. As a result of the growing press attacks on its credibility the IOC felt obliged to investigate the claims, establishing an *ad hoc* Commission of Inquiry under the chairmanship of IOC Vice-President, Dick Pound of Canada. This was initially concerned only with Salt Lake City, but later widened its scope to include bidding for all Olympic Games since 1996. Meanwhile, the Salt Lake Organising Committee (SLOC) established a Board of Ethics to investigate the claims, reporting in February 1999 (Board of Ethics of the Salt Lake Organizing Committee, 1999), the United States Olympic Committee (USOC) also established an inquiry, which reported in early March 1999 (United States Olympic Committee Special Bid Oversight Commission, 1999), the FBI began investigations to determine whether criminal acts had taken place (Magnay, 1999), and the US Congress began holding hearings on the matter (Riley, 1999).

The IOC Commission sought information from SLOC, USOC, NOCs, all cities involved in Games bids since 1996 and IOC members against whom accusations of improper behaviour had been made. It produced two reports, in January and March 1999 (IOC, 1999a, b). In relation to the Salt Lake City bid, it investigated claims of payments totalling more than $US400,000 (IOC, 1999a, b; Lusetich 1999). Typical of the claimed unethical activities involving IOC members and the Salt Lake Bid Committee (SLBC) were:

- payments to support members' children while at university or working in USA;
- payments of tens of thousands of dollars for travel and hotel costs of members and their families to holiday in Utah and for 'side-trips' to the 1995 'Superbowl' in Florida and 'stop-offs' in Paris;
- payment of medical costs for members on trips to Salt Lake City;
- direct cash payments, later claimed to have been passed on to NOCs or other sporting organisations in members' home countries;
- cash payments for consultancy services;
- provision of gifts valued at well above the IOC limit of $US250;
- request for favours for relatives and/or colleagues, such as places in universities.

---

[1]   Fédération Internationale de Ski.

Individual members defended themselves by claiming: that they were unaware of the payments in question, especially when they involved relatives; that they had been led to believe that the payments were from private individuals or sponsoring companies, not from the SLBC itself; that SLBC representatives had persuaded them to accept gifts and favours against their own wishes; or that various of the trips at issue were not actually made during the period of Salt Lake City's candidature. Commentators have also pointed out that a number of the accused members were from countries where practices which would be seen as corrupt in most Western cultures are seen as quite acceptable - indeed, the Commission itself, in reflecting on the practice of gift-giving, declared:

> When passing judgement on what has been characterized as 'improper gift giving', one cannot overlook the fact that gifts viewed as 'improper' in some parts of the world are looked upon with a totally different perception in many others. .. Although such behaviour may create the appearance of misconduct and potential conflicts of interest (and for this reason must be strictly regulated), gift giving should not reflexively be labelled a 'flourishing culture of improper gifts'. In many societies, these exchanges are viewed as an honourable tradition and are not corrupt'. (IOC, 1999b: 11)

The Commission adjudicated on 19 IOC members, recommending that seven be 'excluded from the IOC', ten be warned about their behaviour (ranging from 'warning' to 'serious warning' to 'most serious warning') and two be exonerated. A number of members were duly excluded or resigned (see Appendix 4.1).

At the same time, the Commission was critical of a number of the practices of the Salt Lake City Bid Committee and USOC and other enquiries are on-going in the United States at the time of writing. A number of IOC investigations of further allegations against members, in relation to Salt Lake City and other bids, are also on-going.

The Commission's report therefore fully vindicated Hodler and a number of other critics. In addition to adjudications on individual members, it made three recommendations to the IOC: 1. that changes be made to the bidding process, beginning with the 2006 Winter Games; 2. that limitations be placed on members' travel to bid cities; and 3. that an *Ethics Commission* be established. The first and third of these recommendations were acted on immediately: the Ethics Commission was established in April 1999 (see chapter 4); and bidding procedures are being reviewed by the newly established 80-member *IOC 2000 Commission*, which is to report by October 1999.

The timing of the bribery revelations hampered the efforts of the 2000 and 2002 Games organisers in seeking sponsorship. And existing sponsors, at world and national levels, expressed concern and indicated that sponsorship funds might no longer be forthcoming if the IOC failed to 'clean up its act'. For example, General Motors Holden, one of the 2000 Olympics major sponsors acknowledged that the present situation had undermined its support. Its public relations manager noted, 'We obviously are a bit disturbed .. It is difficult for a sponsor in the current environment to maximise its association with the Games as long as these revelations keep coming to the surface' (quoted in Evans: 1999). One of the most influential of Olympic sponsors, McDonald's Restaurants, has consistently sought, through sport sponsorship, to promote a public image of itself as a wholesome corporate citizen. It could not therefore afford to be aligned with a partner which did not have an appropriately wholesome image. Thus, the head of marketing of the McDonald's German subsidiary said, 'If the corruption suspicions are confirmed, McDonald's will ask itself if sponsorship of the games still has a place in the group's image' (Hans Munichhausen, quoted in Korporaal and Evans, 1999:3). TOP member John Hancock's withdrawal of a multi-million dollar Olympic theme advertising campaign on NBC (the US Olympic broadcaster) was an indirect message to the IOC and one which NBC will, no doubt, have delivered to the IOC. Although sponsors have, to date, stood behind the Olympic Games, the implicit threat of their withdrawal will remain with the IOC until the scandal has been dealt with.

Ironically, therefore, the IOC's very success in raising sponsorship to lessen its dependence on television networks increases its vulnerability, given the resultant increase in the number of influential stakeholders who have a vested interest in how the IOC conducts its business. There is a sense of the wheel coming full circle and a sense of irony when commercial interests, long associated by many, as discussed above, with the debasement of Olympic values, now seek to purify the Olympic Movement. But some would see a degree of hypocrisy in such calls for moral purity from the business sector which uses quite similar practices to do business on a regular basis.

What reforms are being suggested to ensure that such practices do not recur? We have already noted that an Ethics Commission has been established to monitor IOC activity in general. As regards the phenomenon which has given rise to most of the bribery and corruption activity, the bidding process, there is little talk of the permanent site solution discussed above. Rather, it is likely that visits to bid cities will be restricted to members of the Evaluation Commissions, with members still being involved in voting to select the host city.

But longer term reform will involve a reconstitution of the IOC itself, to make it more representative, bringing its structure in line with other modern international corporate organisations. This would entail replacing the current somewhat *ad hoc* and self-perpetuating membership selection system with a more democratic, representational process. At the time of writing it is believed that the IOC intends to invite a number of athletes to become full members. It is notable, however, that the IOC membership already includes a substantial number of retired athletes, whose presence has not prevented the irregular practices which have recently come to light. Whether active Olympians, with busy training and competition schedules, and probably limited experience of the world of business and politics, will be in a position to have a significant impact on the culture of the organisation remains to be seen. Eventually a representative membership structure based on the International Sporting Federations and the National Olympic Committees seems inevitable. How the 40 or so recognised IFs, and the 200 NOCs will be represented will be a matter for considerable negotiation. The results of such a move would be to make the IOC more clearly accountable to the Olympic Movement, to the sporting community as a whole and to other stakeholders.

The Past, Present and Future of the Olympic Games

In this book we have attempted to provide a broad overview of the Olympic Games phenomenon, from their ancient beginnings, via their nineteenth century revival to the modern multi-million dollar, world-wide phenomenon which the Games have now become. In particular, we have sought to illustrate the multi-faceted nature of the Games - while they remain primarily a sporting event, they are also undoubtedly a major media event, a tourism event, an event with significant political dimensions and a major economic enterprise. We are sure that the future of the games, in all their dimensions, is assured. But the nature of that future remains to be seen - offering endless opportunities for future research and speculation.

Appendix I: Web-sites, Films, Videos and CDs

Web-sites

Athens 2004 Organising Committee: www.athens.olympic.org/en
British Olympic Association: www.olympics.org.uk
Centre for Olympic Studies, Barcelona: www.blues.uab.es/olympc.studies
Centre for Olympic Studies, London, Ontario: www.uwo.ca/olympic
Centre for Olympic Studies, Sydney: www.arts.unsw.edu.au/olympic
Commonwealth Games Federation: www.commonwealthgames.org.au
Gay Games: www.gaygames.org
International Olympic Committee: www.olympic.org
International Paralympic Committee: www.paralympic.org
Los Angeles Amateur Athletic Foundation: www.aafla.com
NBC site: www.nbcolympics.com
Olympic Museum, Lausanne, on-line library catalogue: www.rero.ch/vtls/english
Salt Lake City Organising Committee (Winter Games 2002): www.slc2002.org
Torino Organising Cttee (Winter Games 2006): www.torino2006.it/ita/index.asp
Tufts University: www.perseus.tufts.edu/olympic
United States Olympic Committee: www.olympic-usa.org
UTS Olympic Bibliography: www.business.uts.edu.au/leisure/research/olympic.html
    (updates of these web-site addresses will be included in the bibliography)

Films, videos and CDs

The Ancient Games

- *Olympia: 2,800 Years of Athletic Games*, Finatec Multimedia (CD ROM)
- *The Ancient Olympics: Athletes, Games and Heroes*, The Institute for Mediterranean Studies, Ohio (video).
- Tufts University: *'Perseus Project' Olympic exhibit*, 1997: at www.perseus.tufts.edu/index.html

The Revival

- *Modern Olympic Movement http://www.olympics.org.uk/* (British Olympic Association)
- Murray, G., 1996, *The Golden Flame: the Story of the Olympic Revival,* Athens: Efstathiadis Group (CD)
- *Olympia: 2,800 Years of Athletic Games,* Finatec Multimedia (CD)
- *Olympic Gold: A Hundred Year History of the Summer Olympic Games*, Discovery Channel, Multimedia (CD)
- *Olympic Century #2, Myths and Legends*, IOC, Lausanne (Video)

General

- *Olympia*, 1938, Director: Leni Reifenstahl (Germany)
- *Olympic Games in White*, 1948, Director: Torgny Wickman (Switzerland)
- *The Bob Mathias Story*, 1954, Director: Francis Lyon (USA)
- *Wee Geordie*, 1955, Director: Frank Launder
- *Tokyo Olympiad,* 1965, Director: Kon Ichikawa (Japan)
- *Walk, Don't Run*, 1966, Director: Charles Walkers (USA)
- *The Games*, 1970, Director: Michael Winner (USA)
- *Visions of Eight*, 1973, Directors: various (USA)
- *Great Moments at the Winter Games*, 1979, Director: Bud Greenspan (USA)
- *Dawn,* 1979, Director: Ken Hannam (Australia)
- *Goldengirl*, 1979, Director:Joseph Sargeant (USA)
- *Ice Castles*, 1979, Director: Donald Wrye (Australia)
- *Chariots of Fire*, 1981, Director: Hugh Hudson (Great Britain)
- *Personal Best*, 1982, Director: Robert Towne (USA)
- *16 Days of Glory*, 1986, Director: Bud Greenspan (USA)
- *16 Days of Glory: Seoul '88*, 1989: Director: Bud Greenspan (USA)
- *Barcelona '92 Olympic Games,* 1992: NBC Sports (USA)
- *16 Days of Glory: Barcelona '92,* 1993: Director: Bud Greenspan (USA)
- *Cool Runnings*, 1993, Director: Jon Turtletaub (USA)
- *16 Days of Glory: Lillehammer '94,* 1994, Director: Bud Greenspan (USA)

References

Abad, J. M. (1995) 'Introduction: a summary of the activities of the COOB '92', in De Moragas and Botella, *op. cit.*, pp. 11-17.

Addkison-Simmons, D. (1996) 'Sapporo, 1972', in Findling and Pelle, *op. cit.*, pp. 284-288.

Aguilar-Darriba, A. (1988) 'The Olympic Games in Mexico - 1968: a long-term investment strategy', in EAAPP, *op. cit.*, pp. 265-280.

Alam, M. B. (1996) 'Tokyo, 1964: the Games of the XVIIIth Olympiad', in Findling and Pelle, *op. cit.*, pp. 135-138.

Alexandrakis, A. and Krotee, M. L. (1988) 'The dialectics of the IOC', *International Review for the Sociology of Sport*, Vol. 23, No. 4, pp. 325-344.

Arbena, J. L. (1991) 'Sport, development and Mexican nationalism, 1920-1970', *Journal of Sport History*, Vol. 18, pp. 350-364.

Arbena, J. L. (1996) 'Mexico City, 1968: the Games of the XIXth Olympiad', in Findling and Pelle, *op. cit.*, pp. 139-147.

Ashwell, T. (1996) 'Squaw Valley, 1960', in Findling and Pelle, *op. cit.*, pp. 263-269.

Atlanta Organizing Committee of the Olympic Games (1997) *The Official Report of the Games of the XXVI Olympiad*, Atlanta, GA: Peachtree Publishers.

Attwood, A. (1996) 'Now, let the fun and Games begin', *The Age*, August 6, accessed (8.6.99) at: www.smh.com.au/atlanta/.

Audit Office of New South Wales (1998) *Performance Audit Report: The Sydney 2000 Olympic and Paralympic Games: Review of Estimates*, Sydney: Audit Office of New South Wales.

Auf der Maur, N. (1976) *The Billion-Dollar Game: Jean Drapeau and the 1976 Olympics*, Toronto: James Lorimer.

'Aussies lead outcry over drug cheats' (1998) *The Advertiser* (Adelaide) 16 January, p. 1.

Australian Centre for Independent Journalism (1993) *Reportage*, September.

Australian Parliament (1980) *Parliamentary Debates (House of Representatives), Hansard Vol. 117, 20 February*, Canberra: Commonwealth Government Printer.

Australian Sports Commission and the Office of the Status of Women (1985) *Women, Sport and the Media, Report to the Federal Govenment from the Working Group on Women in Sport*, Canberra: AGPS.

Bacon, W. (1993) 'Watchdog's bark muffled', *Reportage: Newsletter of the Australian Centre for Independent Journalism*, (UTS, Sydney), September, pp. 3-5.

Baka, R. (1976) 'Canadian federal government policy and the 1976 summer Olympics', *Canadian Association for Health, Physical Education and Recreation Journal*, Vol. 42, No. 1, pp. 52-60.

Baker, N. (1994a) 'The Games that almost weren't: London 1948', in Barney and Meier, *op. cit.*, pp. 107-116.

Baker, N. (1994b), 'Olympics or Tests: the disposition of the British sporting public, 1948', *Sporting Traditions*, Vol. 11, No. 1, pp. 57-74.

Bandy, S. J. (1988) 'The Olympic celebration of the arts', in Segrave and Chu *op. cit.*, pp. 163-169.

Bannister, R. (1988) 'The Olympic Games: past, present and future', in Segrave and Chu, *op. cit.*, pp. 419-426.

Barnes, M. (1997) *Observance or Repudiation? Australia's Role in the Modern Olympic Movement as it Relates to the Olympic Charter*, MA thesis, School of Leisure abd Tourism Studies, University of Technology, Sydney.

Barnett, C. R. (1996) 'St. Louis, 1904: the Games of the IInd Olympiad', in Findling and Pelle, *op. cit.*, pp. 18-24.

Barney, R. K. (1998) 'The great transformation: Olympic victory ceremonies and the medal podium', *Olympika*, Vol. 7, pp. 89-112.

Barney, R. K. and Meier, K. V. (eds) (1992) *Proceedings of the First International Symposium for Olympic Research*, London, Ontario: Centre for Olympic Studies, University of Western Ontario.

Barney, R. K. and Meier, K. V. (eds) (1994) *Critical Reflections on Olympic Ideology, Second International Symposium for Olympic Research*, London, Ontario: Centre for Olympic Studies, University of Western Ontario.

Barney, R. K., Wamsley, K. B., Martyne, S. G. and MacDonald, G. H. (eds) (1998) *Global and Cultural Critique: Problematizing the Olympic Games*, London, Ontario; International Centre for Olympic Studies, University of Western Ontario.

Barrett, N. (1980) *Olympics 1980*, London: Piper Books.

Barthes, R. (1983) *Mythologies,* London: Paladin.

Barton, L. (1983) *The American Olympic Boycott of 1980: The Amalgam of Diplomacy and Propaganda in Influencing Public Opinion*, PhD dissertation, Boston University.

'Battle against drugs goes on, with new weapons and old hopes' (1996) 9 August, http://167:29.8/olympics/odxg031.htm.

Beck, P. J. (1980) 'Politics and the Olympics: the lessons of 1924', *History Today*, Vol. 20, July, pp. 7-9.

Beder, S. (1993) 'Sydney's toxic green Olympics', *Current Affairs Bulletin*, Vol. 70, No. 6, pp. 12-18.

Berlioux, M. (ed.) (1972) *Olympism*, Lausanne: International Olympic Committee.

Bilder, R. (n. d.) 'Drug testing in sport', www.gemini.co.uk/biopages/

Biles, F. R. (1984) 'Women and the 1984 Olympics', *Journal of Physical Education, Recreation and Dance*, Vol. 55, No. 1, pp. 64-65, 72.

Birrell, S. and Cole, C. (1994) *Women, Sport and Culture*, Champaign, Illinois: Human Kinetics.

Birrell, S. and Theberge, N. (1994) 'Biological control of women in sport', in Costa, D. M. and Guthrie, S. R. (eds) *Women and Sport: Interdisciplinary Perspectives*, Champaign, Illinois: Human Kinetics, pp. 341-360.

Blair, T. (1998) 'An athletic about face', *Time Australia,* 10 August, p. 63.

Blue, A. (1988) *Faster, Higher, Further: Women's Triumphs and Disasters at the Olympics*, London: Virago Press.

Board of Ethics of the Salt Lake Organizing Committee (1999) *Report to the Board of Trustees*, Salt Lake City, Utah: Salt Lake Organizing Committee for the Olympic Winter Games of 2002, SLOC web-site: www.slc2002.org/news/html/report.html.

Booker, C. (1981) *The Games War: A Moscow Journal*, London: Faber and Faber.

Booth, D. and Tatz, C. (1994a) 'Sydney 2000: the games people play', *Current Affairs Bulletin*, Vol.70, No.7, Jan. pp. 4-11.

Booth, D. and Tatz, C. (1994b) 'Swimming with the big boys'? The politics of Sydney's Olympic bid', *Sporting Traditions*, Vol.11, No.1, pp. 3-23.

Borgers, W. (1996) *Olympic Torch Relays 1936-1994*, Kassel, Germany: Agon Sportverlag.

Botella, M. (1995) 'The political games: agents and strategies in the 1992 Barcelona Olympic Games', in De Moragas and Botella (eds) *op. cit.*, pp. 139-148.

Boutilier, M.A. and San-Giovanni, L.F. (1991) 'Ideology, public policy and female Olympic achievement: a cross-national analysis of the Seoul Olympic Games', in Landry *et al., op. cit.*, pp. 396-409.

Brain, P. and Manolakos, J. (1991) 'The 1996 Melbourne Olympics: an economic evaluation', *National Economic Review*, Vol.14, No. 1, pp. 14-21.

Brichford, M. (1996) 'Munich, 1972: the Games of the XXth Olympiad', in Findling and Pelle, *op. cit.*, pp. 148-152.

British Olympic Association (n.d.) *The Modern Olympic Movement* - available under 'History' at: www.olympics.org.uk/

British Olympic Association (1998) *Official Web-site,* at: www.olympics. org.uk/.

British Olympic Council (1908) *The Olympic Games of 1908 in London: A Reply to Certain Criticisms*, London: BOC.

Brohm, J.-M. (1978) 'The Olympic opiate', 'The Olympic Games and the imperialist accumulation of capital', 'The anti-Olympic appeal of the *Ecole Emancipé*' and 'Draft appeal for the setting up of an Anti-Olympic Committee', in *Sport: A Prison of Measured Time*, (Tr. Ian Fraser), London: Ink Links, pp. 102-174.

Brown, D. and MacDonald, G. (1996) 'Grenoble, 1968', in Findling and Pelle, *op. cit.*, pp. 276-283.

Brown, P. (1994) 'The 'containment' of women in the Australian sporting press from 1890-1990', *ACHPER Healthy Lifestyles Journal*, Autumn, pp.4-8.

Bruce, J. (1999) *The Olympic Games: Sydney 2000 Special Edition*, St Leonards, NSW: Dorling Kindersley.

Brundage, A. (1966) 'The Olympic movement: objectives, and achievements', *Gymnasion*, Vol. 3, No. 1, pp. 3-4.

Brunet, F. (1993) *Economy of the 1992 Barcelona Olympic Games* (Trans. Adapta Traductions), Lausanne: International Olympic Committee/Centre d'Estudis Olímpics.

Brunet, F. (1995) 'An economic analysis of the Barcelona '92 Olympic Games: resources, financing and impact', in De Moragas and Botella *op. cit.*, pp. 203-237.

Bryson, L. (1987) 'Sport and the maintenance of masculine hegemony, *Women's Studies International Forum,* Vol. 10, pp. 349-360.

Bryson, L. (1990) 'Challenges to male hegemony in sport' in Messner, M. A. and Sabo, D. F. (eds), *Sport, Men and the Gender Order: Critical Feminist Perspectives*, Champaign, Illinois: Human Kinetics, pp. 173-184.

Burkhardt, A., Toohey, K. and Veal, A. J. (1995) *The Olympic Games: A Bibliography*, Lindfield, NSW: Centre for Leisure and Tourism Studies, University of Technology, Sydney [See also Veal *et al.* (1998]

Burns, J. P. A., Hatch, J. H. and Mules, T. J. (eds) (1986) *The Adelaide Grand Prix: The Impact of a Special Event*, Adelaide: Centre for South Australian Economic Studies.

Bury, J. (1967) *A History of Greece to the Death of Alexander the Great* (3rd edn), New York: Macmillan.

Buschman, J. and Lennartz, K. L. (1996) 'From Los Angeles (1932) to Melbourne (1956): the Olympic Torch's protagonism in ceremonies', in De Moragas, M., MacAloon, J. and Llines, M. (eds) *Olympic Ceremonies: Historical Continuity and Cultural Exchange*, Lausanne: International Olympic Committee

Butler, B. S. (1992) 'Muscular Marxism and the Chicago Counter-Olympics of 1932', *International Journal of the History of Sport*, Vol.9, No.3, pp. 397-410.

Byong-Ik, Kok (ed.) (1990) *Toward One World Beyond All Barriers*, Seoul Olympiad Anniversary Conference, Seoul: Seoul Olympic Sports Promotion Foundation.

Cable, C. (1982) *Architecture of the Olympics (1960-1980*, Bibliography A-706, Monticello, Illinois.: Vance Bibliographies.

Cagigal, J. M. (1975) 'The pedagogic evaluation of the Olympic Games: a survey', *FIEP Bulletin*, Vol.45, pp. 48-56.

Cahill, J. (1998) 'The Olympic flame and torch: running towards Sydney 2000', in Barney *et al.,* pp. 181-190..

Cahill, J. (1999a) 'Political influence and the Olympic flame', *Journal of Olympic History*, Vol. 7, No. 1, pp. 29-32.

Cahill, J. (1999b) *Running Towards Sydney 2000: The Olympic Flame and Torch*, Sydney: Walla Walla Press.

Cahill, S. (1986) *Olympic Spirit*, Melbourne: Australian Gallery of Sport.

Cahill, S. (1989) *'Friendly Games'? The Melbourne Olympic Games in Australian Culture (1946-1956)*, MA thesis, University of Melbourne.

Cahill, S. (1993) 'Lies, damned lies and Olympics', *Sydney Morning Herald: Good Weekend*, 18 Sept., pp. 22-30.

Cameron, J. (1995) 'Blazer and black tie dinners: some aspects of the marginalisation of women in New Zealand sport', *ANZALS Leisure Research Series* Vol. 2, pp. 26-42.

Canadian Ministry for Fitness and Amateur Sport (1986) *Economic Impact of the 1988 Winter Olympic Games*, Ottawa: Ministry of Fitness and Amateur Sport.

Canavan, J. (1997) 'Sex frauds vs doping cheats', *Sport Health*, Vol. 15, 4 Dec., pp. 16-17.

Cashman, R. (1995) 'When the bid party's over: Sydney's problem of delivering the Games', *Australian Quarterly*, Vol. 67, No. 1, pp. 49-54.

Cashman, R. (1999) 'The greatest peacetime event', in Cashman and Hughes, *op. cit.*, pp. 3-17.

Cashman, R. and Hughes, A. (1998) 'Sydney 2000: cargo cult of Australian sport?', in Rowe, D. and Lawrence, G. (eds) *Tourism, Leisure, Sport: Critical Perspectives*, Rydalmere, NSW: Hodder, pp. 216-225.

Cashman, R. and Hughes, A. (eds) (1998) *The Green Games: A Golden Opportunity*, Sydney: Centre for Olympic Studies, University of New South Wales.

Cashman, R. and Hughes, A. (eds) (1999) *Staging the Olympics: The Event and its Impact*, Sydney: University of New South Wales Press.

Chalip, L. (1990) 'The politics of Olympic theatre: New Zealand and Korean cross-national relations', in Byong-Ik, *op. cit.*, pp. 408-433.

Cheek, N. and Burch, W. (1976) *The Social Organisation of Leisure in Human Society*, New York: Harper and Rowe.

Cherfas, J. and Lewin, R. (eds) (1980) *Not Work Alone: A Cross-cultural View of Activities Superfluous to Survival*, London: Temple Smith.

Chomsky, N. (1987) *Necessary Illusions*, Montreal: CBC Enterprises.

Chorbajian, L. and Mosco, V. (1981) '1976 and 1980 Olympic boycott coverage', *Arena Review*, Vol. 5, No. 3, pp. 3-28.

City of Calgary and Alberta Tourism and Small Business (1985) *Economic Impacts of the XV Olympic Winter Games*, Calgary: City of Calgary and Alberta Tourism and Small Business.

Clarke, A. and Clarke, J. (1982) 'Highlights and action replays' - ideology, sport and the media' in J. Hargreaves, ed., *Sport, Culture and Ideology*, London: Routledge and Kegan Paul, pp. 62-87.

Clarke, S. (1997) 'Olympus in the Cotswolds: The Cotswold Games and continuity in popular culture, 1612-1800', *International Journal of the History of Sport*, Vol. 14, No. 2, pp. 40-66.

Coakley, J. J. (1992) *Sport in Society: Issues and Controversies*, St. Louis, Missouri: Mosby

Coates, J. R. (1996) 'London, 1908: the Games of the IIIrd Olympiad', in Findling and Pelle, *op. cit.*, pp. 26-40.

Cockerill, M. (1996) 'Barcelona beats Atlanta by a bull's roar', *Sydney Morning Herald*, August 6, accessed (8.6.99) at: www.smh.com.au/atlanta/.

Commission Royale Enquête (1977) The Report of the Inquiry into the cost of the 21st Olympiad, Quebec: Commission Royal Enquête.

Commonwealth Games Federation (1997) Web-site: www.commonwealthgames.org.au.

Corral, C. (1994) *Pierre de Coubertin: The Humanist*, Lausanne: International Olympic Committee.

Cotton, C. (1989) 'Sports versus news reporting: television-entertainment versus journalism', in Jackson and McPhail, *op. cit.*, pp. 3.11-3.14.

Coubertin, P. de (1988) 'Why I revived the Olympic Games', in Segrave and Chu, *op. cit.*, pp. 101-106 (originally published 1908).

Cox, G., Darcy, M. and Bounds, M. (1994) *The Olympic Games and Housing: A Study of Six International Events and Analysis of Potential Impacts of the Sydney 2000 Olympics*, Campbelltown, NSW, Housing and Urban Studies Research Group, University of Western Sydney and Shelter NSW.

Crawford, S. A. G. M. (1991) 'The 1904 Olympics: a study of contemporary news sources', *Journal of Sports Philately*, Vol. 29, No. 4, pp. 3-7.

Crawford, S. A. G. M. (1996) 'Olympic feature films', in Findling and Pelle, *op. cit.* pp. 415-420.

Crompton, J. L. (1996) 'The potential contributions of sports sponsorship in impacting the product adoption process', *Managing Leisure*, Vol. 1, No. 4, pp. 199-212.

Cronau, P. (1993a) 'Social impact of Games under wraps', *Reportage: Newsletter of the Australian Centre for Independent Journalism*, (UTS, Sydney), September, pp.16-19.

Cronau, P. (1993b) 'City's poor left behind in race for Olympic gold', *The Australian*, 21 Oct.

Crossman, J. and Lappage, R. (1992) 'Canadian athletes' perceptions of the 1980 Olympic boycott', *Sociology of Sport Journal*, Vol.9, No.4, pp. 354-371.

Cuyàs, R. (ed.) (1992) *Official Report of the Games of the XXV Olympiad, Barcelona 1992*, (4 Vols.) Barcelona: COOB'92 (Barcelona Olympic Organising Committee).

Czula, R. (1978) 'The Munich Olympics assassinations: a second look', *Journal of Sport and Social Issues*, Vol.2, No. 1, pp. 19-23.

Da Costa, L. (1998) 'Olympism and the equilibrium of man', in Müller, N. (ed.) *Coubertin and Olympism: Questions for the Future*, Report of the Congress, 17-20 September, 1997, Le Havre, Niederhausen, Germany: Schors/Strasbourg, France: C.R.E.E.E.C./Sydney: Walla Walla Press, pp. 188-199.

244   *The Olympic Games*

Daddario, G. (1994) 'Chilly scenes of the 1992 Winter Games: the mass media and the marginalisation of female athletes', *Sociology of Sport Journal*, Vol. 11, No. 3, pp.275-288.

Darcy, S. and Veal, A. J. (1994) 'The Sydney 2000 Olympic Games: the story so far', *Leisure Options: Australian Journal of Leisure and Recreation*, Vol. 4, No. 1, pp. 5-14.

Davenport, J. (1996) 'Athens, 1896: The Games of the Ist Olympiad', in Findling and Pelle, *op. cit.*, pp. 3-11.

Davies, E. L. (1996) 'Rome, 1960: the Games of the XVIIth Olympiad', in Findling and Pelle, *op. cit.*, pp. 128-134.

Davison, G. (1997) 'Welcoming the world: the 1956 Olympic Games and the re-presentation of Melbourne', in J. Murphy and J. Smart (eds) *The Forgotten Fifties: Aspects of Australian Society and Culture in the 1950s*, Australian Historical Studies No. 109, Melbourne: Melbourne University Press, pp. 64-76.

De Frantz, A. L. (1988) 'The long-term impact of the Los Angeles Olympics', in EAAPP, *op. cit.*, pp. 55-62.

De Lange, P. (1998) *The Games Cities Play*, Monument Park, South Africa: C.P. de Lange Inc.

De Moragas, M. and Botella, M. (eds) (1995) *The Keys to Success: The Social, Sporting, Economic and Communications Impact of Barcelona '92*, Barcelona: Centre d'Estudis Olimpics i del Esport, Universitat Autonoma de Barcelona.

De Moragas, M., MacAloon, J. and Llines, M. (eds) (1996) *Olympic Ceremonies: Historical Continuity and Cultural Exchange*, Lausanne: International Olympic Committee.

Deakin, E. (1993) 'Sydney Olympics 2000: Issues for social impact assessment and management', in Office on Social Policy, *op. cit.*, pp. B1-B53.

Deane, J. (1985) 'The Melbourne press and the Moscow Olympics', *Sporting Traditions*, Vol.1, No.2, pp. 27-42.

Dewar, J. D. (1976) 'Montreal: preparing for the 1976 Olympics', in Killanin and Rhodda, op. cit.

Donald, K. and Selth, D. (1957) *Olympic Saga: The Track and Field Story, Melbourne 1956*, Sydney: Futurian Press.

'Drug cheats stay ahead of the game' (1996) 2 August, www.afnews.org/newsroom/sports/ol.

Duncan, M. C. (1986) 'A hermeneutic of spectator sport: the 1976 and 1984 Olympic Games', *Quest*, Vol. 38, No. 1, pp. 50-77.

Duncan, M. C. (1990) 'Sports photographs and sexual differences: images of women and men in the 1984 and 1988 Olympic Games', *Sociology of Sport Journal*, Vol. 7, No. 1, pp. 22-43.

Duncan, M., Messner, M., Williams, L., Jensen, K. and Wilson. (1994) 'Gender stereotyping in televised sports', in Birrell, S. and Cole, C. (eds) *Women, Sport and Culture*, Champaign, Illinois: Human Kinetics, pp 249-272.

Dunkelberger, R. (1996) 'Sarajevo, 1984', in Findling and Pelle, *op. cit.*, pp. 302-309.

Dunn, K. M. and McGuirk, P. M. (1999) 'Hallmark events' in Cashmore and Hughes, *op. cit.* pp. 18-34.

Durantez, C. (1988) *The Olympic Flame: The Great Olympic Symbol*, Lausanne: International Olympic Committee.

Durick, W. (1996) 'Berlin, 1916: the Games of the VIIth Olympiad', in Findling and Pelle, *op. cit.*, pp. 47-53.

Dyreson, M. (1994) 'From civil rights to scientific racism: the variety of American responses to the Berlin Olympics, the legend of Jesse Owens and the 'Race Question", in Barney and Meier, op. cit., pp. 46-54.

Dyreson, M. L. (1996) 'Scripting the American Olympic story-telling formula: the 1924 Paris Olympic Games and the American media', *Olympika*, Vol. 5, No. 1, pp. 45-80.

'Early alerts on Beijing blooms were ignored' (1998) *Sydney Morning Herald*, 16 January, p.40.

East Asian Architecture and Planning Program (1988) *Hosting the Olympics: the Long-Term Impact, Conference Report*, Seoul: East Asian Architecture and Planning Program, MIT and Graduate School of Environmental Studies, Seoul National University.

Economics Research Associates (1984) *Community Economic Impact of the 1984 Olympic Games in Los Angeles and Southern California, (report to the Los Angeles Olympic Organizing Committee)*, Los Angeles: Economics Research Associates.

Edwards, H. (1981) 'Crisis in the modern Olympic movement', in Segrave and Chu, *op. cit.*, pp. 227-241.

Edwards, H. (1984) 'The free enterprise Olympics', *Journal of Sport and Social Issues*, Vol. 8, pp. i-iv.

Embrey, L., Hall, A. and Gunter, A. (1992) 'Olympians facing the media', *Refractory Girl*, Vol. 43, Winter, pp. 10-13.

Engelbrecht, A. (1996) 'Cortina d'Ampezzo, 1944', in Findling and Pelle, *op. cit.*, pp. 246-247.

Espy, R. (1979) *The Politics of the Olympic Games*, Berkeley, California: University of California Press.

Evans, L. (1998) 'Get that sport into the Games!', *The Olympic Club Magazine: The Official Club of the Sydney 2000 Olympic Games*, Issue 3, pp. 16-18.

Evans, L. (1999) 'Tainted IOC must draw the line to save itself', *Sydney Morning Herald*, 29 January, p. 28.

Farrell, T. B. (1989) 'The 1984 Winter Olympics as an American media event: an 'official' rhetorical crtiticism', in Jackson and McPhail, *op. cit.*, pp. 6.3-6.6.

Fasting, K. and Tangen, J. (1983) 'Gender and sport in Norwegian mass media, *International Review of Sport Sociology*, Vol. 18, No. 1, pp. 61-70.

Fea, J. (1996a) 'Lake Placid, 1932', in Findling and Pelle, *op. cit.*, pp. 232-236.

Fea, J. (1996b) 'Lake Placid, 1980', in Findling and Pelle, *op. cit.*, pp. 295-301.

Federation of Gay Games (1996) *A Brief History of the Gay Games*, San Francisco, CA., Federation of Gay Games, web-site at: www.gaygames.org/ purpose.htm.

Ferkins, L. (1992) *New Zealand Women in Sport: An Untapped Media Resource.* Masters Thesis, Victoria University of Wellington, New Zealand.

Figler, S and Whitaker, G. (1995) *Sport and Play in American Life*, Madison, Wisconsin: Brown and Benchmark.

Findling, J. (1996) 'Nagano, 1998', in Findling and Pelle, *op. cit.*, pp. 335-336.

Findling, J. and Pelle, K. D. (eds) (1996) *Historical Dictionary of the Modern Olympic Movement*, Westport, Connecticut: Greenwood Publishing.

Franks, C. E. S. (1988) 'Sport and Canadian diplomacy', *International Journal*, Vol. 43, No. 4, pp. 665-682.

Fuller, L. K. (1996) 'Olympic documentary films', in Findling and Pelle, *op. cit.*, pp. 405-414.

Furbank, M., Cromarty, H. and McDonald, G. (1996) *William Penny Brooks and the Olympic Connection,* Much Wenlock: Wenlock Olympian Society.

Gallico, P. (1940) *A Farewell to Sport*, New York: Alfred A. Knopf.

Geitner, P. (1997) 'The price of East German gold fever', *Sydney Morning Herald*, 7 October, p. 40.

Georgiadis, K. (1992) 'International Olympic Academy: the history of its establishment, aims and activities', in IOA, *op. cit.*, pp. 57-61.

Gibbs, J. (1898) *A Cotswold Village*, London: John Murray.

Gibson, R. (1976) *Avery Brundage: Professional Amateur*, Ph.D. dissertation, Kent State University.

Glasser, E. (1978) *Amateurism and Athletics*, West Point, New York: Leisure Press.

Goksøyr, M., Lippe, G. von der, and Mo, K. (eds) (1996) *Winter Games, Warm Traditions*, Norwegian Society of Sports History, Sankt Augustin, Norway: Academia Verlag.

Goldlust, J. (1987) *Playing for Keeps: Sport, Media and Society*, Melbourne: Longman Cheshire.

Goldman, B. and Klatz, R. (1992) *Death in the Locker Room: Drugs and Sport*, Chicago: Elite Sports Medicine Publications.

Goldstein, E. S. (1996) 'Amsterdam, 1928: the Games of the Xth Olympiad', in Findling and Pelle, *op. cit.*, pp. 68-74.

Gordon, H. (1994) *Australia and the Olympic Games*, St Lucia, Queensland: Queensland University Press.

Gordon, S. and Sibson, R. (1998) 'Global television: the Atlanta Olympics opening ceremony', in Rowe and Lawrence, *op. cit.*, pp. 204-215.

Gotlieb, M. (1972) 'The American controversy over the Olympic Games', *American Jewish Historical Quarterly*, Vol. 61, pp. 181-213.

Graham, C. (1986) *Leni Riefenstahl and Olympia*, Metuchen, New Jersey: Scarecrow Press.

Graham, C. (1989) 'Leni Riefenstahl's film coverage of the 1936 Olympics', in Jackson and McPhail, *op. cit.*, pp. 2.3-2.6.

Graham, P.J. and Ueberhorst, H. (eds) (1976) *The Modern Olympics*, West Point, New York: Leisure Press.

Gratton, R. (1999) 'The media', in Cashman and Hughes, *op. cit.*, pp. 121-131.

Gray, W. and Knight-Barney, R. (1990) 'Devotion to whom? German-American loyalty on the issue of participation in the 1936 Olympic Games', *Journal of Sport History*, Vol.17, No.2, pp. 214-231.

Greek Ministry of Culture (1996) *Mind and Body; The Revival of the Olympic Idea 19th-20th Century*, Athens: Greek Ministry of Culture.

Green Games Watch 2000 (1999) *Second Environmental Performance Review of the Green Games*, Sydney: Green Games Watch 2000 Inc.

Groussard, S. (1975) *The Blood of Israel: The Massacre of the Israeli Athletes, The Olympics ,1972* (Tran. H. J. Salemson), New York: William Morrow.

Gruneau, R. (1984) 'Commercialism and the modern Olympics', in Tomlinson and Whannel, *op. cit.*, pp. 1-15.

Gruneau, R. (1989) 'Television, the Olympics, and the question of ideology', in Jackson and McPhail, *op. cit.*, pp.7.23-7.34.

Gruneau, R., and Cantelon, H. (1988) 'Capitalism, commercialism and the Olympics', in Segrave and Chu, *op. cit.*, pp. 345-364.

Guegold, W. K. (1996) *One Hundred Years of Olympic Music: Music and Musicians of the Modern Olympic Games, 1896-1996*, Mantua, Ohio: Golden Clef.

Guttman, A. (1984) *The Games Must Go On: Avery Brundage and the Olympic Movement*, New York: Columbia University Press.

Guttman, A. (1988a) 'The modern Olympics: a sociopsychological interpretation', in Segrave and Chu, *op. cit.*, pp. 433-443.

Guttman, A. (1988b) 'The Nazi Olympics', in Segrave and Chu, *op. cit.*, pp. 201-220.

Guttmann, A. (1992) *The Olympics: A History of the Modern Games*, Urbana, Illinois: University of Illinois Press.

Haag, H. (1994) 'Alternate ways of assessing performance - a new look at the results from the 1992 Albertville Olympic Games', in Barney and Meier, op. cit., pp. 159-174.

Haag, H. and Riesinger, G. (1988) 'Comparative analysis of the results of the 1984 Los Angeles Summer Olympic Games', in E. F. Broom, *et al.* (eds) *Comparative Physical Education and Sport*, Vol.5, Champaign, Illinois: Human Kinetics, pp. 83-89.

Hall, A. (1992) 'The Barcelona Olympics: a gender specific analysis of the print media', *Newsletter of the Consultative Committee of Women in Leisure and Recreation* (Melbourne), 17 Dec., pp. 8-9.

Hall, A. (1996a) *Feminism and Sporting Bodies- Essays on Theory and Practice*, Champaign, Illinois: Human Kinetics.

Hall, A. W. (1996b) 'Cortina d'Ampezzo', in Findling and Pelle, *op. cit.*, pp. 258-262.

Hall, A., Cullen, D. and Slack, T. (1990) *The Gender Structure of National Sports Organisations*, Occasional Paper No.1, Sport Canada: Ottawa.

Hall, C. M. (1994) *Hallmark Tourist Events: Impacts, Management and Planning*, London: Belhaven.

Hall, C. M. and Hodges, J. (1996) 'The party's great, but what about the hangover? The housing and social impacts of mega-events with special reference to the

2000 Sydney Olympics', *Festival Management and Event Tourism,* Vol.4, No. 1, pp. 13-20.

Hall, C. M. and Hodges, J. (1998) 'The politics of place and identity in the Sydney 2000 Olympics: 'Sharing the spirit of corporatism", in M. J. Roche (ed.) *Sport, Popular Culture and Identity,* Aachen, Germany: Meyer and Meyer, pp. 95-112.

Hargreaves, J. (1994) *Sporting Females: Critical Issues in the History and Sociology of Women's Sports,* London: Routledge.

Hart-Davis, D. (1988) *Hitler's Olympics: the 1936 Games,* Sevenoaks, Kent: Coronet.

Haxton, P. (1993) *A Post-Event Evaluation of the Social Impacts and Community Perceptions of Mega-Events,* Honours Thesis, Townsville, Queensland: James Cook University.

Hazan, B. (1982) *Olympic Sports and Propaganda Games: Moscow 1980,* New Brunswick, New Jersey: Transaction Books.

Hegel, G. W. F. (1953) *Reason in History* (Trans. R. S. Hartman), New York: Liberal Arts Press.

Heinemann, K. (1992) 'The economic impact of the Olympic Games', in International Olympic Academy, *op. cit.,* pp. 147-156.

Henahan, S. (1996) 'Olympics '96: new tests, newer drugs' 20 July, www.gene.com/ae/ww/su/testing.htm (Access Excellence USA).

Henderson, K. (1994) 'Broadening an understanding of women, gender and leisure', *Journal of Leisure Research,* Vol. 26, No. 1, pp. 1-7.

Henderson, P. (1989) 'Toronto's 1996 bid', in Jackson and McPhail, *op cit.,* pp. 10.9-10.11.

Hendy, P. (1993) 'Olympic marketeers, minders and closures', *Reportage: Newsletter of the Australian Centre for Independent Journalism* (UTS, Sydney), September, pp. 6-7.

Hendy, P. and Kjaerbye, M. (1993) 'Olympic waters: algae threat to canoeing lakes', *Reportage: Newsletter of the Australian Centre for Independent Journalism,* (UTS, Sydney), September, p.15.

Henry, W. M. (1984) *An Approved History of the Olympic Games,* Los Angeles: Southern California Committee of the Olympic Games.

Herman, D. and Chomsky, N. (1988) *Manufacturing Consent: The Political Economy of the Mass Media,* Pantheon: New York.

Herodotus (1962) *The Histories of Herodotus of Halicarnassus* translated by Harry Carter, London: Oxford Press.

Heroux, M. (1996) 'Finding Olympic Games information online', *Database,* June/July pp. 63, 71.

Herr, P. B. (1988) *Hosting the Olympics: the Long-Term Impact, Summary Report of the Conference,* Seoul: East Asian Architecture and Planning Program, MIT and Graduate School of Environmental Studies, Seoul National University (see also, EAAPP).

Herz, D. and Altman, A. (1996) 'Berlin, 1936: the Games of the XIIth Olympiad', in Findling and Pelle, *op. cit.,* pp. 84-94.

Hewitt, J. (1996) 'A grim challenge to world summit on terrorism', *Sydney Morning Herald*, July, 29, p.11.

Higgs, C. and Weiller, K. (1994) 'Gender bias and the 1992 Summer Olympic Games: an analysis of television coverage', *Journal of Sport and Social Issues*, Vol. 18 , No. 3, pp.234-246.

Hill, C. R. (1995) *Olympic Politics*, 2nd edn, Manchester: Manchester University Press.

Hiller, H. (1990) 'The urban transformation of a landmark event: the Calgary Winter Olympics', *Urban Affairs Quarterly*, Vol. 16, No.1, pp. 118-137.

Hinds, R. (1996) 'Second when a city lost its soul', *Sydney Morning Herald*, July 29, p. 8.

Hoberman, J. (1986) *The Olympic Crisis: Sport, Politics, and the Moral Order*, New Rochelle, New York: Ariste D. Carataz.

Holmes, J. (1971) *Olympiad 1936: Blaze of Glory for Hitler's Reich*, New York: Ballantine.

Holmes, P. (1979) *The Olympic Games in Athens 1896: The First Modern Olympics*, New York: Grove Press.

Homebush Bay Development Corporation (1992) *The Cost of Developing Homebush Bay, Homebush Bay Information Sheet 16*, East Sydney, NSW: NSW Government Property Services Group.

Hooker Research (1993a) *The Olympic Corridor: Residential Development at the Starting Block*, Sydney: Hooker Research.

Hooker Research (1993b) *Sydney: Olympics 2000 - Impact on Property*, Sydney: Hooker Research.

Hopkins, J. (1966) *The Marathon*, London: Stanley Paul.

Hornbuckle, A. R. (1996) 'Helsinki, 1952: the Games of the XVIth Olympiad', in Findling and Pelle, *op. cit.*, pp. 109-118.

Horton, P.A. (1994) 'The modern Olympic Games and the cause of black nationalism', in Barney and Meier, *op. cit.,* pp. 55-60.

Houlihan, B. (1994) *Sport and International Politics*, Hemel Hempstead, UK: Harvester.

House of Representatives Standing Committee on Legal and Constitutional Affairs and Australian Sports Commission (1991) *A Chance to have a Say: Equity for Women in Sport. Hansard Report*, Canberra: Parliament House.

Howell, M. (1994) 'Comments on 'Swimming with the big boys", *Sporting Traditions*, Vol. 11, No. 1, pp. 31-35.

Howell, M. (1996) 'Sydney, 2000: the Games of the XVIIth Olympiad', in Findling and Pelle, *op. cit.*, pp. 201-205.

Howell, R. A. and Howell, M. L. (1996) 'Paris, 1900: the Games of the IInd Olympiad', in Findling and Pelle, *op. cit.*, pp. 12-17.

Hruska, B. (1996) 'High tech and high drama', *TV Guide*, Vol. 44, No. 29, July 20-26, pp 8-10.

Hugman, B. and Arnold, P. (1988) *The Olympic Games: Complete Track and Field Results 1896-1988*, New York: Facts on File.

Huguet, J. A. A. (1988) 'Introduction to the 1992 Olympics: Barcelona', in EAAPP, *op. cit.*, pp. 33-40.

Hulme, D. L. (1988) *The Viability of International Sport as a Political Weapon: the 1980 US Olympic Boycott*, PhD dissertation, Fletcher School of Law and Diplomacy.

Hulme, D. L. (1990) *The Political Olympics: Moscow, Afghanistan, and the 1980 US Boycott*, New York: Praeger.

Humphreys, J. M. and Plummer, M. K. (1992) *The Economic Impact on the State of Georgia of Hosting the 1996 Olympic Games*, Atlanta: Commission for the Olympic Games Inc. (at: www.selig.uga.edu/forecast/olympics/olympics.htm).

Humphreys, J. M. and Plummer, M. K. (1993) 'The 1996 Olympic Games - a $5.1 billion prize', *Urban Land*, Vol. 52, May, pp. 10-12.

Hyup, C. (1990) 'The Seoul Olympiad and the Olympic ideals: a critical evaluation', in Byong-Ik, *op. cit.*, pp. 345-356.

International Olympic Academy (1992) *International Olympic Academy: Thirty-Second Session, 17th June - 2nd July 1992*, Lausanne: International Olympic Committee.

International Olympic Committee (1987) *The Olympic Movement*, Lausanne: IOC.

International Olympic Committee (1992) *Manual for Cities Bidding for the Olympic Games*, Lausanne: IOC.

International Olympic Committee (1995) *The Olympic Charter*, Lausanne: IOC. Available at: www.olympic.org.

International Olympic Committee (1996a) 'The IOC Medical Commission and the fight against doping', *IOC Medical Code*, Lausanne: IOC, available at: www. olympic.org/medical/eddop.htm.

International Olympic Committee (1996b) *The IOC Companion,* Lausanne: IOC.

International Olympic Committee (1997) *Manual on Sport and the Environment*, Lausanne: IOC.

International Olympic Committee (1998a) *The IOC Directory*, Lausanne: IOC.

International Olympic Committee (1998b) *Olympic Marketing Matters,* Lausanne: IOC.

International Olympic Committee (1998c) *Olympic Media Fact File, Winter 1998,* Lausanne: IOC.

International Olympic Committee (1998d) *Preliminary Nagano Global Television Audience Results,* unpublished report, Lausanne: IOC.

International Olympic Committee (1998e) *Olympic Marketing Fact File Winter 1998*, Lausanne: IOC.

International Olympic Committee (1999a) *Highlights of the Week's Olympic News,* No. 353, 5 February, Lausanne: IOC

International Olympic Committee (1999b) *Report of the IOC ad hoc Commission to Investigate the Conduct of Certain IOC Members and to Consider Possible Changes in the Procedures for the Allocation of the Games of the Olympiad and the Olympic Winter Games*, (Presented to the Executive Board, January 24), Lausanne: IOC (accessed 29 April 1999 from: www.olympic.org).

International Olympic Committee (1999c) *Second Report of the IOC ad hoc Commission to Investigate the Conduct of Certain IOC Members and to Consider Possible Changes in the Procedures for the Allocation of the Games of the Olympiad and the Olympic Winter Games*, (Presented to the Executive Board, March 11), Lausanne: IOC (accessed 29 April 1999 from: www.olympic.org).

International Olympic Committee (1999d) 'International Olympic Committee announces Ethics Commission members', *IOC Press Release*, 9 April, Lausanne: IOC, available at: www.olympic.org./flat/news/press/pr109_e.html. (accessed: 26.4.99)

International Olympic Committee (1999e) *Manual for Candidate Cities for the XX Olympic Winter Games 2006*, Lausanne: IOC, available at: www.olympic.org (accessed: 29.4.99).

International Olympic Committee (1999f) 'IOC Ethics Commission debates principles for a Code of Ethics', *IOC Press Release*, 3 May, Lausanne: IOC, available at: www.olympic.org/ (accessed: 22.5.99).

International Olympic Committee (n.d.) *Official web-site*, at: www.olympic.org/

International Olympic Committee, City of Sydney, Australian Olympic Committee (1993) *Host City Contract for the Games of the XXVII Olympiad in the Year 2000*, Monte Carlo, Monaco: IOC, City of Sydney, AOC (typescript).

International Olympic Committee, Department of International Cooperation (1998) *Women in the Olympic Movement*, unpublished document, May, IOC: Lausanne.

International Paralympic Committee (n.d.) *Official Web-site*, at: www.paralympic.org.

Iton, J. (1978) *The Economic Impact of the 1976 Olympic Games, Report to the Organising Committee of the 1976 Games*, Montreal: Office of Industrial Research, McGill University.

Iton, J. (1988) 'The longer-term impact of Montreal's 1976 Olympic Games', in EAAPP, *op. cit.*, pp. 195-224.

Jackson, R. and McPhail, T. (eds) (1989) *The Olympic Movement and the Mass Media: Past, Present and Future Issues, International Conference Proceedings*, University of Calgary, Feb. 15-19, Calgary: Hurford Enterprises.

Jeffrey, N. (1997) 'The scandal we had to have', *Weekend Australian*, 17 January, p. 21.

Jennings, A. (1996) *The New Lords of the Rings*, London: Pocket Books.

Jeung, G.H., Jafari, J., and Gartner, W.C. (1990) 'Expectations of the 1988 Seoul Olympics: a Korean perspective', *Tourism Recreation Research*, Vol.15, No.1, pp. 26-33.

Jobling, I. (1994) 'Olympic proposals and bids by Australian cities', *Sporting Traditions*, Vol.11, No.1, pp. 37-56.

Jobling, I. (1996) 'Melbourne, 1956: the Games of the XVIth Olympiad', in Findling and Pelle, *op. cit.*, pp.119-127.

Johnson, W. (1980) 'Avery Brundage, the man behind the mask', *Sports Illustrated*, 4 August, pp. 48-63.

Johnston, C. (1993) 'Sydney Olympics 2000: Approach to assessment and management of social impacts', in Office on Social Policy *op. cit.*, pp. A1-A44.

Jokl, E. (1956) *Sports in the Cultural Pattern of the World: A Study of the Olympic Games 1952 at Helsinki*, Helsinki: Institute of Occupational Health.

Joynt, J., Sten, O. and Steward, T. (1989) 'The XV Winter Olympics Games Organizing Committee (OCO '88) communications plans', in Jackson and McPhail, *op cit.*, pp. 15.3-15.7.

Kane, M. and Parks, J. (1992) 'The social construction of gender difference and hierarchy in sports journalism- few new twists on very old themes', *Women's Sport and Physical Activity Journal*, Vol. 1, No. 1, pp. 49-83.

Kang, H. (1988) 'Accelerating the future-state: urban impact of hosting the 1988 Seoul Olympic Games', in EAAPP, op. cit., pp. 17-32.

Kanin, D.B. (1981) *A Political History of the Olympic Games*, Boulder, Colorado: Westview Press.

Kass, D.A. (1976) 'The issue of racism at the 1936 Olympics', *Journal of Sport History*, Vol.3, pp. 223-235.

Kennedy, J. J. Jr. (1996a) 'Innsbruck, 1964', in Findling and Pelle, *op. cit.*, pp. 270-275.

Kennedy, J. J. Jr. (1996b) 'Innsbruck, 1976', in Findling and Pelle, *op. cit.*, pp. 289-294.

Kent, H. and Merritt, J. (1986) 'The Cold War and the Melbourne Olympic Games', in A. Curthoys and J. Merritt (eds) *Australia's First Cold War: Vol. 2, Better Red than Dead*, Sydney: Allen and Unwin, pp. 170-185, 207-210.

Kew, F. (1997) *Sport: Social Problems and Issues*, Oxford: Butterworth-Heinemann.

Kidd, B. (1980) 'The Popular Front and the 1936 Olympics', *Canadian Journal of History of Sport and Physical Education*, Vol.11, No.1, pp. 1-18.

Kidd, B. (1990a) '.. and Ben Johnson: Canada at the 1988 Olympics', in Byong-Ik, *op. cit.*, pp. 442-454.

Kidd, B. (1990b) 'Seoul to the world, the world to Seoul', in Byong-Ik, *op. cit.*, pp. 434-441.

Kidd, B. (1992a) 'Culture wars of the Montreal Olympics', *International Review for the Sociology of Sport*, Vol. 27, No.2, pp. 151-164.

Kidd, B. (1992b) 'The Toronto Olympic commitment: towards a social contract for the Olympic Games', *Olympika*, Vol.1, pp. 154-167.

Kidd, B. (1994), 'Comments on 'Swimming with the big boys", *Sporting Traditions*, Vol.11, No.1, pp. 25-29.

Kidd, B. (1996) 'Montreal, 1976: the Games of the XXIInd Olympiad', in Findling and Pelle, *op. cit.*, pp. 153-160.

Killanin, L. and Rhodda, J. (eds) (1976) *The Olympic Games*, New York: Collier.

Kim, J.-G. (1988) 'The potential impact of the Seoul Olympic on national development', in EAAPP, *op. cit.*, pp. 319-326.

Kim, U. (1990) *The Greatest Olympics: from Baden-Baden to Seoul*, Seoul: Si-sa-yong-o-sa.

Kirshenbaum, J. (1972) 'A sanctuary violated', *Sports Illustrated*, 15 September, pp. 24-26.

Kirsty, D. (1995) *Coubertin's Olympics: How the Games Began,* Minneapolis: Lerner Publications.

Kjaerbye, M. (1993) 'More than simply 'Sharing the Spirit', *Reportage: Newsletter of the Australian Centre for Independent Journalism*, September, pp. 8-11.

Korporaal, G. and Evans, M. (1999) "Games people play', *Sydney Morning Herald*, 11 February, p. 2.

KPMG Peat Marwick (1993) *Sydney Olympic 2000: Economic Impact Study*, Two Volumes, Report to Sydney Olympics 2000 Bid Ltd, Sydney.

Krippendorff, K. (1980) *Content Analysis: An Introduction to its Methodology*, Beverly Hills, California: Sage Publications.

Krotee, M.L. (1988) 'An organizational analysis of the International Olympic Committee', in Segrave and Chu, *op. cit.*, pp. 113-148.

Krüger, A. (1990) 'The Seoul Olympic Games in the German press: a divided nation views another', in Byong-Ik, *op. cit.*, pp. 311-330.

Krüger, A. (1996) 'The history of the Olympic Winter Games: the invention of a tradition', in Goksøyr, M., Lippe, G. von der, and Mo, K. (eds) *Winter Games, Warm Traditions*, Norwegian Society of Sports History, Sankt Augustin, Norway: Academia Verlag, pp. 101-122.

Krüger, A. (1998) 'The Ministry of Popular Enlightenment and Propaganda and the Nazi Olympics of 1936', in Barney *et. al., op. cit.*, pp. 33-48.

Kumar, K. (1995) *From Post-industrial to Post-modern Society*, Oxford: Blackwell.

Landry, F., Landry, M. and Yerlès, M. (eds) (1991) *Sport .. The Third Millenium: Proceedings of the International Symposium, Quebec City, May 21-25 1990*, Sainte-Foy, Quebec: Presses de l'Université Laval.

Lapchick, R. E. (1975) *The Politics of Race and International Sport: The Case of South Africa*, Westport, Connecticut: Greenwood.

Larson, J. F. (1989) 'Seoul Olympics television concerns: 'Seoul to the world, the world to Seoul' - television as the essence of the 1988 Summer Olympics', in Jackson and McPhail, *op. cit.*, pp. 12.3-12.4.

Larson, J. F. and Rivenburgh, N. K. (1991) 'A comparative analysis of Australian, US and British telecasts of the Seoul Olympic opening ceremony', *Journal of Broadcasting and Electronic Media*, Vol. 35, No. 1, pp. 75-94.

Laura, R. and White, S. (1991) *Drug Controversy in Sport: the Socio-Ethical and Medical Issues*, Sydney: Allen and Unwin.

Lawrence, G. and Rowe, D. (eds) (1986) *Power Play: Essays in the Sociology of Australian Sport*, Sydney: Hale and Iremonger.

Lawrence, G. (1986) 'The race for profit: commercialism and the Los Angeles Olympics', in Lawrence and Rowe, *op. cit.*, pp. 204-214.

Lawrence, R. Z., and Pellegrom, J. (1990) 'Fool's gold: how America pays to lose in the Olympics', *Television Quarterly*, Vol. 24, pp. 93-101.

Lee, J.-S. (1989) 'Seoul Olympics - television concerns', in Jackson and McPhail, *op. cit.*, pp. 12.5-12.9.

Leigh, M. (1974) *The Evolution of Women's Participation in the Summer Olympic Games: 1900-1948*, PhD dissertation, Ohio State University.

Leiper, J. M. (1976) *The International Olympic Committee: its structure and function, past and present problems, and future challenges*, PhD Dissertation, University of Alberta.

Leiper, J. M. (1981) 'Political problems in the Olympic Games', in Segrave and Chu, *op. cit.*, pp. 104-117.

Leiper, N. and Hall, C. M. (1993) *The 2000 Olympics and Australia's Tourism Industries*, submission to the House of Representatives standing Committee on Industry, Science and Technology Inquiry into Implications for Australian Industry Arising from the Year 2000 Olympic Games, Canberra.

Lellouche, M. (1996) 'Albertville and Savoie, 1992', in Findling and Pelle, *op. cit.*, pp. 318-325.

Lenk, H. (1976) 'The 1972 Munich Olympic Games: a dilemma?' in Graham and Ueberhorst, *op. cit.*, pp. 199-208.

Lenskyj, H. J. (1992) 'More than games: community involvement in Toronto's bid for the 1996 Summer Olympics', in Barney and Meier, *op. cit.*, pp. 78-87.

Lenskyj, H. J. (1994) 'Buying and selling the Olympic Games: citizen participation in the Sydney and Toronto bids', in Barney and Meier, *op. cit.*, pp. 70-77.

Lenskyj, H. (1997) 'Sydney 2000, Olympic sport and the Australian media', paper presented to *Everyday Wonders Conference on Popular Culture*, June, Brisbane.

Lenskyj, H. (1998a) 'Green Games or empty promises? Environmental issues and Sydney 2000', in Barney *et al., op. cit.*, pp. 173-179.

Lenskyj, H. (1998b) 'Sport and corporate environmentalism: the case of the Sydney 2000 Olympics', *Review for the Sociology of Sport*, Vol. 33, No. 4, pp. 341-354.

Levitt, S. (1990) *1984 Olympic Arts Festival: Theatre*, PhD dissertation, University of California, Davis.

Loder, C. (1997) *Politics and the Olympic Games: Beyond Athletic Endeavours*, BA in Human Movement Studies (Hons) thesis, University of Technology, Sydney.

Loland, S. (1994) 'Pierre de Coubertin's ideology of Olympism from the perspective of the history of ideas', in Barney and Meier, *op. cit.*, pp. 26-45.

Los Angeles Times (1936) 23 July, p. 7; 25 July, pp. 13, 17, 25; 26 July, p. 1.

Lucas, J. A. (1980) 'American involvement in the Athens Olympic Games', *Stadion*, Vol.6, pp. 217-228.

Lucas, J. A. (1981a) 'A decalogue of Olympic Games reform', in Segrave and Chu, *op. cit.*, pp. 148-164.

Lucas, J. A. (1981b) 'The genesis of the modern Olympic Games', in Segrave and Cuu, *op. cit.*, pp. 22-41.

Lucas, J. A. (1982) 'Prelude to the Games of the Tenth Olympiad in Los Angeles, 1932', *Southern California Quarterly*, Vol. 64, No. 4, pp. 313-317.

Lucas, J. A. (1983) 'American preparations for the first post World War Olympic Games, 1919-1920', *Journal of Sport History*, Vol.10, No.2, pp. 30-44.

Lucas, J. A. (1988a) 'The genesis of the modern Olympic Games', in Segrave and Chu *op. cit.*, pp. 89-99.

Lucas, J. A. (1988b) 'A decalogue of Olympic Games reform', in Segrave and Chu, *op. cit.*, pp. 427-432.

Lucas, J. A. (1992) *The Future of the Olympic Games*, Champaign, Illinois: Human Kinetics.

Lucian (1905) *The Works of Lucian of Samosata,* (trans. W. H. Fowler and F. G. Fowler), Oxford: Clarendon Press.

Ludwig, J. (1976) *Five Ring Circus: The Montréal Olympics*, Toronto: Doubleday.

Lusetich, R. (1999) 'The buying Games', *Weekend Australian*, 16-17 January, p. 22.

Lyberg W. (1996) *Fabulous 100 Years of the IOC: Facts, Figures and Much More*, Lausanne: International Olympic Committee.

Lynch, P. G. and Jensen, R. C. (1984) 'The impact of the XII Commonwealth Games on the Brisbane region', *Urban Policy and Research*, Vol. 2, No. 1, pp. 11-14.

Lynch, R., McDonnell, I., Thompson, S. and Toohey, K. (eds) (1996) *Sport and Pay TV - Strategies for Success*, Sydney: School of Leisure and Tourism Studies, University of Technology, Sydney.

MacAloon, J. J. (1991) 'Comparative analysis of the Olympic ceremonies, with special reference to Los Angeles', in Commision Interministerial de Ciencia y Tecnologia, *International Syposium on Olympic Games, Media and Cultural Exchanges*, Barcelona: Commision Interministerial de Ciencia y Tecnologia. pp. 35-54.

MacAloon, J. J. (1989) ' Festival, ritual and television', in Jackson and McPhail, *op. cit.*, pp. 6.21-6.40.

MacAloon, J. J. (1990) 'Korean nationalism, the Seoul Olympics, and contemporary anthropology', in Byong-Ik, *op. cit.*, pp. 117-159.

MacAloon, J.J. (1995) 'Barcelona '92: the perspective of cultural anthropology', in De Moragas and Botella (eds) *op. cit.*, pp. 181-187.

MacDonald, G. (1992) 'Regime change and the International Olympic Committee', in Barney and Meier, *op. cit.*, pp. 14-27.

MacDonald, G. (1998) 'A colossal embroglio: control of amateur ice hockey in the United States and the 1948 Olympic Winter Games', *Olympika*, Vol. 7, pp. 43-60.

MacDonald, G. and Brown, D. (1996) 'Oslo, 1952', in Findling and Pelle, *op. cit.*, pp. 252-257.

Magdalinski, T. (1998) 'Recapturing Australia's glorious sporting past: drugs and Australian identity', *Bulletin of Sport and Culture*, 14 March, pp. 1, 6-8.

Magnay, J. (1999) 'FBI grills IOC members over bribes', *Sydney Morning Herald*, 21 June, p. 2.

Magnay J. and Hinds, R. (1996) 'Terror: bomb blast hits Atlanta Games', *Sydney Morning Herald*, July 28, pp. 1, 7.

Magnay, J. and Korporaal, G. (1999) 'Rich sports nobble Olympic drugs fight', *Sydney Morning Herald*, 5 February, p. 1.

Mahon, T. (1993) 'Drugs in Sport', *ACHPER Journal*, Vol. 40, No. 1, pp. 13-16.

Mâitre, H. J. (1980) *The 1980 Moscow Olympics: Politics and Polity*, Palo Alto, California: Hoover Institution on War, Revolution and Peace, Stanford University.

Malec, M. (1996) 'Usenet news groups: another internet resource', *Journal of Sport and Social Issues,* pp. 106-109.

Mallon, B. (1984) *The Olympics: A Bibliography*, New York: Garland.

Mallon, B. (1992) *The Unofficial Report of the 1920 Olympics*, Durham, North Carolina.

Mallon, B. (1998) *The 1900 Olympic Games: Results for all Competitors in All Events*, Jefferson, North Carolina: McFarland.

Mallon, B. and Widlund, T. (1998) *The 1896 Olympic Games: Results for all Competitors in All Events*, Jefferson, North Carolina: McFarland.

Maloney, L. (1996) 'Barcelona, 1992: the Games of the XXVth Olympiad', in Findling and Pelle, *op. cit.*, pp. 185-193.

Maloney, L. (1996a) 'Lillehammer, 1994', in Findling and Pelle, *op. cit.*, pp. 326-334.

Maloney, L. (1996b) 'Atlanta, 1996: the Games of the XXVIth Olympiad', in Findling and Pelle, *op. cit.*, pp. 194-200.

Mandell, R. (1971) *The Nazi Olympics*, New York: MacMillan.

Mandell, R. (1976a) *The First Modern Olympics,* Berkeley, California: University of California Press.

Mandell, R. D. (1976b) 'The Modern Olympic Games: a bibliographic essay', *Sport-wissenschaft*, Vol. 6, No. 1, pp. 89-98.

Mandell, R. D. (1978) 'Sportsmanship and Nazi Olympism', in B. Lowe, D. B. Kanin and A. Strenk (eds) *Sport and International Relations*, Champaign Il.: Stipes, pp. 135-152.

Mandell, R. D. (1991) *The Olympics of 1972, A Munich Diary*, Chapel Hill, North Carolina: University of North Carolina Press.

Mangan, J. A. (ed.) (1985) *Proceedings of the XIth HISPA International Congress*, Glasgow: Jordan Hill College.

Manning, M. J. (1996) 'London, 1944: the Games of the XIVth Olympiad', in Findling and Pelle, *op. cit.*, pp. 101-102.

Marsan, J.-C. (1988) 'Expo '67, The 1976 Olympic Games and Montreal urban design', in EAAPP, *op. cit.*, pp. 225-244.

Martin, D. and Gynn, R. (1979) *The Marathon Footrace*, Springfield, Illinois: Charles C.Thomas.

Martueci, D. (1988) 'The London Olympics 40 years on', *Olympic Review*, No. 253, pp. 653-656.

Marvin, C. (1982) 'Avery Brundage and American participation in the 1936 Olympic Games', *Journal of American Studies*, Vol. 16, No. 1, pp. 81-105.

Masumoto, N. (1993) 'Revival of 'Olympia': reflections of body by Leni Riefenstahl', *Journal of Philosophy and Principles of Physical Education*, Vol. 23, No. 1, pp. 1-15.

Masumoto, N. (1994) 'Interpretation of the filmed body: an analysis of the Japanese version of Leni Riefenstahl's 'Olympia", in Barney and Meier, *op. cit.*, pp. 146-158.

Matthews, G. R. (1980) 'The controversial Olympic Games of 1908 as viewed by the *New York Times* and the *Times* of London', *Journal of Sport History*, Vol. 7, No. 2, pp. 40-53.

Maxwell, L. and Howell, R. (1976) 'The 1952 Helsinki Olympic Games: another turning point?', in Graham and Ueberhorst, *op. cit.*, pp. 187-198.

May, V. (1995) 'Environmental implications of the 1992 Winter Olympic Games', *Journal of Tourism Management*, Vol. 16, No. 4, pp. 269-276.

Mazitelli, D. (1985) 'Major events', in Hartung, G. and Miller, T. (eds), *Australian Sport: A Profile*, Department of Sport, Recreation and Tourism/Australian Sports Commission, Canberra: AGPS, pp. 64-73.

Mazitelli, D. (1988) 'Melbourne's Olympic inheritance: subsequent impacts', in EAAPP, *op. cit.*, pp. 171-194.

Mbaye, K. (ed.) (1996) *Centennial Olympic Congress, Congress of Unity, Study Commission: Final Report, Atlanta, July 1996*, Lausanne: IOC.

McCollum, R. H. and McCollum, D. F. (1981) 'Analysis of the ABC-TV coverage of the 21st Olympiad Games', in Segrave and Chu, *op. cit.*, pp. 127-139.

McCoy, J. (1997) 'Radio sports broadcasting in the United States, Britain and Australia (1920-1956 and its influence on the Olympic Games', *Journal of Olympic History*, Vol. 5, No. 1, pp. 20-25.

McGeoch, R. with Korporaal, G. (1994) *The Bid: How Australia Won the 2000 Games*, Melbourne: William Heinemann Australia.

McIntyre, N. (1995) 'The legacy of Lillehammer', in C. Simpson and B. Gidlow (eds) *Australian and New Zealand Association for Leisure Studies: Second Conference: Leisure Connections*, Canterbury, NZ: Lincoln University, pp. 391-394.

McKay, J. (1991) *No Pain, No Gain? Sport and Australian Culture*, Sydney: Prentice-Hall.

McKay, J. (1992) *Why so few? Women Executives in Australian Sport*, Report to the Applied Sports Research Program of the Australian Sport Commission, Canberra.

McMurty, J. (1973) 'A case for killing the Olympics', *Maclean's*, January, pp. 34, 57-57, 60.

Meadow, R. G. (1989) 'The architecture of Olympic broadcasting', in Jackson and McPhail, *op cit.*, pp. 6.7-6.20.

Meenaghan, T. (1997) *Olympic Market Research: Analysis Report*, Lausanne: International Olympic Committee.

Messinesi, X. L. (1973) *A Branch of Wild Olive*, New York: Exposition Press.

Messinesi, X. L. (1976) *History of the Olympics,* New York: Drake Publications.

Messner, M. and Sabo, D. (eds) (1990) *Sport, Men and the Gender Order: Critical Feminist Perspectives*, Champaign, Illinois: Human Kinetics.

Miller, D. (1996) *The Olympic Revolution*, London: Pavilion.

Millet i Serra, L. (1995) 'The games of the city', in De Moragas and Botella (eds) *op. cit.*, pp. 188-202.

Mohsen, S. and Alexandraki, A. (1989) Organisation of the 1988 Calgary Winter Olympic Games', in Jackson and McPhail, *op. cit.*, pp. 11.55-11.60.

Moore, M. (1998) 'Games sponsor blasts delay in hotel room allocations', *Sydney Morning Herald*, 2 February, p. 3.

Moore, M. (1999) 'How SOCOG learned the score', *Sydney Morning Herald*, 14 August, p. 47.

Moore, M. and Magnay, J. (1998) 'In hot water', *Sydney Morning Herald*, 17 January, p. 35.

Moore, M. and Korporaal, G. (1998) 'Whatever it costs', *Sydney Morning Herald*, 19 December, p. 27.

Morrison, R. L (1983) *Government Documents Relating to the 1980 Olympic Games Boycott: A Contents Analysis Bibliography*, Washington, D. C.: US Government Printing Office.

Morrow, D. (1992) 'Grace without pressure: Canadian scintillation and the media in the Amsterdam Olympic Games', in Barney & Meier, *op. cit.*, pp. 125-134.

Mount, J. and Leroux, C. (1994) 'Assessing the effects of a mega-event: a retrospective study of the impact of the Olympic Games on the Calgary business sector', *Festival Management and Event Tourism*, Vol. 2, No. 1, pp. 15-23.

Murdock, G. (1990) 'Television and citizenship', in A. Tomlinson (ed.), *Consumption. Identity and Style: Marketing, Meanings and Packaging of Pleasure*, London: Comedia/Routlege, pp. 77-101.

Murray, W. J. (1992a) 'Berlin in 1936: old and new work on the Nazi Olympics', *International Journal of the History of Sport*, Vol. 9, No. 1, pp. 29-49.

Murray, W. J. (1992b) 'France, Coubertin and the Nazi Olympics: the response', *Olympika*, Vol.1, pp. 46-69.

Nader, J. C. (1992) *Prentice-Hall's Illustrated Dictionary of Computing*, Englewood Cliffs, New Jersey: Prentice-Hall.

Nafziger, J. A. (1980) 'Diplomatic fun and the Games: a commentary on the United States boycott of the 1980 Summer Olympics', *Williamette Law Review*, Vol. 17, pp. 67-81.

National Institute of Economic and Industry Research (1990) *The Melbourne Olympics: An Economic Evaluation, report to the Melbourne Olympic Candidature 1996 Committee*, Clifton Hill, Victoria: NIEIR.

Naul, R. (ed.) (1997) *Contemporary Studies in the National Olympic Games Movements, Sport Sciences International*, Vol. 2, Frankfurt: Peter Lang.

Neale, S. (1982) 'Chariots of Fire: images of men', *Screen*, Vol. 23, pp. 3-4.

Network 10 (1984) *XXIII Olympic Games: The Official Pictorial History, Los Angeles,* Sydney: Australian Olympic Federation.

New York Times, 8 December, 1934, p. 20;15 July, 1936, p.15; 24 July, 1936, p. 21; 25 July, 1936, p. 7; 3 August, 1936, p. 19; 9 August, 1936, sect V., p. 2.

Newsleads Australia (1994) *Melbourne Olympic Candidature 1996*, Melbourne: Newsleads Australia.

Nixon, H. (1988) 'The background, nature and implications of the organization of the 'Capitalist Olympics", in Segrave and Chu, *op. cit.*, pp. 237-252.

Noak, D. (1996) 'The sporting world', *Internet World*, August, pp. 49-52.

North, R. (1963) *Content Analysis: A Handbook with Applications for the study of International Crises*, Evanston, Illinois: Northwestern University Press.

NSW Treasury and the Centre for Regional Economic Analysis (1997) *The Economic Impact of the Sydney Olympic Games*, Sydney: New South Wales Treasury.

Office on Social Policy (1993) *Sydney Olympics 2000: Approaches and Issues for Management of Social Impacts*, Sydney: NSW Government: Office on Social Policy.

Olympic Coordination Authority (1996) *State of Play: A Report on Sydney 2000 Olympics Planning and Construction*, Sydney: OCA.

Onigman, M. (1976) 'Discontent in the Olympic Winter Games, 1980-1980', in Graham and Ueberhorst, *op. cit.*, pp. 226-244.

Organising Committee for the Games of the XVI Olympiad (1958) *Official Report of the Organising Committee for the Games of the XVI Olympiad, Melbourne 1956*, Melbourne: Government Printer.

Oswald, D. (1993) 'Doping: the sports movement leads the way. Plea for a different approach to the problem of doping', *Olympic Review*, No. 303, Jan/Feb., pp. 34-37.

Palenski, R. (1996) 'Seoul, 1988: the Games of the XXIVth Olympiad', in Findling and Pelle, *op. cit.*, pp. 178-184.

Pattengale, J. A. (1996) 'Tokyo/Helsinki, 1940: the Games of the XXIIth Olympiad', in Findling and Pelle, *op. cit.*, pp. 95-100.

Pausanias (1962) *Guide to Greece*, Translated by W. Jones, Cambridge, Massachusetts: Harvard University Press.

Perelman, R. (ed.) (1985) *Olympic Retrospective: the Games of Los Angeles*, Los Angeles: Los Angeles Olympic Organising Committee.

Phillips, D. (1990) 'Australian women at the Olympics: achievement and alienation', *Sporting Traditions*, Vol. 6, No. 2, pp. 181-200.

Phillips, D. H. (1992) *Australian Women at the Olympic Games: 1912-92,* Kenthurst, NSW: Kangaroo Press.

Phillips, M. G. (1997) *An Illusory Image: a report on the media coverage and portrayal of women's sport in Australia (1996)*, Canberra: Women's Sport Unit, Australian Institute of Sport.

Philostratis (1987) 'On athletics', in Sweet, W. (ed.) *Sport and Recreation in Ancient Greece: A Sourcebook with Translations*, New York: Oxford University Press, p. 125.

Pieroth, D. H. (1996a) *Their Day in the Sun: Women of the 1932 Olympics*, Seattle: University of Washington Press.

Pieroth, D. (1996b) 'Los Angeles, 1932: the Games Xth Olympiad', in Findling and Pelle, *op. cit.*, pp. 75-83.

'Plan to set up 'super' web-site for Sydney' (1988) *Sydney Morning Herald*, 15 May, p. 14.

Pound, R. W. (1994) *Five Rings over Korea: the secret negotiations behind the 1988 Olympic Games in Seoul*, Boston: Little, Brown.

Pound, E. T. and Johnson, K. (1999) 'Pricey project sheds light on courting of Samaranch', *USA Today*, 17 March, pp. 1A-2A.

Powell, J. T. (1994) *Origins and Aspects of Olympism*, Champaign, Illinois: Stipes.

Prasad, D. (1999) 'Environment', in Cashman and Hughes, *op. cit.*, pp. 83-92.

Preuss, H. (1998) 'Problematizing arguments of the opponents of Olympic Games', in Barney *et al., op. cit.*, pp. 197-218.

Pujadas, X. and Santacana, C. (1992) 'The popular Olympic Games: Barcelona 1936: Olympians and anti-fascists', *International Review for the Sociology of Sport*, Vol. 27, No. 2, pp. 139-150.

Rabkin, Y. M. and Franklin, D. (1989) 'Soviet/Canadian press perspectives on the Montréal Olympics', in Jackson and McPhail, *op. cit.*, pp. 4.29-4.38.

Rauter, M. (1991) *A History of the International Olympic Committee's TOP-ISL Program*, Masters thesis, Pennsylvania State University.

Real, M., Mechikoff, R. and Goldstein, D. (1989) 'Mirror images: the Olympic Games in Cold War rhetoric: US and Soviet press coverage of the 1980 and 1984 Summer Olympics', in Jackson and McPhail, *op. cit.*, pp. 4.39-4.46.

Redmond, G. (1981) 'Prologue and transition: the 'pseudo-Olympics' of the nineteenth century', in Segrave and Chu, *op. cit.*, pp. 7-21.

Redmond, G. (1988) 'Towards modern revival of the Olympic Games: the various 'pseudo-Olympics of the 19th century', in Segrave and Chu, *op. cit.*, pp. 71-87.

Reich, K. (1986) *Making it Happen: Peter Ueberroth and the 1984 Olympics*, Santa Barbara, California: Capra Press.

Reich, K. (1989) 'L. A. Organising Committee and press relations', in Jackson and McPhail, *op. cit.*, pp. 4.3-4.6.

Renson, R. (1985) 'From the trenches to the track: the 1920 Antwerp Olympic Games', in N. Müller and J. K. Rül (eds) *Olympic Scientific Congress, 1984 Official Report: Sport History*, Niederhausen, Germany, pp. 234-244.

Renson, R. (1996a) 'Antwerp, 1920: the Games of the VIIth Olympiad', in Findling and Pelle, *op. cit.*, pp.47-60.

Renson, R. (1996b) *The Games Reborn: the VIIth Olympiad - Antwerp 1920*, Ghent: Pandora.

Renson, R. M., Lämmer, M., Riordan, J. and Chassiotis, D. (eds) (1991) 'The Olympic Games through the ages: Greek antiquity and its impact on modern sport', *Proceedings of the 13th International HISPA Congress*, HISPA (Hellenic Sports Research Institute), Olympia, Greece, May 22-28, 1989.

Rich, F.C. (1982) 'The legal regime for a permanent Olympic site', *The New York University Journal of International Law and Politics*, Vol. 155, pp. 1-53.

Riggs, K.E., Eastman, S. T. and Golobic, T. S. (1993) 'Manufactured conflict in the 1992 Olympics - the discourse of television and politics', *Critical Studies in Mass Communication*, Vol. 10, No. 3, pp. 253-272.

Riley, M. (1999) 'Atlanta bid files to be scrutinised', *Sydney Morning Herald*, 11 May, p. 5.

Riordan, J. (1984) 'The workers' Olympics', in Tomlinson and Whannel, *op. cit.*, pp. 98-112.

Riordan, J. (1993) 'Soviet-style sport in Eastern Europe: the end of an era', in L. Allison (ed.) *The Changing Politics of Sport*, Manchester: University Press, pp. 37-57.

Riordan, J. (1996) 'Moscow, 1980: the Games of the XXIInd Olympiad', in Findling and Pelle, *op. cit.*, pp. 161-168.

Ritchie, J. R. B. (1990) 'Promoting Calgary through the Olympics: the mega-event as a strategy for community development', in S.H. Fine (ed.) *Social Marketing: Promoting the Causes of Public and Non-profit Agencies*, Boston: Allyn and Bacon, pp. 258-274.

Ritchie, J. R. B. and Lyons, M. (1990) 'Olympulse VI: a post-event assessment of resident reaction to the XV Olympic Winter Games', *Journal of Travel Research*, Vol. 28, No. 3, pp. 14-23.

Ritchie, J. R. B. and Smith, B. (1991) 'The impact of a mega-event on host-region awareness: a longitudinal study', *Journal of Travel Research*, Vol. 30, No. 1, pp. 3-10.

Rivenburgh, N. (1991) 'Learning about Korea - or did we? A multi-national comparison of televised cultural coverage of the Seoul Olympic opening ceremony', in Landry *et al.*, *op. cit.*, pp. 95-97.

Roberts, A. J. and McLeod, P. B. (1989) 'The economics of a hallmark event', in Syme *et al.*, *op. cit.*, pp. 242-9.

Roche, M. (1992) 'Mega-events and micro-modernization: on the sociology of the new urban tourism', *British Journal of Sociology*, Vol. 43, No. 4, pp. 563-600.

Rose, D. (1988) 'Should the Olympic Games be abolished?' in Segrave and Chu, *op. cit.*, pp. 393-406.

Rosenzweig, R. (1997) 'The Nazi Olympics: Berlin 1936', *Journal of Sport History*, Vol. 24, No. 1, pp. 77-80.

Rubien, F. (ed.) (1936) *Report of the American Olympic Committee for the Games of the Xith Olympiad: Berlin, Germany, August 1 to 16, 1936*, New York: American Olympic Committee.

Rühl, J. K. and Keuser, A. (1997) 'Olympic Games in 19th century England with special consideration of the Liverpool Olympics', in Naul, *op. cit.*, pp. 55-70.

Salleh, A. and Kjaerbye, M. (1993a) 'Putting on the Green Glitz', *Reportage: Newsletter of the Australian Centre for Independent Journalism*, September, pp. 12-13.

Salleh, A. and Kjaerbye, M. (1993b) 'Olympic waters: ferries stir up toxic fears', *Reportage: Newsletter of the Australian Centre for Independent Journalism*, September, p. 14.

Salt Lake Organizing Committee for the Olympic Winter Games of 2002 (1999) *Board of Ethics Report to the Board of Trustees*, Salt Lake City, Utah: SLOC (available at: www.slc2002.org/news/).

Samaranch, J. A. (n. d.) *The IOC Medical Commission and the Fight Against Doping*, International Olympic Committee, at: www.olympic.org/medical/eddop.htm.

Sandler, D. M. and Shani, D. (1989) 'Olympic sponsorship vs 'Ambush' marketing: who get the gold?' *Journal of Advertising Research*, Vol. 29, No. 4, pp. 9-14.

Sandler, D.M. and Shani, D. (1993) 'Sponsorship and the Olympic Games: the consumer perspective', *Sport Marketing Quarterly*, Vol. 2, No. 3, pp. 38-43.

Scharenberg, S. (1996) 'Sapporo/St. Moritz/Garmisch-Partenkirchen, 1940', in Findling and Pelle, *op. cit.*, pp. 242-245.

Schor, J. (1991) *The Overworked American*, New York: Basic Books.

Scraton, S. (1992) *Shaping up to Womanhood,* Buckingham: Open University Press.

Segrave, J. O. and Chu, D. (eds) (1981) *Olympism*, Champaign, Illinois: Human Kinetics.

Segrave, J. O. and Chu, D. (eds) (1988) *The Olympic Games in Transition*, Champaign, Illinois: Human Kinetics.

'Send them home' (1998) *The Advertiser* (Adelaide) 16 January, p.19.

Shanklin, B. (1988) *Sport and Politics: the Olympics and the Los Angeles Games*, New York: Praeger.

Sheil, P. (1998) *Olympic Babylon*, Sydney: MacMillan.

Shigeru, I. (1988) 'Urban planning evaluation of the Tokyo Olympics', in EAAPP, *op. cit.*, pp. 91-124.

Simmons, D. C. (1996) 'St. Moritz, 1928', in Findling and Pelle, *op. cit.*, pp. 228-231.

Simmons, D. C. (1996) 'St. Moritz, 1948', in Findling and Pelle, *op. cit.*, pp. 248-251.

Simon, D. (1988) 'Long-term impact of the Olympic Games on Los Angeles', in EAAPP, *op. cit.*, pp. 41-54.

Simri, U. (1977) *A Historical Analysis of the Role of Women in the Modern Olympic ·Games*, Netanya, Israel: Wingate Institute for Physical Education and Sport.

Simson, V. and Jennings, A. (1992) *The Lords of the Rings: Power, Money and Drugs in the Modern Olympics*, London: Simon and Schuster.

Slater, J. (1998) 'Changing partners: the relationship between the mass media and the Olympic Games', in Barney *et al., op. cit.*, pp. 49-68.

Slowinowski, S. (1991a) 'Ancient sport symbols and postmodern tradition', in Renson *et al., op. cit.*, pp. 400-411.

Slowinowski, S. (1991b) 'Burning desire: festival flame ceremony', *Sociology of Sport Journal*, Vol. 8, No. 3, pp. 239-259.

Slowikowski, S. S. and Loy, J. W. (1993) 'Ancient athletic motifs and the modern Olympic Games: an analysis of rituals and representations', in A. G. Ingham and J. W. Loy (eds) *Sport in Social Development*, Champaign, Illinois: Human Kinetics, pp. 21-49.

Smith, R. J. and Gibbs, M. (1993) *Navigating the Internet*, Carmel, Indiana: Sams Publishing.

Snyder, C. D. (1936) 'The real winners in the 1936 Olympic Games', *Scientific Monthly*, Vol. 43, October, pp. 372-374.

Soldatow, S. (1980) *Politics of the Olympics*, North Ryde, NSW: Cassell.

Spa, M., Rivenburgh, N. and Larson, J. (1995) *Television in the Olympics*, London: John Libbey.

Spencer, B. (1966) *High Above the Olympians*, Los Altos, California: Tafnews Press.

Sports Illustrated (1956a) 'In full view of the world', Vol. 15, 3 December, pp. 22-23.

Sports Illustrated (1956b) 'The Battle of Melbourne', December 17, p. 23.

Stauff, J. W. (1996) 'Garmisch-Partenkirchen, 1936', in Findling and Pelle, *op. cit.*, pp. 237-241.

Steadward, R.D. (1996) 'Integration and sport in the paralympic movement', *Sport Science Review*, Vol. 5, No. 1, pp. 26-41.

Stevens, M. (1999) 'Prince of the Past shames the Games', *Weekend Australian*, 6-7 February, p. 19.

Stevens, M. and Stewart, C. (1999) 'IOC bribe inquiry claims new scalp', *Weekend Australian*, 23-24 January, p. 6.

Stevenson, D. (1998) 'The art of the Games: leisure, tourism and the Cultural Olympiad', in Rowe, D. and Lawrence, G. (eds) *Tourism, Leisure, Sport: Critical Perspectives*, Rydalmere, New South Wales: Hodder, pp. 124-134.

Stoddart, B. (1994) *Invisible Games. A Report on the Media Coverage of Women's Sport, 1992.* Canberra: Sport and Recreation Ministers' Council.

Stone, B. (1996) 'Olympiad online: the net takes Olympic reporting to new levels' *Internet World*, August, pp. 41-47.

Strenk, A. (1970) 'Back to the very first day: eighty years of politics in the Olympic Games', *Journal of Sport and Social Issues*, Vol. 2, No. 1, pp. 24-36.

Strenk, A. (1979) 'What price victory? The world of international sports and politics', *Annals of the American Academy of Political and Social Science*, Vol. 445, pp. 128-140.

Stringer, H. (1995) 'China's Great Wall of lies', *Inside Sport*, No. 37, January, pp. 16-27.

Stump, A. J. (1988) 'The Games that almost weren't', in Segrave and Chu, *op. cit.*, pp. 191-200.

Sutcliffe, K. (1994) 'Insight into the media in sport', *Eighth NSW Session of the Australian Olympic Academy*, 13-14 April, North Ryde, NSW: Macquarie University, pp. 6-10.

Swaddling, J. (1980) *The Ancient Olympic Games*, Austin, Texas: University of Texas Press.

Sweeney, Brian, and Associates (1992) *The Olympic Reality: A Survey into Australians' Views on the Barcelona Olympics*, South Melbourne: Brian Sweeney and Associates.

Sweet, W. (1987) *Sport and Recreation in Ancient Greece*, Oxford: Oxford University Press.

'Swimming: Smith says medals come from training, not drugs' (1996) 31 July, www.afnews.org/newsroom/sports/ol.

Switzer, P. *et al.* (1989) 'Calgary Olympics: CTV host broadcaster concerns', in Jackson and McPhail, *op. cit.*, pp. 14.3-14.9.

Sydney Olympic Games Review Committee (1990) *Report to the Premier of New South Wales*, Sydney: Premier's Department.

Sydney Olympic Broadcasting Organisation (1998) *Infosheet*, Sydney: SOBO.

Sydney Olympics 2000 Bid Ltd (1993a) *The Bid by the City of Sydney to Host the Games of the XXVII Olympiad in the Year 2000*, Sydney: SOBL.

Sydney Olympics 2000 Bid Ltd (1993b) *Fact Sheets: A Summary of the Bid by the City of Sydney to Host the Games of the XXVII Olympiad in the Year 2000*, Sydney: SOBL.

Sydney Olympics 2000 Bid Ltd (1993c) *Environmental Guidelines for the Summer Olympic Games*, Sydney: SOBL.

Sydney Organising Committee for the Olympic Games (1997) *Sydney Olympic News*, 9 September.

Sydney Organising Committee for the Olympic Games (1994) *Progress Report to the International Olympic Committee 102nd Session - Lillehammer, February 1994*, Sydney: SOCOG.

Syme, G. J., Shaw, B. J., Fenton, M. D. and Mueller, W. S. (eds) (1989) *The Planning and Evaluation of Hallmark Events*, Aldershot, UK: Avebury.

Takac, A. (1976) 'Forty years for fourteen days', *The Gazette* (Montréal), July 17, p. 2.

'Task of sending the news home was quite a story' (1988) *Australian Olympian*, December, p. 9.

Tewnion, T. (1993) The University of Calgary and the XV Olympic Winter Games, Calgary, Alberta: University of Calgary.

'The Guide' (1992) *Sydney Morning Herald*, 20 July.

The Olympic Almanac, www.andrew.cmu.edu/~mmdg/Almanac/.

Theberge, N. (1988) 'Making a career in a man's world: the experience and orientations of women in coaching', *Arena Review*, Vol. 12, No. 2, pp. 116-127.

Theberge, N. (1991) 'A content analysis of print media coverage of gender, women and physical activity', *Journal of Applied Sports Psychology,* Vol. 3, No. 1, pp. 36-50.

Tomlinson, A. (1984) 'De Coubertin and the modern Olympics', in Tomlinson and Whannel, *op. cit.*, pp. 84-97.

Tomlinson, A. (1989) 'Representation, ideology and the Olympic Games: a reading of the opening and closing ceremonies of the L. A. Olympic Games', in Jackson and McPhail, *op. cit.*, pp. 7.3-7.12.

Toohey, D. and Warning, K. (1981) 'Nationalism: inevitable and incurable?', in Segrave and Chu, *op. cit.*, pp. 118-126.

Toohey, K. (1990a) *The politics of Australian élite sport: 1949-1982*, PhD thesis, Pennsylvania State University.

Toohey, K. (1990b) 'A content analysis of the Australian television coverage of the 1988 Seoul Olympics', paper to the *Ninth Commonwealth and International Conference of Physical Education, Sport, Health, Dance, Recreation and Leisure,* January, Auckland.

Toohey, K. (1993a) 'Educators discuss fair play', *Australian Olympian,* Summer, pp. 13-16.

Toohey, K. (1993b) 'The Olympics, television and equity: the Barcelona Olympics'. Paper presented to *19th Australian Council for Health, Physical Education and Recreation Biennial Conference,* July, Darwin.

Toohey, K. (1997) 'Australian television, gender and the Olympic Games', *International Review for the Sociology of Sport,* Vol. 31, No. 1, pp. 19-29.

Toohey, K. and Warning, P. (1998) 'Olympic flames: analysis of an Olympic internet newsgroup' in Barney *et al., op. cit.,* pp. 141-154.

Tourism Forecasting Council (1998) *The Olympic Effect- Be Part of the Action,* Canberra: TFC.

Truñó E. (1995) 'Barcelona: city of sport', in De Moragas and Botella (eds) *op. cit.,* pp. 43-56.

Tufts University (1997a) 'Did politics ever affect the ancient games?' at: www.-olympics.tufts.edu/pol.html

Tufts University (1997b) 'Spectators at the Games', at: www.olympics.tufts.edu/specs.html

'Two medal winners thrown out of Olympics for drug violations', (1996) 29 July. www.afnews.org/newsroom/sports/ol.

Ueberhorst, H. (1976a) 'The International Olympic Academy: idea and reality', in Graham and Ueberhorst, *op. cit.,* pp. 50-52.

Ueberhorst, H. (1976b) ; 'Conclusion', in Graham and Ueberhorst, *op. cit.,* pp. 245-254.

Ueberhorst, H. (1996) 'Stockholm, 1912: the Games of the IVth Olympiad', in Findling and Pelle, *op. cit.,* pp. 41-46.

Ueberroth, P. (1986) *Made in America,* New York: William Morrow.

United Nations General Assembly (1968) *Official Records of the General Assembly, 34th Session 2 December, Supplement No. 22 (A/34/22)* New York: UN, pp. 114-131.

United States Olympic Committee (1999) *Official web-site,* at: www.olympic-usa.org/games/

United States Olympic Committee, Special Bid Oversight Commission (1999) *Report,* USOC - available at: www.olympic-usa.org/games/

Vamakaris, F. (1997) 'Blood sports', *Inside Sport,* June, pp. 26-39.

Van Wynsberghe, R. and Ritchie, I. (1994) '(Ir)Relevant rings: the symbolic consumption of the Olympic logo in postmodern media culture', in Barney and Meier, *op. cit.,* pp. 124-135.

Veal, A. J. (1994) *Leisure Policy and Planning,* London: Pitman.

Veal, A. J., Burkhardt, A., Toohey, K. and Haxton, P. (1998) *The Olympic Games: A Bibliography*, School of Leisure and Tourism Studies, University of Technology, Sydney, at: www.business.uts.edu.au/leisure/research/olympic.html.

Vegara, J. M. and Salvador, N. (1992) The Economic Impact of the Barcelona '92 Olympic Games, Barcelona: Ajuntament de Barcelona.

Voeltz, R. A. (1996) 'London, 1948: the Games of the XVth Olympiad', in Findling and Pelle, *op. cit.*, pp. 103-108.

Wallechinsky, D. (1992) *The Complete Book of the Olympics*, London: Aurum Press.

Walsh, M. (1992) 'Risible arithmetic on Olympics bid', *Sydney Morning* Herald, 23 Dec. p. 27.

Walsh, M. (1993a) 'Olympic backers fail to count the cost', *Sydney Morning Herald*, April 9, p. 25.

Walsh, M. (1993b), 'Olympic figures just do not add up', *Sydney Morning Herald*, June 25, p. 21.

Walsh, M. (1993c), 'First gold goes to cost concealment', *Sydney Morning Herald*, September 28, pp. 29, 32.

Wamsley, K. B. (1996) 'Calgary, 1988', in Findling and Pelle, *op. cit.*, pp. 310-317.

Wamsley, K. B. and Heine, M. (1994) "Calgary is not a cowboy town' - ideology, the Olympics and the politics of identity', in Barney and Meier, *op. cit.*, pp. 78-83.

Warning, K. (1980) *A Political History of the Modern Summer Olympic Games*, Masters thesis, California State University, Long Beach, California.

Watkins, G. T. (1997) *The Official Report of the Centennial Olympic Games*, (3 Volumes), Atlanta, Georgia: Atlanta Committee for the Olympic Games/ Peachtree Publishers.

Weber, R. (1990) *Basic Content Analysis* (2nd edn), Newbury Park, CA.: Sage .

Welch, P. D. (1996a) 'Paris, 1924: the Games of the VIIIth Olympiad', in Findling and Pelle, *op. cit.*, pp. 61-67.

Welch, P. D. (1996b) 'Chamonix, 1924', in Findling and Pelle, *op. cit.*, pp. 223-227.

Welsh, P. and Costa M. (1994) 'A century of Olympic competition', in Costa, M. and Guthrie, S. (eds) *Women and Sport: Interdisciplinary Perspectives*, Champaign, Illinois: Human Kinetics, pp. 123-138.

Wendl, K. (1998) 'The Route of Friendship: a cultural/artistics event of the Games of the XIX Olympiad,in Mexico City, 1968', *Olympika*, Vol. 7, pp.113-134.

Wenn, S. R. (1991) 'A suitable policy of neutrality? FDR and the question of American participation in the 1936 Olympics', *International Journal of the History of Sport*, Vol. 8, No. 3, pp. 319-335.

Wenn, S. R. (1993) 'Lights! Camera! Little action: television, Avery Brundage and the 1956 Melbourne Olympics', *Sporting Traditions*, Vol. 10, No. 1, pp. 38-53.

Wenn, S. R. (1995) 'Growing pains: the Olympic Movement and television, 1976-1972', *Olympika*, Vol. 4, pp. 1-22.

Wenn, S. R. (1996) 'Television rights negotiations and the 1976 Montreal Olympics', *Sport History Review*, Vol. 27, No. 2, pp. 111-138.

Whannel, G. (1983) *Blowing the Whistle: the Politics of Sport*, London: Pluto Press.

Whannel, G. (1984) 'The television spectacular', in Tomlinson and Whannel, *op. cit.*, pp. 30-43.

Whitson, D. (1998) 'Olympic sport, global media and cultural diversity', in Barney *et al.*, *op. cit.*, pp. 1-10.

Whitson, D. and Macintosh, D. (1993) 'Becoming a world-class city: hallmark events and sport franchises in the growth strategies of Western Canadian cities', *Sociology of Sport Journal*, Vol. 10, No. 3, pp. 221-240.

Whittaker, M. (1993) 'How green the Games?', *The Australian Magazine*, Dec. 11-12, pp. 28-36.

Wilcox, D. A. (1994) 'Lessons for tourism industries from the 1984 Olympics at Los Angeles', paper to the *'THC '94' conference*, Sydney, March.

Wilson, H. R. (1993) *The Golden Opprtunity: A Study of the Romanian Manipulation of the Olympic Movement During the Boycott of the 1984 Los Angeles Olympic Games*, PhD dissertation, Ohio State University.

Wilson, H. R. (1994) 'The golden opportunity: Romania's political manipulation of the 1984 Los Angeles Olympic Games', *Olympika*, Vol.3, pp. 83-98.

Wilson, N. (1988) *The Sports Business: the Men and the Money*, London: Piakas.

Wilson, W. (ed.) (1990) *Gender Stereotyping in Televised Sport*, Los Angeles: Amateur Athletics Foundation of Los Angeles.

Wilson, W. (1996) 'Los Angeles, 1984: the Games of the XXIIIrd Olympiad', in Findling and Pelle, *op. cit.*, pp. 169-177.

'Women, sport and the media', (1988) *Ms Muffet*, No. 35, May, pp. 6-8.

Woodhead, W. R. (1988) 'The legacy of the 1956 Melbourne Olympics', in EAAPP, *op. cit.*, pp. 133-170.

'Wrestling star hits at politics' (1972) *New York Times*, 27 April.

Wright, G. (1978) 'The political economy of the Montreal Olympic Games', *Journal of Sport and Social Issues*, Vol. 2, No. 1, pp. 13-18.

Young, D. C. (1996) *The Modern Olympics: A Struggle for Revival*, Baltimore: Johns Hopkins University Press.

Young, M. (1988) 'The Melbourne press and the 1980 Moscow Olympic boycott controversy', *Sporting Traditions*, Vol. 2, No. 2, pp. 184-200.

Zakus, D. H. (1992) 'The International Olympic Committee: tragedy, farce, and hypocrisy', *Sociology of Sport Journal*, Vol. 9, No. 4, pp. 340-353.

Zuzanek, J. and Veal, A. J. (eds) (1999) 'Time pressure, stress, leisure participation and well-being', special issue of *Loisir et Société*, Vol. 21, No. 2.

Index